NASA Monographs in Systems and Software Engineering

Series editor

Mike Hinchey, Limerick, Ireland

The **NASA Monographs in Systems and Software Engineering** series addresses cutting-edge and groundbreaking research in the fields of systems and software engineering. This includes in-depth descriptions of technologies currently being applied, as well as research areas of likely applicability to future NASA missions. Emphasis is placed on relevance to NASA missions and projects.

More information about this series at http://www.springer.com/series/7055

Emil Vassev · Mike Hinchey

Autonomy Requirements Engineering for Space Missions

 Springer

Emil Vassev
Mike Hinchey
Lero—The Irish Software Engineering
    Research Centre
University of Limerick
Limerick
Ireland

ISSN 1860-0131   ISSN 2197-6597   (electronic)
ISBN 978-3-319-38403-0   ISBN 978-3-319-09816-6   (eBook)
DOI 10.1007/978-3-319-09816-6

Springer Cham Heidelberg New York Dordrecht London

Printed on acid-free paper

Springer is part of Springer Science+Business Media (www.springer.com)

To my beloved wife Slava, "Many women do noble things, but you surpass them all."

Emil Vassev

Preface

Over the years, both ESA and NASA missions have been gradually adding autonomy to flight and ground systems to increase the amount of science data returned from missions, perform new science, and reduce mission costs. In new space exploration initiatives, there is emphasis on both human and robotic exploration. Even when humans are involved in the exploration, human tending of space assets must be evaluated carefully during mission definition and design in terms of benefit, cost, risk, and feasibility. Risk and feasibility are major factors motivating the use of unmanned craft and the use of automation and robotic technologies where possible.

The development of unmanned space exploration missions is closely related to integration and promotion of autonomy in robotic spacecraft. Both ESA and NASA are currently adapting autonomic computing as a valuable paradigm for development of autonomous spacecraft systems where, to tackle autonomy, traditional development approaches are applied. Experience has shown though, that traditional software development is inappropriate to such tasks, because it pays scant attention to autonomy itself, and therefore, new autonomy-aware software development approaches should be employed.

Nowadays, requirements engineering for autonomous systems appears to be a wide open research area with no definitive solution yet. Elicitation and expression of autonomy requirements is one of the most significant challenges autonomous spacecraft engineers need to overcome today. This book presents the Autonomy Requirements Engineering (ARE) approach, intended to help software engineers properly elicit, express, verify, and validate autonomy requirements. ARE is the result of a joint project of Lero—The Irish Software Engineering Research Centre and ESA's ESTEC—the European Space Research and Technology Centre.

Limerick, Ireland

Emil Vassev
Mike Hinchey

Acknowledgments

This book is the result of a joint project funded by the European Space Agency's European Space Research and Technology Centre (ESTEC) under contract number 4000106016. The work performed to obtain the results described in this book was also supported by the European Union FP7 Integrated Project on Autonomic Service-Component Ensembles (ASCENS) and by Science Foundation Ireland grant 03/CE2/I303_1 to Lero—The Irish Software Engineering Research Centre. We are grateful to our collaborators from ESTEC, especially Yuri Yushtein for the thorough discussions and his valuable suggestions during our research. Special thanks also go to Martin Hiller and James Windsor, Kjeld Hjortnaes, and Maria Hernek for their great support and encouragement.

Abbreviations

AC	Autonomic Computing
ACMF	Aircraft Conditioning Monitoring Function
ACS	Avionics Control System
ADMS	Aircraft Diagnostic and Maintenance System
ADP	Antenna Despun Motor
AE	Autonomic Element
AEIP	Autonomic Element Interaction Protocol
AI	Artificial Intelligence
AIT	Assembly, Integration and Testing
AMP	Adaptive Motion Planning
ANTS	Autonomous Nano-Technology Swarm
AP	Atomic Propositions
APM	Antenna Pointing Mechanism
AR	Autonomy Requirements
ARE	Autonomy Requirements Engineering
AREM	Autonomy Requirements Engineering Model
AS	Autonomic System
ASCENS	Autonomic Service-Component Ensembles
ASIP	Autonomic System Interaction Protocol
ASM	Abstract State Machines
ASSL	Autonomic System Specification Language
AUAS	Autonomous Unmanned Aerial System
BELA	BepiColombo Laser Altimeter
BIT	Built-in-Test
C2	Command and Control
CCS	Calculus of Communicating Systems
CI	Collaborative Infrastructure
CMC	Central Maintenance Computer
CPM	Chemical Propulsion Module
CPU	Central Processing Unit

CSP	Communicating Sequential Processes
DDD	Detailed Design Document
DMS	Data Management System
DOBERTSEE	Dependent On-Board Embedded Real-Time Software Engineering Environment
DS-1	Deep Space One Mission
ECM	Elevation Control Mechanism
ELEO	Equatorial Low Earth Orbit
EO-1	Earth Observing Mission-1
ESA	European Space Agency
ESTEC	European Space Research and Technology Center
ETBA	Energy Trace and Barrier Analysis
FDIR	Failure Detection, Isolation and Recovery
FFA	Functional Failure Analysis
FSM	Finite State Machines
GAR	Generic Autonomy Requirements
GAR-SM	GAR for Space Missions
GEO	Geostationary Earth Orbit
GORE	Goal-Oriented Requirements Engineering
GMSEC	GSFC Mission Services Evolution Center
GSFC	NASA Goddard Space Flight Center
HOGC	Higher-Order Graph Calculus
HOOD	Hierarchical Object-Oriented Design
HPC	High Performance Computing
HRT-HOOD	Hard Real-Time HOOD
ICO	Intermediate Circular Orbit
IBM	The International Business Machines Corporation
IEEE	Institute of Electrical and Electronics Engineers
IER	Information Exchange Requirement
INCOSE	International Council on Systems Engineering
ISA	Italian Spring Accelerometer
ISS	International Space Station
ITU-T	International Telecommunications Union-Telecommunications
IVHM	Integrated Vehicle Health Management
JSF	Joint Strike Fighter
KLRF	KnowLang Reward Function
KR	Knowledge Representation
KRC	Knowledge Representation Context
LCMWG	Life Cycle Management Working Group
LEO	Low Earth Orbit
LEXIOR	LEXical analysis for Improvement of Requirements
LTS	Labeled Transition System
LOGOS	Lights out Ground Operations System
MAS	Multi-Agent System

MBSE	Model Based Systems Engineering
MDM	Mercury Dust Monitor
MGA	Medium Gain Antenna
MGNS	Mercury Gamma ray and Neutron Spectrometer
MEO	Medium Earth Orbit
MERMAG	Mercury Magnetometer
MERMAG-MGF	Instrument Science Objective Mercury Magnetometer
MERTIS	Mercury Thermal Infrared Spectrometer
MIXS	Mercury Imaging X-ray Spectrometer
MLI	Multi-Layer Insulation
MMO	Mercury Magnetospheric Orbiter
MORE	Mercury Orbiter Radio Science Experiment
MPO	Mercury Planetary Orbiter
MPPE	Mercury Plasma Particle Experiment
MSASI	Mercury Sodium Atmospheric Spectral Imager
OCA	Orbital Communications Adaptor
OCAMS	OCA Mirroring System
OCL	Object Constraint Language
OOP	Object-Oriented Programming
PBE	Platform Based Engineering
PHEBUS	Probing of Hermean Exosphere by Ultraviolet Spectroscopy
PHM	Prognostics Health Management
PMAC	Policy Management for Autonomic Computing
PWI	Mercury Plasma Wave Instrument
QoS	Quality of Service
RA	Remote Agent
RAISE	Rigorous Approach to Industrial Software Engineering
RAX	Remote Agent Experiment
RC	Requirements Chunk
R&D	Research and Development
RE	Requirements Engineering
ROE	Rules of Engagement
SATCOM	Satellite Communications
SDL	Specification and Description Language
SEAS DTC	UK Systems Engineering and Autonomous Systems Defence Technology Centre
SEPM	Solar Electric Propulsion Module
SERENA	Search for Exosphere Refilling and Emitted Neutral Abundances
SIXS	Solar Intensity Xray Spectrometer
SLO	Service-Level Objectives
SMA	Space Mission Analysis

SMAD	Space Mission Analysis and Design
SOA	Service Oriented Architecture
SSM	Second Surface Mirror
SYMBIOSYS	Spectrometers and Imagers for MPO BepiColombo Integrated Observatory System
TL	Temporal Logic
UAS	Unmanned Aerial System—a fleet of UAVs
UAV	Unmanned Aerial Vehicle
UAV-P	Unmanned Aerial Vehicle Pilot
UHF	Ultra High Frequency
UML	Unified Modeling Language
VDM	Vienna Development Method
XML	Extensible Markup Language

Contents

1 Software Engineering for Aerospace: State of the Art   1
  1.1   Introduction: The Specifics of Aerospace Industry   1
        1.1.1   Emphasis on Safety   2
        1.1.2   Standardization   2
        1.1.3   Complexity   3
        1.1.4   Diversity of Platforms   3
  1.2   Software Engineering Process for Aerospace   3
        1.2.1   Requirements Engineering and Modeling   5
        1.2.2   Managing Safety and Risk   8
        1.2.3   Dealing with Complexity   9
        1.2.4   Design 10
        1.2.5   Implementation 12
        1.2.6   Testing, Verification and Validation 13
  1.3   Methods, Techniques and Architecture Approaches
        for Aerospace 13
        1.3.1   Formal Methods 13
        1.3.2   Software Verification and Validation 14
        1.3.3   SOA 15
        1.3.4   Multi-agent Systems 16
  1.4   Autonomous and Autonomic Aerospace Systems 22
        1.4.1   Autonomy Versus Automation 22
        1.4.2   Autonomic Computing 23
        1.4.3   Engineering Resilient Systems with Adaptability 27
        1.4.4   Integrated Vehicle Health Management 28
        1.4.5   UAV 29
        1.4.6   Formal Methods for Autonomic Computing 32
        1.4.7   Software Engineering Aspects, Conclusions
                and Recommendations 33
  1.5   Approaches to Requirements Engineering for Autonomous
        Systems 35

1.5.1   Goal-Oriented Requirements Engineering   36
1.5.2   The ASSL Approach to Requirements Engineering
           for Autonomic Systems   36
1.5.3   Requirements for Autonomous Unmanned
           Air Systems   38
1.6   Summary   39
References   41

2   Handling Autonomy Requirements for ESA Systems   47
2.1   Introduction   47
2.1.1   Autonomy and Automation.   49
2.1.2   Levels of Autonomy for ESA Missions   49
2.2   Requirements Engineering, Specification Models and Formal
      Methods for Aerospace.   50
2.2.1   Requirements Specification and Modeling   50
2.2.2   Requirements Engineering for Autonomous Systems   51
2.2.3   Generic Autonomy Requirements   51
2.3   Generic Autonomy Requirements for Space Missions.   55
2.3.1   Space Mission Requirements Analysis   55
2.3.2   Earth-Orbiting Missions   57
2.3.3   Interplanetary Missions   64
2.4   Controller Architectures for Robotic Systems   70
2.4.1   Architectural Issues Related to Autonomy   70
2.4.2   Controller Architectures for Robotic Systems   71
2.5   Formal Methods for ARE   74
2.5.1   Goal-Oriented Requirements Engineering   75
2.5.2   Awareness Modeling   78
2.5.3   ASSL   80
2.5.4   KnowLang   83
2.6   Case Studies: Specifying Autonomy Requirements.   90
2.6.1   Handling Autonomy Requirements with KnowLang.   90
2.6.2   Specifying Autonomy Requirements for Voyager
           with ASSL.   94
2.7   Summary   99
References   100

3   Autonomy Requirements Engineering   105
3.1   Introduction   105
3.2   ARE: Autonomy Requirements Engineering   106
3.2.1   GAR: Generic Autonomy Requirements.   107
3.2.2   GORE for ARE   108
3.2.3   Understanding ARE.   108
3.2.4   From Goals to Self-* Objectives   110
3.2.5   Recording Self-* Objectives   118

3.2.6 Variability Points and Degree of Goals Satisfaction
in ARE 121
3.3 The Spacecraft in BepiColombo Mission 126
3.3.1 Planetary Orbiter 127
3.3.2 Mercury Magnetospheric Orbiter 128
3.3.3 Composite Module (MPO and MMO) 130
3.3.4 Transfer Module 130
3.3.5 Carrier Spacecraft 130
3.4 GORE for BepiColombo 131
3.4.1 Mission Objectives 131
3.4.2 Environmental Constraints for BepiColombo 138
3.5 Autonomy Requirements for BepiColombo 139
3.5.1 Applying GAR for Space Missions 140
3.5.2 Goals Model for BepiColombo with Self-* Objectives ... 146
3.5.3 Specifying the Autonomy Requirements
with KnowLang 155
3.6 Summary 170
References 170

4 Verification and Validation of Autonomy Requirements 173
4.1 Introduction 173
4.2 Background 174
4.3 AdaptiV 175
4.3.1 Model Checking 176
4.3.2 Stabilization Science 178
4.3.3 State Space Reduction 180
4.3.4 High Performance Computing 180
4.3.5 Compositional Verification 181
4.3.6 Operational Monitors 182
4.3.7 System Inputs 183
4.4 Summary 183
References 184

5 Summary and Future Work 185

Appendix A: Requirements for Cognitive Capabilities of UAS 189

Appendix B: ASSL Specification of Voyager Image-Processing
Behavior 193

Appendix C: BepiColombo Autonomy Requirements Specification
with KnowLang 229

Index 247

Chapter 1
Software Engineering for Aerospace: State of the Art

Abstract This chapter discusses the state-of-the-art of software engineering for aerospace. To be successful, software engineering for aerospace must take into account the fact that aerospace systems need to meet a variety of standards and high safety requirements, and therefore, the development of aerospace systems emphasizes verification, validation, certification, and testing. This chapter discusses the complexity of software development along with the software engineering process currently employed by leading aerospace organizations such as NASA, ESA, Boeing, and Lockheed Martin. Their software development projects apply a spiral-based methodology where the emphasis is on verification. Methods, techniques, and architectural approaches for aerospace are also discussed. A new class of autonomous aerospace systems (such as UAV and robotic space-exploration systems) is currently emerging to incorporate features like integrated health management, self-monitoring and on-board decision making. The lack of proper, yet dedicated, software engineering for autonomous aerospace systems is the reason for many inherent problems related to requirements, modeling, and implementation. Requirements engineering for autonomous systems appears to be a wide open research area with only a limited number of approaches yet considered.

1.1 Introduction: The Specifics of Aerospace Industry

The Aerospace Industry can be characterized as very complex where manufacturers such as Boeing and Airbus and space programs such as those of ESA and NASA produce long life-cycle products (up to 34 years). Today, it is one of those industries where final products or services result from the cooperation of a huge number of enterprises and the production and design of different parts of aircraft is outsourced or executed in collaboration with other enterprises. For example, Boeing has outsourced more than 70 % of the design and production of the Boeing 787 Dreamliner. Thus, the specifics of the Aerospace Industry require tight cooperation among companies of varying sizes leading to dependencies of different levels. Moreover, the diversity of the production, often results in non-planable R&D cooperation, changing consensus/conflict constellations and many iterations of the design and development

© Springer International Publishing Switzerland 2014   1
E. Vassev and M. Hinchey, *Autonomy Requirements Engineering for Space Missions*,
NASA Monographs in Systems and Software Engineering,
DOI 10.1007/978-3-319-09816-6_1

processes. Thus, manufacturers such as Boeing or Airbus depend on the performance and abilities of their strategic suppliers.

1.1.1 Emphasis on Safety

The Aerospace Industry (e.g., NASA and ESA) follows the "Design for Minimum Risk" strategy, which emphasises safety principles. This is necessary to ensure that an adequate level of safety is properly specified, designed and implemented. The following are basic safety principles and methods common to several industries [49]. These are used to minimize the possibility of accidents and reduce the consequences of an accident should one occur:

- hazard elimination and limitation;
- barriers and interlocks;
- fail-safe design;
- failure risk minimization;
- monitoring, recovery and escape.

Often in combination, these principles and methods, which are the basic elements of a comprehensive safety design program, are used as deemed appropriate.

1.1.2 Standardization

Standards are fundamental to all business aspects of aerospace "as the vehicles for interoperability and interconnectivity; the common requirements to ensure reliability, repeatability, and quality; the basis for safety and certification; and one of the most powerful mechanisms for propagating change" [76]. Standards form the single largest source of technical data used in the global design, build and support of aerospace products. The results of an overly complex, often duplicative aerospace standards system are increased costs associated with the harmonization of regulatory requirements based on competing standards, increased costs associated with multiple conformity assessments and quality management audits due to multiple standards, and increased costs and inefficiencies associated with redundant and overlapping standards and standards infrastructures.

The Aerospace Industries Association Board of Governors provides:

- key requirements for standards systems that are intended to be used to support the global Aerospace Industry;
- major standards development models and organizations used today in light of the defined requirements;
- a set of recommendations for optimum standards required by the Aerospace Industry.

Both NASA and ESA are providing their own standards in particular for Software Engineering. For example, ESA's Software Engineering division, Software Engineering and Standardization section [70] is responsible for software standardisation, both for internal ESA standards through the co-chairmanship of the BSSC (Board for Software Standardisation and Control), and for external software standards—mainly with ECSS (European Cooperation for Space Standardisation) and sometimes with ISO.

1.1.3 Complexity

To cope up with the standards and safety regulations, the software developed for aerospace systems is under constant quality control. For example, ESA has run various initiatives to investigate software issues in projects, mainly related to problems with the time schedule and safety. One of the major discoveries was that the high complexity makes the link between the avionics system and its software very weak [71]. Due to increasing system complexity:

- the system definition (requirements and design) is completed later and later in the project;
- the software requirements are never stable and often software engineers have to implement requirements which are still moving when the software is already in AIT (Assembly, Integration and Testing);
- the software schedule becomes shorter and shorter.

1.1.4 Diversity of Platforms

Aerospace Production uses various operational platforms and runtime environments. For example, ESA uses different operating environments such as IRIX, Solaris, Linux, Windows, etc, for their products. The diversity of platforms introduces another level of complexity to the development process. Here we quote Peter van der Plas, a Simulation Engineer at Modeling & Simulation Group, European Space Agency: *Whenever ESA scientists request new functionality, we make the changes, issue a new version and test it on every platform. The more platforms we had the longer it took.*

1.2 Software Engineering Process for Aerospace

In general, for any software system to be developed, it is very important to choose the appropriate development lifecycle process (software process) for the project at hand because all other activities are derived from the process. The notion of *software process* means a set of activities whose goal is the development or evolution of software. The most generic activities in all kinds of software processes are:

- *specification*—determining the system's functionality and its development constraints;
- *development*—production of the software system;
- *validation*—checking whether the software is what the customer wants;
- *evolution*—changing the software in response to changing demands.

An aerospace software development process must take into account the fact that aerospace systems need to meet a variety of standards and also have high safety requirements. To cope with these aspects, the development of aerospace systems emphasizes verification, validation, certification, and testing. The software development process must be technically adequate and cost-effective for managing the design complexity and safety requirements of aerospace systems and for certifying their embedded software. Decomposing the project life cycle into phases organizes the entire development process into more manageable pieces. *The software development process should provide managers with incremental visibility into the progress being made at points in time that fit with the management and budgetary environments.* For most modern aerospace software development projects tackled by NASA, ESA, Boeing and Lockheed Martin some kind of spiral-based methodology is used over a waterfall process model where the emphasis is on verification [56]. The waterfall process model [61] is considered a classic software life cycle, where software evolution proceeds through an orderly sequence of transitions from one phase to the next in order. Such models resemble finite state machine descriptions of software evolution. The *waterfall model* and its derived versions have been perhaps most useful in helping to structure, staff, and manage large software development projects in complex organizational settings (e.g., NASA and ESA), which was one of its primary purposes [8, 61].

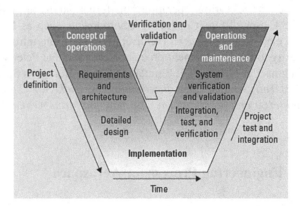

Fig. 1.1 A common view of the NASA/ESA Software Development Process [56]

As shown in Fig. 1.1, a common aerospace development process involves intensive verification, validation, and certification steps to produce sufficiently safe and reliable control systems [68]:

- The "Concept and Operations" phase (at ESA this phase is called "System Software Co-engineering" [68]) is intended to link the software development with the system requirements. System, in this instance, means any spacecraft/aircraft sub-system that generates on-board software requirements (examples: data-handling, attitude control, thermal control, power management).
- The Requirements Engineering and Architecture phase emphasises high-level modeling as a means of enforcing the completeness and consistency of the requirements. The hard real-time nature of most flight software imposes requirements for a thorough schedulability analysis and the use of specific scheduling policies (e.g., Ravenscar [18]).
- Detailed Design is about low-level system modeling. In this phase, modeling languages are also used with design methods, but often with a particular emphasis on hard real-time systems.
- Implementation can be done manually or automatically. Note that modeling allows automation of the life cycle through the automatic generation of flight code and some validation tests. Code is cross-compiled for specific space-qualified processors. The choice of language is influenced by the constraints arising from the use of the hardware in space.
- The Integration, Testing and Maintenance phases comprise a set of activities intended to validate the implementation and maintain the system once in operation. Both testing and verification may discover design and implementation flaws, which may result in repetition of the pre-implementation and implementation steps.

ECSS-E40 [21] is an ESA standard for developing software in the scope of a space system project. ECSS is a cooperative effort of the European Space Agency, national space agencies and European industry associations for the purpose of developing and maintaining common standards. ECSS-E40 emphasises a document-centric process model for developing Dependable On-Board Real Time software (DOBERT). The model is similar to the one shown in Fig. 1.1, where each document is expressed in CASEML, an XML-based description language. ECSS-E40 has been applied to a variety of ESA projects including the DOBERTSEE (Dependent On-Board Embedded Real-Time Software Engineering Environment)/Low-Cost On-Board Software Development Toolkit project [75], intended to produce an affordable and integrated Software Engineering Environment for avionics software.

1.2.1 Requirements Engineering and Modeling

Requirements engineering [5, 69] is the process of eliciting, documenting and communicating requirements. It manages changes to requirements and maintains traceability in requirements documents. Requirements can be written by using quality attributes known as software requirements specification. Software requirements reflect the needs of the users and procurers. Normally, requirements are related to requested services that must be provided by the future system, but they also can be requirements concerning product quality or constraints. Moreover, varying user perception and understanding of the system can result in either extremely abstract statements of services (e.g., "produce reports") or detailed features (e.g., mathematical formulae that should be implemented). Thus, in order to handle requirements properly, requirements engineering strives to classify requirements. There are two major types of requirement: functional and non-functional. Whereas functional requirements determine the operation of the future system, non-functional requirements are said to be about system qualities or constraints. According to the IEEE Recommended Practices for Software Requirements Specifications (known as IEEE Standard 830-1998) these two groups of requirements should address issues such as [42]:

- *Functionality*—Emphasizes the software functions; i.e., services to be delivered to the users.
- *External interfaces*—Covers issues related to how the software will interact with people or with other software and hardware systems.
- *Performance*—Emphasizes performance issues (for the system in general and for particular system functions), such as speed, availability, response time, recovery time, etc.
- *Quality attributes*—Measures of the quality of the future system, e.g., portability, correctness, maintainability, security, etc.
- *Constraints*—Emphasizes design, hardware, cultural, and other issues that may affect the implementation. For example, required standards, implementation language, policies for database integrity, resource limits, operating environments, etc.

1.2.1.1 Specification and Modeling

Practice has shown that formal languages can be extremely useful in *requirements specification and system modeling* in the development of safety-critical systems such as *avionics software* where software failures can easily cause safety hazards. For example, for the development of the control software for the C130J Hercules II, Lockheed Martin applied a correctness-by-construction approach based on formal (SPARK) and semi-formal (Consortium Requirements Engineering) languages [3]. The results have showed that this combination was sufficient to eliminate a large number of errors and brought Lockheed Martin significant dividends in terms of high quality and less costly software. At ESA, requirements specification and system modeling can be related to [34]:

- data typing (in XML or ASN.1);
- data organisation, e.g., in classes and objects;

- behavior—behavioral modeling languages allow for formal representation of the sequence of states and events that the system engages in. These are quite often based on state machines that exchange sequences of events, based on a synchronous or asynchronous model.

Among the most interesting languages for specification and modeling used in the space domain are SDL, Esterel, Lustre, a variety of languages implemented in Mat-Lab/Simulink, etc. In particular, SDL, a standardised language used for formal modeling of concurrent finite state machines, has been primarily used for telecommunication protocols. It has been proved useful for some space applications [69]:

- workbench of a data handling system (Data Management System (DMS) Design Validation—DDV);
- Failure Detection, Isolation and Recovery (FDIR) of the Meteosat Second Generation spacecraft—the on-board software requirements for the avionics reconfiguration were modelled;
- SpaceWire protocol providing a standard for the communication language.

Lustre is a synchronous dataflow programming language [34] for programming reactive systems. Lustre has been successfully applied in the development of automatic control software for critical applications such as the software for Airbus and the fight control software for Rafale fighters [7]. Other formal languages may be used to verify particular functions of the software requirements (e.g., B, VDM, PVS). The advantages emerge from the rigorous mathematical semantics and the high level of abstraction, thus allowing for the development of software tools for automatic verification and validation.

Often, requirements are expressed in a natural language. To correctly process such requirements (e.g., to allow for traceability and to avoid the ambiguity stemming from the use of natural language) natural language analysis is required. A tool providing for natural language analysis is LEXIOR (LEXical analysis for Improvement of Requirements) [16]. The tool includes a database of best practice rules for writing requirements specifications, as well as a lexical analysis and parsing engine for pre-processing, content verification and interactive writing and editing according to a set of predefined best practices.

1.2.1.2 Requirements Metrics

Requirements metrics are an important part of measuring software that is being developed. These include *requirements volatility metric* (how much program's requirements change once coding beings), *requirements traceability metric*, *requirements versioning metric* and *requirements completeness metric*. Measuring requirements manually is a tedious task and automated requirements tools should be used. Such tools might help us to manage requirements in an efficient way. For example, IBM Rational Requisition, Dynamic Object Oriented Requirements Systems and Requirements Use Case Tool are some prominent automated requirements tools used to measure software. Traceability and versioning of requirements is offered by many commercial tools such as DOORS or IRQA. It is also implemented in the DOBERT-SEE [75] software engineering environment.

1.2.1.3 Characteristics of Requirements

To measure the quality of requirements, Requirements Engineering defines characteristics for good requirements. The following is a short description of NASA's classification for attributes of good requirements [5]:

- *Necessary*—The product/system cannot meet the real needs of the user without it.
- *Unambiguous*—If a requirement has multiple interpretations, the system that is built may not match what the user wanted. Clarity is very important.
- *Complete*—It is impossible to know all of a system's future requirements, but all of the known ones should be specified.
- *Consistent*—Requirements must not conflict with each other.
- *Traceable*—The source of each requirement should be identified.
- *Verifiable*—Each requirement must be able to be verified by test, analysis, inspection, or demonstration. Avoid negative requirements where possible, for example, "The component shall not overheat".

1.2.2 Managing Safety and Risk

Requirements for complex electronics come from system and sub-system requirements, safety, and the constraints imposed by the chosen architecture, the technology and tools used, the environment the device will operate in, and the implementation environment. For many NASA systems, safety is an especially important source of requirements. Safety requirements may feed into the system requirements, and then flow down to the complex electronics, or are directly invoked at each level of requirements decomposition.

The development process should help software engineers specify the required level of safety to ensure they design and implement secure systems. NASA engineers can express software safety as a set of features and procedures that ensure predictable system performance under normal and abnormal conditions. Furthermore, when developers specify software safety properly, "the likelihood of an unplanned event occurring is minimized and its consequences controlled and contained" [37]. NASA uses two *software safety standards* [51] that define: (1) four qualitative hazard severity levels-catastrophic, critical, marginal, and negligible; and (2) probability levels-probable, occasional, remote, and improbable. Hazard severity and probability are correlated to derive a risk index for prioritizing risk resolution (see Table 1.1).

One principle of system safety is that every hazard associated with or presented by a system is known and understood fully before it is allowed to operate [49].

Table 1.1 NASA's risk index determination [51]

Hazard severity	Hazard probability			
	Probable	Occasional	Remote	Improbable
Catastrophic	1	1	2	3
Critical	1	2	4	4
Marginal	2	3	4	5
Negligible	3	4	5	5

Automation and autonomic behavior must be explored with all possible hazards. In a study by the NASA Engineering and Safety Center, the following guiding principles were published for use by the teams who are responsible for the safety of design [53]:

- Define a clear and simple set of prioritized program needs, objectives, and constraints, including safety, that form the validation basis for subsequent work.
- Manage and lead the program with a safety focus, simple and easy-to-understand management structures, and clear lines of authority and responsibility among the elements.
- Specify safety and reliability requirements through a triad of fault tolerance, bounding failure probability, and adhering to proven practices and standards.
- Manage complexity by keeping the primary mission objectives as simple and minimal as possible and adding complexity to the system only where necessary to achieve these objectives.
- Conceive the right system conceptual design early in the life cycle by thoroughly exploring risks from the top down, and using a risk-based design loop to iterate the operations concept, the design, and the requirements until the system meets mission objectives at minimum complexity and is achievable within constraints.
- Build the system right by applying a multilayered "defense in-depth" approach of following proven design and manufacturing practices, holding independent reviews, inspecting the end product, and employing a "test like you fly, fly like you test" philosophy.
- Seek and collect warning signs and precursors to safety, mission success, and development risks throughout the life cycle, and integrate those into a total risk picture with appropriate mitigation activities.

1.2.3 Dealing with Complexity

Contemporary aerospace systems are often designed and implemented as multi-component systems, where the components are self-contained and reusable, thus requiring high independency and complex synchronization. Moreover, the components of more sophisticated systems are considered as agents (multi-agent systems) incorporating some degree of intelligence. Note that intelligent agents are considered to be the key to realization of self-adaptive systems [31]. Developing aerospace systems usually involves [89]:

- multi-component systems where you can't always model inter-component interactions and system-level impact;
- elements of AI;
- autonomous systems;
- evolving systems;
- high-risk and high-cost systems, often intended to perform missions with significant societal and scientific impacts;
- rigid design constraints;
- the potential for extremely tight design space;
- highly risk-driven systems, where you can't always capture or understand the risks and uncertainty.

1.2.4 Design

Similar to most organizations working on software projects, ESA and NASA consider preliminary (also called architectural or conceptual) and detailed design. The objective of the design phases (preliminary and detailed) is to create a design that will correctly and completely implement the requirements.

1.2.4.1 Preliminary Design

For the preliminary design, the main goal is to map out how the future system will perform the functions specified in the requirements, within the constraints of the hardware devices, the defined interfaces, and the environment the devices will operate within. At this phase, the software engineers need to maintain a systems perspective and look at the system operations and interactions with the other systems (or subsystems). For example, at ESA the *architectural design* is part of the technical specification as a *top-level architecture* [67]. During preliminary design, a high-level design concept is created, which will implement the complex electronics requirements. This design concept may be expressed as functional block diagrams, design and architecture descriptions, sketches, and/or behavioral description languages.

Some of the traditional space design methods employed by ESA [67] are HOOD4 [28] and HRT-HOOD3 [10] (Hard Real-Time HOOD). Both are based on HOOD (Hierarchical Object-Oriented Design) [57]. With the HOOD4 approach a software engineer can concentrate on the required functionality and does not have to care about a certain hardware configuration which may have to be changed when he has finished the implementation. HOOD4 tackles the problem of software distribution in a threefold manner: Firstly, it introduces clearly defined planes in a design where a cut can easily be done without impacting the logic of the software system. Secondly, the HRTS provides the means needed to establish the communication channels between the physically separated partitions. Thirdly, it allows for the provision of timing information from which a performance prediction can be derived. This allows for the evaluation of the performance of a hardware and software configuration during the design phase. Based on the results of the performance prediction, the optimum hardware configuration can be evaluated in advance. The HRT-HOOD development process is divided into two phases: a logical, followed by a physical architecture phase. The former supports hierarchical decomposition of the functional requirements of the system. This results in a collection of objects of various types and properties. The later addresses a system's non-functional requirements and the constraints of the underlying execution environment. ESA uses HOOD4 for the development of ground systems and HRT-HOOD3 for the development of on-board systems. HOOD4 is also largely used for the on-board systems in Eurofighter and Airbus.

Other methods for preliminary design employed by ESA are [67]:

- UML and packages, generally after a UML requirements modeling. In particular HRT-UML is an adaptation of UML aimed at keeping the design engineering qualities of HOOD. The method has been assessed against the AOCS Framework by an ESA trainee. HRT-UML is evolving towards a profile of UML 2.0
- methods allowing for the expression of the variability of an application domain, and used for generic architectures: design patterns, features, aspects, etc.
- behavioral languages such as SDL, Lustre, Esterel, etc.

Note that the preliminary design is often used to identify *inconsistencies*, *misunderstandings*, and *ambiguities* in requirements.

1.2.4.2 Detailed Design

For avionics, the detailed design phase primarily consists of design synthesis. This process takes the architectural (or conceptual) design models and translates these into a low-level design, which actually defines the software components, modules and interfaces of the system in consideration. In general, detailed design transforms concept alternatives, preliminary physical architectures, design specifications, and technical requirements into final, cross-disciplinary design definitions. These definitions are documented in the Detailed Design Document (DDD). The DDD is a comprehensive specification of the code to be implemented [22].

At this phase, software engineers must first complete the *top–down decomposition* of the software started in the preliminary design phase and then outline the processing to be carried out by each software component. Note that detailed design must continue the structured approach imposed by the preliminary design without introducing unnecessary complexity. A good practice is that software engineers verify detailed designs in design reviews, level by level. *Review of the design by walkthrough or inspection before coding is a more efficient way of eliminating design errors than testing.*

At this stage, design patterns might be applied. A design pattern [27] is an encapsulated set of solutions, alternatives, and rules that lead to solutions, and/or process guidelines for dealing with a design problem arising in a particular context. Each design pattern relies on, results in, and/or interacts with other contexts, problems, and solutions addressed in other patterns. In avionics, patterns are often applied to combine observations, reinterpretations, rational reconstructions, and redesigns of the Avionics Control Systems. An Avionics Control System (ACS) is the main navigation system of an aircraft. An ACS continuously collects sensor data to estimate the actual state of an aircraft, computes desired aircraft state with respect to guidance modes, and performs actions that advise pilots and/or directly manipulate aircraft effectors in ways that bring the actual and desired states in closer agreement. ACS patterns [15] describe domain-specific architecture concerns and steps in the construction of an ACS using a minimal vocabulary (e.g., "components", "interfaces", "functions", "attributes"), and with minimal commitment to how these should be expressed within any particular design method, notation, engineering tool, or development process. However, because of the critical impact of the ACS on human safety, it is essential to capture the resulting designs in appropriate formalisms and semi-formalisms that can be analyzed and reasoned about.

1.2.5 Implementation

To implement the system in question, the design must be translated into a machine readable form. Usually, the formal and semi-formal design models can be used to generate the implementation automatically especially in the presence of detailed design. Alternatively, the implementation is done by developers using implementation languages such as C, C++, Java, ADA, etc. One of the popular implementation languages at ESA is SystemC [1]. SystemC is a set of C++ classes and macros which provide an event-driven simulation kernel in C++, together with signals, events, and synchronization primitives. SystemC is generally applied to system-level modeling, architectural exploration, software development, functional verification, and high-level synthesis.

One of the most widely used programming styles in Avionics is the object-oriented programming (OOP) paradigm. This is especially relevant to software reuse, which allows developers to implement/test/debug complex, task-specific components that then can be trusted to run in other software programs.

1.2.6 Testing, Verification and Validation

From a process perspective, the Verification and Validation Processes may be similar in nature, but the objectives are fundamentally different. Verification shows proof of compliance with requirements that the product can meet—each "shall" statement is proven though performance of a test, analysis, inspection, or demonstration [54]. Validation shows that the system accomplishes the intended purpose in the intended environment, i.e., it meets the expectations of the customer and other stakeholders as shown through performance of a test, analysis, inspection, or demonstration. Verification testing relates back to the approved requirements set and can be performed at different stages in the product life cycle. The approved specifications, models, design and other configuration documentation establish the configuration baseline of the implemented system, which may have to be modified at a later time. Without a verified baseline and appropriate configuration controls, later modifications could be costly or cause major performance problems.

1.3 Methods, Techniques and Architecture Approaches for Aerospace

1.3.1 Formal Methods

Formal methods originate from formal logic and refer to a plethora of mathematically-based activities where both notations and tools with mathematical basis are used. Formal notations (also known as formal languages) are used to precisely and unambiguously specify system requirements or to model system design. Formal tools provide the needed formal support to prove correctness of specified system properties and eventually correctness of their implementation.

Formal methods provide a vast family of formal notations in the form of formal specification languages (sometimes called modeling languages). In general, we use these to precisely describe, with the logical underpinning of mathematics, features of the system under consideration at a higher level of abstraction than the one provided by the implementation. Thus, formal languages are used to provide a formal and neutral, i.e., implementation-independent, representation (often called formal specification) of systems. In avionics, formal methods are used for requirements specification, system modeling and code generation, and validation. However, in order to define an appropriate basis for reasoning about formal specifications, formal languages must have both a well-defined context-free grammar and a well-defined formal semantics. Whereas grammars help formal methods to process sentences written in a formal language, a formal semantics provides the meaning of those sentences. Here a formal semantics provides logical rules of truth-conditions expressed in terms of truth relative to various parameters, thus allowing for automated reasoning. In general, we classify formal specification languages into three main classes:

- *Model-oriented* formal languages support specification and construction of a mathematical model of the system under consideration. The goal is the derivation of an explicit model of the system's desired behavior in terms of abstract mathematical objects. Note that the model-oriented approach (also called constructive) is typically associated with the use of definitions. The approach is exemplified by formal languages such as ASM (Abstract State Machines), B-Method, RAISE (Rigorous Approach to Industrial Software Engineering), VDM (Vienna Development Method), ASSL (Autonomic System Specification Language), the Z notation, etc.
- *Property-oriented* formal languages have syntax identical to (or close to) a formal logic syntax providing some formal mathematical baseline. This class of languages (also called descriptive) is generally associated with the use of axioms. Thus, property-oriented formal languages rely on a special axiomatic semantics (probably expressed with first-order predicate logic) to express pre-conditions and post-conditions of operations over abstract data types, and on an algebraic semantics (based on multi-sorted algebras) to relate properties of a system over its entities. Some examples of property-oriented languages are Larch and the OBJ family of languages (including CafeOBJ).
- Formal languages considered as *process algebras*. These have evolved to meet the needs of concurrent, distributed, and real-time systems. They usually describe the behavior of such systems by describing their algebras of communicating processes. Such languages are CSP (Communicating Sequential Processes) and CCS (Calculus of Communicating Systems).

However, not all formal languages can be classified in just one of the categories above. For example, the RAISE development method is based on extending a model-based specification language (specifically, VDM-SL) with concurrent and temporal aspects.

1.3.2 Software Verification and Validation

Formal methods have been considered as software engineering practices helping to create reliable software and software that maximizes the probability of meeting the requirements. This is due to the fact that formal methods usually come with both a formal notation and a toolset. Whereas the former helps to define aspects of a system mathematically, the latter allows for automatic (or semi-automatic) reasoning about that system. The family of formal methods tools includes theorem provers and model checkers. Principle verification techniques for software (or hardware) systems are *simulation, testing, deductive verification*, and *model checking*. For both simulation and testing we need executable prototyping models of the system, where the evaluation is based on certain inputs and expected outputs. Deductive verification usually refers to the use of axioms and logical reasoning and is usually performed manually by a verification expert.

A promising, and lately one of the most popular, verification technique is *model checking* [14], a formal verification technique for automated software validation where automatic reasoning is provided to verify that a specification model meets the system requirements and that the algorithms are specified (or implemented) properly. The approach advocates formal verification tools whereby software programs are automatically checked for specific flaws by considering correctness properties expressed in a temporal logic [14]. Model checking strives to check the desired correctness properties by performing exhaustive testing on a special state graph (often called a labeling transition system) representing the system under consideration as a finite state machine. Note that temporal logics are used because they provide operators, which when associated with models, convey different notions of time. Thus, they allow for formalization of rules related to system evolution over time. Numerous formal tools allowing verification by model-checking have been developed, such as Spin, Emc, Cwb, Tav, Mec, Jack, Concurrency Factory, etc. However, despite best efforts and the fact that it has proved to be a revolutionary advance in addressing the correctness of critical systems, model checking for large and highly-complex systems such as spacecraft or aircraft is still a tedious task. The most serious drawback of model checking is the so-called state explosion. In general, complex systems can have extremely large state graphs and systems with infinite state spaces cannot be handled.

Note that formal methods do not eliminate the need of testing, but rather may provide a new means of testing. Formal methods can be used to create formal specifications, which subsequently can be used for automatic test case generation. In this approach, usually, test generation techniques partition the input domain into a set of sub-domains where the specified behavior is considered uniform [39]. Test cases are generated from each sub-domain or can be generated from a few related sub-domains. Practice has shown that model-oriented formal languages generally help in writing model-based specifications, which are appropriate for test case generation. Specifications written in the Z notation, B, or VDM have been used to derive test cases. However, test case generation often requires powerful analysis, which can be provided by formal tools such as theorem provers. In addition, a test case, generated from a formal specification of a state-based system, may require the determination of a sequence of operations to set up the internal state of the system in question.

1.3.3 SOA

Service Oriented Architecture (SOA) based on Web Services technology [90] provides flexibility, reuse and loose coupling. The main goal of SOA is to achieve loose coupling among interacting components providing services. A service is a unit of work, implemented and offered by a service provider, to achieve desired results for a service consumer. Both provider and consumer are roles played by software agents (systems or subsystems). The basic idea of SOA is to increase the *interoperability*, *flexibility*, and *extensibility* of the designed system and their individual components. In the implementation of any system, we may want to be able to reuse components of existing systems, however doing that we usually introduce additional dependencies between the components. SOA strives to minimize these dependencies by using loosely coupled components. SOA achieves loose coupling among interacting components by employing two architectural constraints:

1. Use only a small set of simple and ubiquitous interfaces to all participant components with only generic semantics encoded in them.
2. Each interface can send on request descriptive messages explaining both its functionality and capabilities. These messages define the structure and semantics of the services provided.

These constraints depart significantly from that of OOP, which strongly suggests that you should bind data and its processing together. When some component needs a functionality not provided by itself, it asks the system for the required service. If another component of the system has this capability, their location will be provided and finally the client component can consume the service using the common interface in the provider component. The interface of a SOA component must be simple and clear enough to be easily implemented in different platforms, both hardware and software.

NASA Goddard Space Flight Center (GSFC) successfully utilizes SOA in its GSFC Mission Services Evolution Center (GMSEC), an integrated effort across multiple GSFC organizations to provide GSFC mission services through the year 2017 [52]. The advantages are increased scalability, reusability, and flexibility in IT systems. This can result in better solutions at lower costs delivered faster compared to traditional development methods.

Moreover, SOA might be used to provide loose technology coupling needed to support the vast supplier networks of the Aerospace Industry. Flexibility and reuse is needed because globally distributed supplier network partners in aerospace can change over time; loose technology coupling is required since different companies use different applications running on different platforms for managing their work.

1.3.4 Multi-agent Systems

The basic idea behind a Multi-Agent System (MAS) is that of a society of autonomous software agents acting independently, but interacting to achieve user and system-wide goals. By giving each agent the ability to act independently of the others, many of the common disadvantages associated with large-scale distributed computing such as *synchronization, single point of failure* and *difficulty of modifying the system at runtime* can be mitigated. MASs deal with problems which are beyond the capabilities of an individual agent. Because the capacity of an individual agent is limited by its knowledge, its computing resources and its perspective, the goal of multi-agent systems research is to find methods that help software engineers to build complex systems composed of autonomous agents that operate on both local and distributed knowledge and overcome their individual limitations through cooperative work and shared goals. Note that to study and develop a MAS properly, we must go beyond the individual intelligence of a single agent and pay attention to the problem-solving capabilities of the entire system, i.e., problem-solving that has social aspects [74]. As Durfee and Lesser point out in [20], a MAS can be defined as a loosely coupled network of problem solvers that interact to solve problems that are beyond the individual capabilities or knowledge of each problem solver.

Definitions of "agent" have been the subject of much debate and as a result, the computer science community has come up with various such definitions [26, 35, 47, 62, 94]. Although all the definitions referenced above are different, they all share a basic set of concepts: the notion of an agent, its environment, and autonomy. For example, according to Wooldridge's definition [94], an agent is "a software (or hardware) entity that is situated in some environment and is able to autonomously react to changes in that environment". Going into more detail [62], an agent can be viewed as an entity that perceives its environment through special sensors and acts upon that environment through actuators (also called effectors). As shown in Fig. 1.2 illustrating this definition, an agent interacts with the surrounding environment by using sensors in order to observe certain aspects of its environment and actuators to perform actions and eventually change the environment.

Ideally, the environment is everything external to the agent. The environment may be physical (e.g., the computer hardware) or it may be the computing environment (e.g., data sources, computing resources, and other agents). Moreover, an agent is not only situated in its environment, but it may also act autonomously in response to environmental changes [94]. The concept of autonomy means that an agent exercises control over its own actions, thus eventually resulting in scheduling certain actions for execution. Thus, a common agent function f maps the perceptions to actions performed in the environment, i.e., an agent program runs to produce f:

$$[f : P* \rightarrow A] \tag{1.1}$$

Note that the clear borderline between the two notions—agent and environment, leads to the conclusion that agents are inherently distributable.

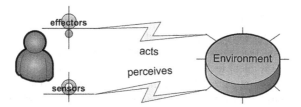

Fig. 1.2 An agent perceives and acts in its environment

1.3.4.1 Core Attributes of Agents

Despite the diversity of the definitions of agents, there are some essential attributes typical for all the agents called the "notions of agency" [95]. These attributes are divided into three categories: weak, stronger and optional. The weak notions, listed below, are considered essential:

- *Autonomy*. Autonomous agents may respond unpredictably (or later, or not at all) to external influence, such as messages from other agents; agents can say "no". Thus, most practical agents include some kind of thread of control.
- *Reactivity*. Agents are typically situated in a rich and dynamic environment. Environmental changes are detected using sensors, and changes are affected using actuators (or effectors). Agents are "reactive", in that they will respond in a timely way to certain environmental conditions.
- *Proactivity*. An agent will select appropriate programmer-defined actions or plans, and execute them in order to achieve its goals. Actions and plans may fail, because the environment may change at any time. Thus, agents must be prepared to adapt.
- *Social ability*. MAS use social concepts, such as speech-like communication, cooperation, and competition, in order to organize their activities effectively.

The stronger notion of agency represents a much narrower definition: the agent's internal state should be described or implemented in human or "mentalistic" terms. So an agent may have knowledge, belief, desires, intentions, capabilities, trust and even emotions. The optional notions are:

- *Rationality*. An agent will always act to achieve its goals.
- *Veracity*. An agent will never deliberately mislead.
- *Benevolence*. An agent will never adopt directly conflicting goals.
- *Mobility*. An agent may migrate between hosts across a network.

1.3.4.2 Intelligent Agents

Intelligent agents are a special category of autonomous agents providing additional concepts that may help us realize intelligent systems, e.g., systems capable of self-management. This is the reason why a great deal of research effort is devoted to developing intelligent agent technology, which has become a rapidly growing area of research and new application development. Although very popular, there is no commonly agreed definition of the term "intelligent agent". Probably the most popular definition is the one given by IBM research as:

> Intelligent agents are software entities that carry out some set of operations on behalf of a user with some autonomy and employ either knowledge or representation of the user's goals and desires. [30]

However, there is consensus that *autonomy*, i.e., the ability to act without human intervention or such of other systems, is the key feature of an intelligent agent.

Table 1.2 Agent characteristics

Agent	Autonomous
	Able to communicate with other agents and user
	Monitors the state of its execution environment
Intelligent agent	Able to use symbols and abstractions
	Able to exploit significant amounts of domain knowledge
	Capable of adaptive goal-oriented behavior
	Capable of operation in real-time
	Able to learn from the environment
	Able to communicate with the user

Table 1.2 presents some common features of agents and those of intelligent agents as presented in the Agent Builder toolkit [2], a framework for constructing intelligent agents.

As shown in Table 1.2, the central idea of agents is delegation of tasks that an agent can autonomously perform on behalf of the user who delegates those tasks. Thus, in order to be operational, an agent must be able to communicate with the user to receive instructions and provide results back to the same. Based on the level of intelligence, we distinguish four basic types of intelligent agents (increasing intelligence) [62]:

- simple reflex agents;
- model-based reflex agents;
- goal-based agents;
- utility-based agents;
- learning agents.

1.3.4.3 Agent Interconnections in Aerospace Systems

Agents exist in a collaborative world established by the MAS they are part of. Considering the agents' collaborative nature and the specifics of the aerospace systems (recall the emphasis is on safety), there are some conclusions that agents can affect each other in three distinct ways [91].

1. Safety requirements that affect multiple agents are incorporated into the mechanism design as system constraints, and define the feasible set of solutions that the agents can agree to.
2. The costs incurred by each agent depend on the choice of feasible solution, and can vary greatly depending on the way in which a solution is selected.
3. It is important to consider the fairness of a solution concept, as agents will likely evaluate their outcome relative to the outcomes achieved by other agents, affecting

the satisfaction with which they view the overall process and the likelihood that they will continue to participate as expected.

Note that, in order to enforce system constraints without violating the independence of individual agents, a distributed or decentralized algorithm shall be used. A distributed algorithm is one in which the agents are given the opportunity to signal their intended course of action, and a central authority coordinates the process in order to achieve agreement as to a feasible solution to implement. A decentralized algorithm, on the other hand, does not include any component of central coordination, and relies on a protocol of peer-to-peer communication to ensure an appropriate solution is found. In this sense, decentralized algorithms are also distributed, where the central authority performs the trivial task of not affecting the mechanism.

1.3.4.4 MAS in Aerospace

The Livingstone Project

Livingstone [55] is a MAS developed at NASA Ames [93] as a health monitoring system. It uses a special symbolic, qualitative model of a physical system, such as a spacecraft, to infer its state and diagnose faults. Livingstone is one of the three parts of the Remote Agent (RA), an autonomous spacecraft controller developed by NASA Ames Research Center jointly with the Jet Propulsion Laboratory. The two other components are called Planner and Smart Executive. Whereas the former generates flexible sequences of tasks for achieving mission-level goals, the latter commands spacecraft systems to achieve those tasks. Remote Agent was demonstrated in flight on the Deep Space One mission (DS-1) in May 1999, which made it the first case where the control of an operational spacecraft was taken over by AI software [48]. Moreover, Livingstone is used in other control applications such as the control of a propellant production plant for Mars missions [13], the monitoring of a mobile robot [66], and Intelligent Vehicle Health Management (IVHM) for the X-37 experimental space transportation vehicle.

The structure and operation of Livingstone is illustrated in Fig. 1.3 [55]. As shown, the Mode Identification module (MI) estimates the current state of the system by tracking the commands issued to the device. It then compares the predicted state of the device against observations received from the actual sensors. If a discrepancy is noticed, Livingstone performs a diagnosis by searching for the most likely configuration of component states that are consistent with the observations. Using this diagnosis, the Mode Recovery module (MR) can compute a path to recover to a given goal configuration.

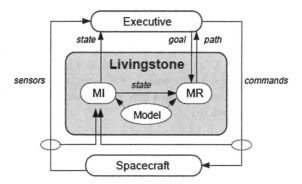

Fig. 1.3 Livingstone mode identification (MI) and mode recovery (MR) [55]

NASA's OCA Mirroring System

Orbital Communications Adaptor (OCA) Flight Controllers, in NASA's International Space Station Mission Control Center, use different computer systems to uplink, downlink, mirror, archive and deliver files to and from the International Space Station (ISS) in real time. The OCA Mirroring System (OCAMS) [65] is a MAS that is operational in NASA's Mission Control Center. From a MAS perspective, the OCAMS system is divided into three separate distributed agents running in a separate and special Brahms Hosting Environment [65]. Such an environment can run on any desired computer and network configuration, making the architecture easily adaptable to the computer architecture and network. The communication between the OCAMS components is established by using the so-called NASA Collaborative Infrastructure (CI). The CI is an infrastructure that provides an application programming interface and a set of services that allows components to:

- interact with structured messages (transport service);
- find one another (directory service);
- share data via a publish/subscribe service (data distribution service);
- be managed using a common interface (management service).

The components that make use of the CI are called agents or actors. The CI, in addition, provides process management tools to manage the *startup*, *monitoring*, and *shutdown* of actor hosting environments and their actors.

Lights out Ground Operations System

The Lights out Ground Operations System (LOGOS) is a prototype MAS developed by NASA to automate ground operations for satellites. LOGOS relies on a community of cooperative intelligent agents that perform ground operations by replacing human operators and using traditional ground system software tools, such as orbit generators, schedulers and command sequence planners [60]. In general, LOGOS provides a comprehensive environment that supports the development, deployment, and evaluation of evolving agent-based software concepts in the context of lights-out operations. Moreover, LOGOS supports evaluation of information visualization concepts and cognitive studies. Additionally LOGOS helps researchers realize how agents being "tool users" can be integrated into an agent community responsible for running ground control operations.

1.4 Autonomous and Autonomic Aerospace Systems

Over the years, both ESA and NASA missions have been gradually adding autonomy to flight and ground systems to increase the amount of science data returned from missions, perform new science, and reduce mission costs. In new space exploration initiatives, there is emphasis on both human and robotic exploration. Even when humans are involved in the exploration, human tending of space assets must be evaluated carefully during mission definition and design in terms of benefit, cost, risk, and feasibility. Risk and feasibility are major factors motivating the use of unmanned craft and the use of automation and robotic technologies where possible.

1.4.1 Autonomy Versus Automation

Both *autonomy* and *automation* refer to processes that may be executed independently from start to finish without any human intervention. *Automated processes* simply replace routine manual processes with software/hardware ones that follow a step-by-step sequence that may still include human participation. *Autonomous processes*, on the other hand, have the more ambitious goal of emulating human processes rather than simply replacing them.

An example of an automated ground data trending program would be one that regularly extracts from the data archive a set list of telemetry parameters, performs a standard statistical analysis of the data, outputs in report form the results of the analysis, and generates appropriate alerts regarding any identified anomalies. So, in contrast to an autonomous process, in this case the ground system performs no independent decision-making based on real-time events, and a human participant is required to respond to the outcome of the activity [79].

On the other hand, the more elaborate process of autonomy is displayed by a ground software program that independently identifies when communication with a spacecraft is possible, establishes the link, decides what files to uplink, uplinks those files, accepts downlinked data from the spacecraft, validates the downlinked data, requests retransmission as necessary, instructs the freeing-up of onboard storage as appropriate, and finally archives all validated data. This would be an example of a fully autonomous ground process for uplink/downlink [79].

1.4.2 Autonomic Computing

Autonomic Computing (AC) [40] emerged as the new multi-agent paradigm where the agents are cooperative (i.e., share common objectives) but also *autonomous* and capable of *self-management* [43]. In general, AC is a concept to describe computing systems that are intrinsically intended to reduce complexity through automation. Today, many researchers agree on the fact that AC provides the set of capabilities required to make computing systems self-managing via inherent *self-adaptation*. Typically, *adaptive systems* are contingent upon varying environments where they can reason about the environment and adapt to changing situations [29]. In that context, AC emphasizes adaptive features and other self-managing ones to provide solutions to one or more real world problems in one or more domains spanning intra or inter-domain applications. The "Vision of Autonomic Computing" [43] defines the concept of self-management as comprising four basic policies—*self-configuring*, *self-healing*, *self-optimizing*, and *self-protecting*. In addition, in order to achieve these *self-managing objectives* (behavior policies), an *autonomic system* (AS) must constitute the following self-* properties:

- *self-awareness*—aware of its internal state;
- *self-situation* (context awareness)—environment awareness, situation and context awareness;
- *self-monitoring*—able to monitor its internal components;
- *self-adjusting* (self-adaptiveness)—able to adapt to the changes that may occur.

Thus, despite their differences in terms of application domain and functionality, all ASs are capable of self-management and are driven by one or more self-management objectives. Note that this requirement automatically involves: (1) *self-diagnosis* (to analyze a problem situation and to determine a diagnosis), and (2) *self-adaptation* (to repair the discovered faults). The ability to perform adequate self-diagnosis depends largely on the quality and quantity of system knowledge. Moreover, AC recognizes two modes of self-healing: *reactive* and *proactive*. In reactive mode, an AS must effectively recover when a fault occurs, identify that fault, and when possible repair the same. In proactive mode, an AS monitors vital signs to predict and avoid health problems or reach undesirable risk levels.

1.4.2.1 Autonomic Element: The New Concept of Intelligent Agent

A key concept in the AC paradigm is the so-called *autonomic element* (AE). A widely accepted architecture for ASs considers AEs as the system's building blocks [40]. By its nature, an AE extends programming elements (i.e., objects, components, services) to define a *self-contained piece of software* with specified interfaces and explicit context dependencies. Essentially, an AE encapsulates rules, constraints and mechanisms for self-management, and can dynamically interact with other AEs of the AS in question to provide or consume computational services. As stated in [40], the basic structure of an AE is a special *control loop*. The latter is described as a

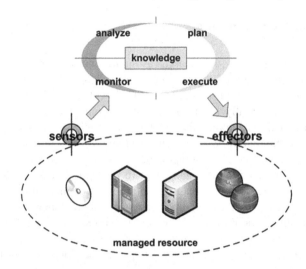

Fig. 1.4 Generic AE architecture

set of functionally related units: *monitor, analyzer, planner,* and *executor* where all share *knowledge*. By sharing knowledge, those units form an intelligent control loop that forms the self-managing behavior of the AE in question. A closer look at the generic structure of an AE is presented in Fig. 1.4. As depicted, an AE operates over a special *managed resource*. The latter is a generic presentation of software that can be managed by the control loop in order to leverage its functionality to a self-managing level. Here, through its control loop, an AE monitors the managed resource details, analyzes those details, plans adjustments, and executes the planned adjustments. It is important to mention that for these activities, an AE can use information from humans (administrators) as well as rules and policies defined (by humans) and learned by the AS [40]. Thus, a control loop helps an AE make decisions and controls the managed resource through monitoring and intensive interaction. Note that the managed resource is highly scalable [40], i.e., it can be any software system such as a file, a server, a database, a network, a middleware software, a standalone software application, a business object, etc.

A key factor in the success of AE self-management is the shared solution knowledge. Note that the lack of solution knowledge is a drawback for self-management. For example, today there are a number of maintenance mechanisms for installation, configuration, and maintenance. The vast diversity in system administration tools and distribution packaging formats creates unexpected problems in the administration of complex systems. In addition, the same problems are leveraged by the use of dynamic environments where application functionality can be added and removed dynamically. Here, common solution knowledge removes the complexity introduced by diversity in formats and installation tools. Moreover, when acquired in a consistent way, this very knowledge is used by the AE's control loop in contexts other than configuration and maintenance, such as *problem formation and optimization*.

1.4.2.2 Autonomic Computing Requirements

The first step towards development of a new computer system is to determine the system's requirements, which includes both elicitation and specification of the same. In general, requirements fall into two categories: *functional* and *non-functional*. Whereas the former define the system's functionality the latter emphasize system's qualities (e.g. performance) and constraints under which a system is required to operate. Like any computer system, ASs also need to fulfill specific requirements from these two categories. However, unlike other systems, the development of an AS is driven by the so-called *self-management objectives* and *attributes* (see Sect. 1.4.2), which introduce special requirements termed *self-* requirements* [88]. Despite their differences in terms of application domain and functionality, all s*autonomic systems* are capable of self-management and are driven by one or more self-management objectives.

Knowledge

In general, an AS is intended to possess awareness capabilities based on well-structured knowledge and algorithms operating over the same. Conceptually, knowledge can be regarded as a large complex aggregation composed of constituent parts representing knowledge of different kind. Every kind of knowledge may be used to derive knowledge models of specific domains of interest.

Awareness

One of the success factors for an AS is to employ its knowledge and become aware system. Such a system is able to sense and analyze its components and an environment where it operates. A primary task is to determine the state of each component and the status of the service-level objectives. Thus, an aware system should be able to notice a change and understand the implications of that change. Therefore, both self-monitoring and monitoring of the environment are key issues in awareness. Moreover, an aware system should be able to apply both pattern analysis and pattern recognition to determine normal and abnormal states.

Monitoring

Since monitoring is often regarded as a prerequisite for awareness, it constitutes a subset of awareness. For ASs, monitoring is the process of obtaining knowledge through a collection of sensors instrumented within the AS in question.

Adaptability

The core concept behind adaptability is the general ability of an AS to change its observable behavior and structure. This requirement is amplified by self-adaptation (or automatic adaptation). Self-adaptation helps an AS decide on-the-fly about an eventual adaptation on its own.

Autonomy

As the term AC already suggests, autonomy is one of the essential characteristics of ASs. AC aims at freeing human administrators from complex tasks, which typically requires a lot of decision making without human intervention.

Dynamicity

Dynamicity shows the system's ability to change at runtime. Whereas adaptability refers to the conceptual change of certain system aspects (this does not necessarily imply the change of components or services), dynamicity is about the technical ability to remove, add or exchange services and components.

Robustness

Robustness is a requirement that is claimed for almost every system. ASs should benefit from robustness since this may facilitate the design of system parts that deal with self-healing and self-protection. In addition, the system architecture could ease the application of measures in cases of errors and attacks.

Resilience

Adaptability may be considered as a quality attribute that is a prerequisite for *resilience* and *system agility* [46]. Resilience is a system quality attribute important to the Aerospace Industry. Resilience enables aerospace systems to bounce back from unanticipated disruptions as well as to equip aging systems with the ability to respond to changing operational requirements.

Mobility

Mobility enfolds all parts of the system: from mobility of code on the lowest granularity level via mobility of services or components up to mobility of devices or even mobility of the overall system.

1.4.3 Engineering Resilient Systems with Adaptability

Adaptability has been identified as a highly desirable and vital system key characteristic in ensuring that a system is not only agile but resilient as well [46]. A key research challenge in making aerospace systems resilient is addressing *affordability*, *adaptability*, and *effectiveness simultaneously*. Taking the development of system resilience as an inherent property into consideration, software engineers need to first examine how to quantify adaptability by identifying the elements of system adaptability as *adaptation*, the ability to *repurpose a system*, and the ability to *reconfigure a system* [58].

The adaptability elements (or adaptation factors) will identify how a system might be designed to take on an expected number of adaptations. The trade-off that is likely to be experienced with the adaptation factors is limiting design and innovation to save cost and reduce risk.

In [58] a framework for resilience is presented. The framework is based on two engineering approaches: Platform Based Engineering (PBE) and Model Based Systems Engineering (MBSE). The International Council on Systems Engineering (INCOSE) Life Cycle Management Working Group (LCMWG) has identified *acquisition*, *technology*, *regulatory*, *process adaptation*, *knowledge management*, and *key decision points* as some of the key perspectives of the a System Engineering Lifecycle for resilient systems [45].

1.4.3.1 Platform-Based Engineering

Platform-Based Engineering (PBE) has been offered as a cost-effective, risk-mitigated systems development approach that employs a common structure from which high-quality derivative products can be rapidly deployed. The PBE concept provides the means to deploy systems that are modular with the flexibility of adaptation for future advances in technology and evolution of the operational environment. While PBE is advantageous in providing adaptability, it is not without cost. Such costs can range from stifling innovation through standardization and limiting supply sources to costly research in maximizing the design of the initial platform to reach desired requirements across a wide spread spectrum of use.

1.4.3.2 Model-Based System Engineering

Model-Based System Engineering was conceived to overcome the drawbacks of *document-based system engineering*. While model-based approaches have been successfully employed for years in various fields of engineering, MBSE is relatively new. System design and communication is greatly enhanced through the use of MBSE which employs a unified model to integrate system requirements, design, analysis, and verification models. MBSE employs an integrated model that replaces individual, disjoint models.

1.4.4 Integrated Vehicle Health Management

Integrated Vehicle Health Management (IVHM) uses measurable system data in order to generate information which is used in the operational and maintenance decisions for a vehicle or fleet of vehicles. The current state of IVHM development is focused on putting a variety of sensor systems onboard spacecraft/aircraft along with intelligent software to automatically interpret the various sensor output streams. These data provide inputs to prognostic systems that then assess issues such as structural integrity and remaining component/subsystem life. Two state-of-the-art hardware health management systems are Honeywell's Aircraft Diagnostic and Maintenance System (ADMS) and the Joint Strike Fighter (JSF) Prognostics Health Management (PHM) System. ADMS is a fault propagation modeling system that is used in the Boeing 777 [72].

ADMS is an avionics system that has been designed to be scalable and extensible to various aircraft, and as such represents the next generation in modular avionics systems. The ADMS is an evolution of several maintenance features used in previous systems, and is comprised of the Central Maintenance Computer (CMC), Aircraft Conditioning Monitoring Function (ACMF), and the built-in-test (BIT) functionality of the various systems on the aircraft. The system performs root cause diagnostics to eliminate cascading faults and provide correlation between system faults and flight deck effects.

The JSF Program [38] has incorporated prognostics health management (PHM) into its design using sensors, advanced processing and reasoning, and a fully integrated system of information and supplies management. The on-board JSF PHM system is hierarchical, dividing the aircraft into areas such as propulsion and mission systems. Area data are generated by a mixture of dedicated, purpose-built sensors and analysis on existing control sensors to identify degradation and failures, which are compiled and correlated by area reasoners and then correlated by system-level model-based reasoners. Maintenance data links transmit vehicle health data to ground-based information systems focused on maintenance and management of the supply chain. *Prognostic events* are detected by prognostic built-in-tests, automated post-flight trending, and reasoning with an emphasis on disambiguating sources of degradation rather than failure. An *autonomic logistics information system* provides logistic support to the end-user and also provides off-board trending across the entire JSF fleet.

Note that the implementation of an IVHM system on a vehicle goes beyond just the technical challenges of the sensor placement. As IVHM has an effect on the operational and maintenance decisions these aspects must also be taken into account. Although the examples shown here represent significant achievements in IVHM, it is widely acknowledged that more work is required to build reliable and effective health management systems that build upon fundamental breakthroughs in detection, diagnostics, and prognostics to enable safe and efficient implementation of mitigation strategies. The following key areas are defined by the JSF Program as needing improvement and attention, including the development of tools and technologies to [38]:

- understand the physics of failure;
- improve state awareness;
- understand the dynamics of incipient crack growth;
- understand fault and failure progression rates;
- understand material properties under different loading conditions;
- develop better data fusion methods;
- understand the effects of failures across the vehicle.

1.4.5 UAV

An unmanned aerial vehicle (UAV), commonly known as a *drone*, is an aircraft without a human pilot on board. Its flight is either *controlled autonomously* by on-board computerized systems or remotely by a navigator on the ground or in another vehicle. Pre-planned contingency approaches with more intensive mathematical algorithms have produced very precise agility in small UAVs, suitable for complex maneuvers in unpredictable or crowded environments such as urban canyons or under jungle canopies. Auto-formation algorithms have allowed for aircraft to fly in optimal geometries used in triangulation when geo-locating targets of interest.

Current control approaches require disproportionate manpower to operate a single UAV. Scripted route planners used in support of *autonomous missions* are often hindered by unanticipated obstacles, unplanned events, or off-course drift. Adaptive Motion Planning (AMP) [36] is an approach encompassing a class of algorithms and feedback loops focused on the layer of motion between autopilot and mission planning (see Fig. 1.5). When applied, AMP has the potential to significantly reduce manpower for command and control of multiple UAVs. AMP provides an approach to trajectory planning for reactive movement to external events, enabling a loose control over multiple UAVs.

1.4.5.1 IVHM for UAS

To be efficient an IVHM system for UAS (unmanned aerial system—a fleet of UAVs) must consider factors often very specific to the UAV in question, such as [36]:

- Configuration, mission and payload(s) of the UAS: A UAS designed for combat will have different configuration, flight profile and payloads compared to a UAS designed for surveillance.
- National and international regulations applicable to the UAS.

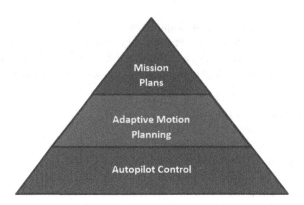

Fig. 1.5 Layers of motion control in UAV

- Level of Autonomy in the UAS: The higher the level of autonomy the more reliance is placed on the outputs from the sensors and thus the outputs must be of sufficient quality and reliability.
- Existing sensors in the UAS: All sensors and not those specifically used for monitoring systems, as it may be possible to use the existing sensors to capture health data even if it was not its original purpose. Additional sensors are used to capture operational conditions in order to set health data in context.
- A new UAS or modification of an existing UAS: Whether or not the UAS is a completely new design, evolution of an existing design or a modification to an existing fleet will have an impact on many aspects, such as the life cycle costs, whether there is usage history, allowable weight.
- The crew of the UAS: Pilots (UAV-P), maintenance personnel, etc.
- Health data users: Current (e.g., maintenance) and possible users of health data (e.g., designers of the next generation of UAS).
- Composition of the UAS: The number of UAVs, any launch equipment, etc.
- Size and weight of the individual UAV.
- Safety assessments.
- Costs of the UAS: Purchase cost, lifecycle costs, etc.

1.4.5.2 IVHM Requirements for UAS

Once information about the UAS and its operation has been gathered the system functions needed for the UAS to accomplish its mission need to be identified. When considering these functions it is often easy to focus on one aspect, predominantly the technical side. It can be all too easy to look at the technical problems for an IVHM system, such as: what parameters of a system can be monitored, and not considering if monitoring a system will help preserve the functionality of the UAS. In order to combat this tunnel vision it is useful to think of the IVHM requirements as a series of interrelated sub-sets of requirements: *business and operational, user, technical,* and *legal* [36]. Splitting the requirements into these four groups should help the designer of the IVHM system keep an overview of the complexity evolved, keeping them from focusing on the technical solution, without considering the wider impacts. Additionally it helps the designer to identify groups of people she should seek for input in their respective themes: UAV-Ps as users, Lawyers as legal experts, etc.

Business and Operational Health Monitoring Requirements

The business and operational health monitoring requirements group focuses on the company's view point of what the IVHM system needs to do in order for the UAS to accomplish its mission. For example, for a UAV the mission could be to conduct flights in order to run experiments. As well as ensuring flight of the UAV the IVHM should also monitor the health of the experiments onboard, as if the experiments fail the mission also fails. The health information could possibly be used to explain anomalous reading/data from the experiments. This means that the IVHM system must have the capability for additional input for heath data from systems (experiments). The health data and information should also be stored in an easily accessible (but secure) database to allow the relevant staff access. As most of the other vehicles of the UAS are likely to change, the IVHM should be concerned about the other UAVs as well.

User Health Monitoring Requirements

The user health monitoring requirements group focuses on the needs of people using the UAS and the people using the health data generated by the IVHM system. For a UAV the users of health data and information from the IVHM system would be the UAV-P and the personnel conducting the experiment, the number of which may vary between experiments/flights. As the turnover of staff is likely to be high, the way the information is presented to them should be in an easy-to-comprehend and intuitive manner.

Technical Health Monitoring Requirements

The technical health monitoring requirements group focuses on identifying the system's functionalities related to the UAS equipment, physical aspects (e.g. size, weight) of the components of the IVHM system, and the technologies and techniques available to the designer. These requirements will become much more defined as the design progresses and trade-off studies are performed. For a UAV the main technical health monitoring requirement is that the IVHM system is of as little weight as possible, so the UAV is close to its maximum take-off weight. There must also be clear boundaries defined between the systems on the UAV.

Legal Health Monitoring Requirements

The legal health monitoring requirements group focuses on legal matters concerned with the IVHM system. This does not just include the compliance with the relevant standards and certification documentation, but also covers contracts with customers, import and export regulations, and who owns or has the rights to the health data generated from the IVHM system.

1.4.6 Formal Methods for Autonomic Computing

Formal methods may facilitate the development of ASs. AC formalisms help developers with a well-defined formal semantics that makes the AC specifications a base from which developers may design, implement, and verify ASs. However, an AC formalism should not only provide a means of describing a system's behavior but also should tackle the vital self-* requirements (see Sect. 1.4.2.2).

Formalisms dedicated to AC have been targeted by a variety of industrial and university projects. IBM Research developed a framework called Policy Management for Autonomic Computing (PMAC) [41]. The PMAC formalism emphasizes the specification of special self-managing policies encompassing the scope under which those policies are applicable.

The so-called Specification and Description Language (SDL) is an object-oriented, formal language defined by the International Telecommunications Union—Telecommunications Standardization Sector (ITU-T) [92]. SDL is dedicated to real-time systems, distributed systems, and generic event-driven systems. The basic theoretical model of an SDL system consists of a set of extended finite state machines, running in parallel and communicating via discrete signals, thus making SDL suitable for the specification of self-management behavior.

Cheng et al. introduce a specification language for self-adaptation based on the ontology from system administration tasks and built over the underlying formalism of utility theory [12]. In this formalism, special self-adaptation actions are described as architectural operators, which are provided by the architectural style of the targeted system.

Formalism for ASs is also provided by the so-called chemical programming represented by the Gamma Formalism [6] which uses the chemical reaction metaphor to express the coordination of computations. The Gama Formalism describes computation in terms of chemical reactions (described as rules) in solutions (described as multi-sets of elements).

Andrei and Kirchner present a biologically-inspired formalism for AC called Higher-Order Graph Calculus (HOGC) [4]. This approach extends the Gama Formalism with high-level features by considering a graph structure for the molecules and permitting control on computations to combine rule applications. HOGC borrows various concepts from graph theory, in particular from graph transformations, and uses representations for graphs that have already been intensively formalized.

Autonomic System Specification Language (ASSL) is a declarative specification language for ASs with well-defined semantics [86]. It implements modern programming language concepts and constructs like inheritance, modularity, type system, and high abstract expressiveness. Conceptually, ASSL is defined through formalization tiers. Over these tiers, ASSL provides a multi-tier specification model that is designed to be scalable and exposes a judicious selection and configuration of infrastructure elements and mechanisms needed by an AS. ASSL defines ASs with special self-managing policies, interaction protocols, and autonomic elements.

1.4.7 Software Engineering Aspects, Conclusions and Recommendations

1.4.7.1 Software Engineering for Autonomic Aerospace Systems

Leading aerospace organizations like NASA, ESA, Boeing and Lockheed Martin are currently approaching AC recognizing in its paradigm a valuable approach to the development of aerospace systems capable of self-management and self-adaptation. However, the Aerospace Industry does not currently employ any development approaches that facilitate the development of autonomic features. Instead, the software engineering development process for AC is identical to the one used for the development of normal software, thus causing inherent problems like:

- requirements expressed in a traditional way are not verifiable;
- models are difficult to set up and use;
- implementation hardly complies with the limited resources of embedded systems.

1.4.7.2 Behavior Engineering

One of the most challenging yet poorly defined aspects of engineering an autonomic aerospace system is behavior engineering, including definition, specification, design, implementation, and verification and validation of the system's behaviors. This is especially true for behaviors of highly autonomous and intelligent systems.

1.4.7.3 Intelligent Swarms

Artificial Intelligence (AI) emerged over 50 years ago when Alan Turing described his test for intelligent machines. For over five decades, AI research has gone over tremendous evolution conceiving research fields such as natural language processing (including speech recognition and speech generation), data mining, machine learning, automated reasoning, neural networks, genetic algorithms, fuzzy logic, etc. *Intelligent agents* (see Sect. 1.3.4.2) provide both concepts and technologies that are products of this very evolution. Today, intelligent agents are considered one of the key concepts that may help us to realize autonomous systems. This is the reason why a great deal of research effort is devoted to developing intelligent agent technology, which has become a rapidly growing area of research and new application development. An extension of the "intelligent agent" paradigm (see Sect. 1.3.4.2) are the so-called intelligent swarm systems [9], where intelligent agents are considered to be autonomous entities that interact either cooperatively or non-cooperatively (on a selfish base). Intelligent swarm systems are MASs based on biologically-inspired concepts. By their nature, such systems are complex MASs, where the individual members of the swarm imply independent intelligence. Traditionally, a swarm-based system offers many advantages compared with the single-agent system, such as: *greater redundancy, reduced costs and risks,* and the *ability to distribute the overall work among the swarm members,* which may result in *greater efficiency and performance.* A good example of an intelligent swarm system is the NASA ANTS (Autonomous Nano-Technology Swarm) mission, a swarm-based exploration mission representing a new class of concept exploration missions based on the cooperative nature of hive cultures [78]. A mission of this class necessitates special autonomous mobile agents exhibiting both self-organizing and self-adapting features. Note that a swarm-based space-exploration system has the ability to explore regions of space where a single large spacecraft would be impractical.

1.4.7.4 Automation of Human–Machine Interaction

This is a very interesting problem tackled by [24]. If such automation is targeted by R&D, a number of different points should be emphasised, such as:

- the mismatch between the assumptions of the design team about the operators' skills and the operators' performance in a given operational environment;
- interaction interfaces may hinder understanding of automation or machine status, thus causing reaction in unexpected ways, i.e., when the operator is unable to keep track of the state of the device automation she may perform inappropriate actions or omit necessary actions.

1.4.7.5 Smart Communication Gateway

In autonomous spacecraft several communication links may be available, for instance RF links, SATCOM links, or wireless links. However, not all links may be available at the same time, and moreover the cost of using each link could be completely different. Depending on the flight (or usage) stage and application some of the links may be more appropriate than others. Therefore, in a flexible architecture it should be possible to dynamically choose the most convenient or reliable network link. For example, a special communication manager (or gateway) may monitor all communication links and routes the traffic between the vessel and the ground base station through one or more communication links. Network capabilities, their link quality (bandwidth and latency), the required throughput and the usage cost (both economical and power requirements) should be taken into account. The gateway should have enough intelligence to select the appropriate routing decision in a real-time and autonomous way. One of the key elements of such a communication gateway is the fact that it may provide an abstraction that hides the actual infrastructure used at any time. A data router at the entry point of the base station and another at the Mission Computer will redirect all traffic between the vessel and the ground segments through the best available link

1.5 Approaches to Requirements Engineering for Autonomous Systems

An autonomous system is able to monitor its behavior and eventually modify the same according to changes in the operational environment, thus being considered as self-adaptation (see Sect. 1.2.1). As such, autonomous systems must continuously monitor changes in its context and react accordingly. But what aspects of the environment should such a system monitor? Clearly, the system cannot monitor everything. And exactly what should the system do if it detects less than optimal conditions in the environment? Presumably, the system still needs to maintain a set of *high-level goals* that should be satisfied regardless of the environmental conditions, e.g., mission goals of unmanned spacecraft used for space exploration. But non-critical goals could be not that strict [82], thus allowing the system a degree of flexibility during operation. These questions (and others) form the core considerations for building autonomous systems.

Traditionally, requirements engineering is concerned with what a system should do and within which constraints it must do it (see Sect. 1.2.1). Requirements engineering for autonomous systems (and self-adaptive systems), therefore, must address what adaptations are possible and under what constraints, and how those adaptations are realized. In particular, questions to be addressed include: (1) *What aspects of the environment are relevant for adaptation?*; and (2) *Which requirements are allowed to vary or evolve at run-time, and which must always be maintained?*. Requirements engineering for autonomous systems must deal with uncertainty, because the execution environment often is dynamic and the information about future execution environments is incomplete, and therefore the requirements for the behavior of the system may need to change (at run-time) in response to the changing environment.

Requirements engineering for autonomous systems appears to be a wide open research area with only a limited number of approaches yet considered. The Autonomic System Specification Language (ASSL) [85–87] is a framework providing for a formal approach to specifying and modeling autonomous (autonomic) systems by emphasizing the self-* requirements (see Sect. 1.4.2.2). Cheng and Atlee [11] report on work on specifying and verifying adaptive software. In [25, 63], research on run-time monitoring of requirements conformance is described. In [73], Sutcliffe,

S. Fickas and M. Sohlberg demonstrate a method (called PC-RE) for personal and context requirements engineering that can be applied to autonomous systems. In addition, some research approaches have successfully used goal models as a foundation for specifying the autonomic behaviour [44] and requirements of adaptive systems [33].

1.5.1 Goal-Oriented Requirements Engineering

A major breakthrough of the past decade in (Software) Requirements Engineering is the goal-oriented approach to capturing and analyzing stakeholder intentions to derive functional and non-functional (hereafter quality) requirements [17, 50]. In essence, this approach has extended upstream the software development process by adding a new phase (*early requirements analysis*) that is also supported by engineering concepts, tools and techniques.

The fundamental concepts used to drive the goal-oriented form of analysis are those of *goal* and *actor*. To fulfill a stakeholder goal, the Goal-Oriented Requirements Engineering (GORE) [81] approach provides for analyzing the *space of alternatives*, which makes the process of generating functional and non-functional (quality) requirements more systematic in the sense that the designer is exploring an explicitly represented space of alternatives. It also makes it more rational in that the designer can point to an explicit evaluation of these alternatives in terms of stakeholder criteria to justify her choice.

The basis of the *early requirements analysis* are goal models that represent stakeholder intentions and their refinements using formally defined relationships. Functional stakeholder goals are modeled in terms of hard goals (or simply goals, when there is no ambiguity). For example, *schedule task* and *fulfill every critical task* are functional goals that are either fulfilled (satisfied) or not fulfilled (denied). Other stakeholder goals are qualitative and are hard to define formally. For instance, *have fulfilled satisfactory requirements* are qualitative goals and they are modeled in terms of *soft goals*. A soft goal by its very nature doesn't have a clear-cut criterion for its fulfillment, and may be fully or partially satisfied or denied.

There has been interest in trying to apply GORE to tackle requirements for ASs [44]. The basic idea is to build goal models that can help us to consecutively design autonomous systems.

1.5.2 The ASSL Approach to Requirements Engineering for Autonomic Systems

ASSL [85–87] is a model-oriented specification language for ASs (autonomic systems (see Sect. 1.4.2). The language is highly expressive and provides modern

```
I. Autonomic System (AS)
   * AS Service-level Objectives
   * AS Self-managing Policies
   * AS Architecture
   * AS Actions
   * AS Events
   * AS Metrics
II. AS Interaction Protocol (ASIP)
   * AS Messages
   * AS Communication Channels
   * AS Communication Functions
III. Autonomic Element (AE)
   * AE Service-level Objectives
   * AE Self-managing Policies
   * AE Friends
   * AE Interaction Protocol (AEIP)
     - AE Messages
     - AE Communication Channels
     - AE Communication Functions
     - AE Managed Elements
   * AE Recovery Protocol
   * AE Behavior Models
   * AE Outcomes
   * AE Actions
   * AE Events
   * AE Metrics
```

Fig. 1.6 ASSL multi-tier specification model

programming-language concepts such as *inheritance*, *modularity*, *type system*, and *domain-specific constructs*. In general, ASSL considers ASs, as composed of autonomic elements (AEs) (see Sect. 1.4.2.1) interacting over special *interaction protocols*. Recall that AEs are known to be the highest abstraction of autonomic system component. To specify ASs, ASSL uses a multi-tier specification model that is designed to be scalable and to expose a judicious selection and configuration of infrastructure elements and mechanisms needed to model an AS. By their nature, the ASSL tiers are levels of abstraction of different aspects of the AS under consideration.

Figure 1.6 represents the tiers in ASSL. As we can see, the ASSL specification model decomposes an AS in two directions: (1) into levels of functional abstraction; and (2) into functionally related sub-tiers.

ASSL is designed to tackle the so-called *self-* requirements* (see Sect. 1.4.2.2). To do so, the framework imposers a requirements engineering approach where self-* requirements are specified as special "policy models" [85, 86]. ASSL has been used in a variety of projects targeting functional prototypes of autonomous NASA space exploration missions [83, 84].

1.5.3 Requirements for Autonomous Unmanned Air Systems

In [32], Gillespie and West (from Defence Science & Technology Laboratory, UK) elaborate on the problem of engineering requirements for autonomous UAS (see Sect. 1.4.5). The approach follows research programs on ways of introducing more *autonomy into decision processes*. Examples can be seen in the results from the UK Systems Engineering and Autonomous Systems Defence Technology Centre (SEAS DTC) [80] conferences. Note that in this approach, autonomy is considered to be the introduction of machine intelligence (or AI—Artificial Intelligence) into decision making in the Command and Control (C2) system. According to the authors of [32], AI is clearly relevant and will be of increasing importance to UAS, but in a military C2 context, AI systems will probably remain as decision aids for a human commander. Although desirable, this condition (or assumption) is not 100 % applicable to the space-exploration missions where even the human commander is present at the ground station, the connection with long-range spacecraft may experience a considerable delay.

The questions that drive the requirements engineering in this approach are [32]:

- How do we make an autonomous system recognize that it does not have sufficient information to make a decision which can be justified under current Rules of Engagement (ROE—delineation of the circumstances and limitations within which the system may operate to achieve its objectives)?
- Can an autonomous system decide what information it needs to make a decision and decide how to find it?
- How can the autonomous system ensure that the humans in the C2 chain have sufficient information for them to make a better, more informed, decision?

Thoms has developed a three-part model of decision-making process to capture the human cognitive contributions to delivering the system's purpose [77]. It is used in [32] to derive a method to convert the human role to one provided by an autonomous decision-making system. The three cognitive capabilities are:

- *Awareness*—Perceiving the current operational position and context. This is the assimilation of all available sensor and other information relevant to the UAS and its mission.
- *Understanding*—Recognizing the relationships in the information, and their significance.
- *Deliberation*—Choosing between the various options available, based on an understanding of them and their consequences. It includes making the decision within the known constraints and acting on it; i.e., it is a decision point in the command chain.

Figure 1.7 shows Thoms's three cognitive capabilities. The input data to the Awareness block has been separated into:

- sensor data on the current situation;
- context data from pre-mission sources and their updates;

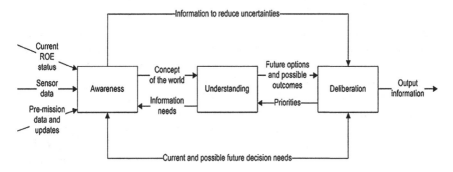

Fig. 1.7 Three-part model of human decision-making process [32, 77]

- ROE constraints.

Dynamic mission changes (e.g., UAS being targeted by hostile weapons) will change the applicable part of the ROEs. Thoms's cognitive capabilities model provides a useful context for UASs as it partitions the decision process into sub-systems which can be specified in engineering terms.

Appendix A presents engineering requirements for each of the three capabilities as: *function*, *inputs*, and *outputs*. These provide a conceptual basis to assess whether a specific technology can be used to meet the requirements and whether a technology needs more development work for justifiable autonomous decision-making. Note that each function will need a clear test strategy when implemented in a system that can be linked directly to a safety case. Derivation of information requirements with confidence levels for classifications should be achievable. Appendix A also presents criteria for: making a decision and issuing appropriate commands; requesting more information in order to make a decision; or referring the decision to another authorized entity and giving it sufficient information for a rapid, informed decision.

1.6 Summary

Aerospace Software Engineering develops new software technologies and applications for use in aviation, defense systems, and space exploration, often specializing in areas such as structural design, guidance, navigation and control, instrumentation and communication, or production methods. A successful *software development process for aerospace* must take into account the fact that aerospace systems have to meet a variety of standards and also have high safety requirements. To cope with these aspects, the development of aerospace systems emphasizes *verification*, *validation*, *certification*, and *testing*.

Today, leading aerospace organizations like NASA, ESA, Boeing and Lockheed Martin for their software development projects apply a *spiral-based methodology* used over a *waterfall process model* where the emphasis is on verification. In this model, requirements engineering is identified as one of the weak points of the software development process. Many space project reviews identify weakness in the software requirements in the early development. Requirements solicitation, analysis, and management are key elements of a successful and safe development process for aerospace systems. The importance of having consolidated software requirements makes desirable the use of special *specification and modeling techniques* that help the software engineers to achieve complete and consistent requirements. Moreover, *requirements metrics* are important part of measuring software that is being developed. These include: *requirements volatility metric* (how much program's requirements change once coding beings), *requirements traceability metric*, *requirements versioning metric*, and *requirements completeness metric*.

Similar to most organizations working on software projects, ESA and NASA consider *preliminary* and *detailed design*. The objective of the design phases (preliminary and detailed) is to create a design that will correctly and completely implement the requirements. Next, to implement the system in question, the design must be translated into a machine readable form. Usually, the formal and semi-formal design models can be used to generate the implementation automatically especially in the presence of detailed design. Testing, verification, and validation are software engineering techniques used to approve specifications, models, design, implementation and deployment configuration to establish the baseline of the implemented system, which may have to be modified at a later time.

Formal methods may assist in the development of aerospace systems. The provided formal notations might be used to precisely and unambiguously specify system requirements or to model system design. Moreover, formal tools provide the needed formal support to prove correctness of specified system properties and eventually correctness of their implementation.

Modern aerospace systems increase their performance, resilience and agility by benefiting from contemporary architecture models like SOA and MAS. Moreover, a new class of *autonomous and autonomic aerospace systems* (like UAV and robotic space-exploration systems) is currently emerging to incorporate AC features like: *self-adaptation*, *self-management*, and *self-awareness*. These features allow for the realization of unmanned spacecraft with integrated health management, self-monitoring, and on-board decision making. However, the Aerospace Industry does not currently employ any development approaches that facilitate the development of autonomic features. Instead, these are identical to the one used for the development of normal software, which is the reason for many inherent problems related to requirements, modeling and implementation. Moreover, requirements engineering for autonomous systems appears to be a wide open research area with only a limited number of approaches yet considered.

References

1. Accellera Systems Initiative: Technical tutorial: An introduction to IEEE 1666–2011, the new systemc standard. media.systemc.org (2007). http://media.systemc.org/ieee16662011/index.html
2. Acronymics Inc: AgentBuilder: An integrated toolkit for constructing intelligent software agents—reference manual—ver. 1.4. agentbuilder.com (2004). http://www.agentbuilder.com/Documentation/ReferenceManual-v1.4.pdf
3. Amey, P.: Correctness by construction: Better can also be cheaper. CrossTalk Mag.: J. Def. Softw. Eng. **6**, 24–28 (2002)
4. Andrei, O., Kirchner, H.: A Higher-order graph calculus for autonomic computing. In: Graph Theory, Computational Intelligence and Thought. Lecture Notes in Computer Science, pp. 15–26. No. 5420. Springer, Berlin (2008)
5. Assurance Process for Complex Electronics, NASA: Requirements engineering. hq.nasa.gov (2009). http://www.hq.nasa.gov/office/codeq/software/ComplexElectronics/l_requirements2.htm
6. Bantre, J.P., Fradet, P., Radenac, Y.: Programming self-organizing systems with the higher-order chemical language. Int. J. Unconv. Comput. **3**(3), 161–177 (2007)
7. Benveniste, A., Caspi, P., Edwards, S., Halbwachs, N., Guernic, P.L., Simone, R.D.: The synchronous languages twelve years later. Proc. IEEE **91**(1), 64–83 (2003)
8. Boehm, B.: Software engineering. IEEE Trans. Comput. **25**(12), 1226–1241 (1976)
9. Bonabeau, E., Thraulax, G.: Swarm smarts. Sci. Am. **282**, 72–79 (2000)
10. Burns, A., Wellings, A.: HRT-HOOD: A Structured Design Method for Hard Real-Time Systems. Elsevier, Amsterdam (1995)
11. Cheng, B., Atlee, J.: Research directions in requirements engineering. In: Proceedings of the 2007 Conference on Future of Software Engineering (FOSE 2007), pp. 285–303. IEEE Computer Society, Minneapolis (2007)
12. Cheng, S.W., Garlan, D., Schmerl, B.: Architecture-based self-adaptation in the presence of multiple objectives. In: Proceedings of the 2006 International Workshop on Self-adaptation and Self-managing Systems (SEAMS'06), pp. 2–8 (2006)
13. Clancy, D., Larson, W., Pecheur, C., Engrand, P., Goodrich, C.: Autonomous control of an insitu propellant production plant. In: Proceedings of the Technology 2009 Conference, Miami, USA (1999)
14. Clarke, E., Grumberg, O., Peled, D.: Model Checking. MIT Press, Cambridge (2002)
15. Coglianese, L., Tracz, W., Batory, D., Goodwin, M., Shafer, S., Smith, R., Szymanski, R., Young, P.: Collected Papers of the Domain-Specific Software Architectures (DSSA) Avionics Domain Application Generation Environment (ADAGE). Document ADAGE-IBM-93-09, IBM Federal Sector Company (1994)
16. Cortim: LEXIOR: LEXIcal analysis for improvement of requirements. cortim.com (2007) http://www.cortim.com
17. Dardenne, A., van Lamsweerde, A., Fickas, S.: Goal-directed requirements acquisitions. Sci. Comput. Program. **20**, 3–50 (1993)
18. de la Puente, J.A., Ruiz, J.F., Zamorano, J.: An open Ravenscar real-time kernel for GNAT. In: Reliable Software Technologies- Ada-Europe 2000. Lecture Notes in Computer Science, No. 1845, pp. 5–15. Springer, Berlin (2000)
19. Devedzic, V., Radovic, D.: A framework for building intelligent manufacturing systems. IEEE Tran. Syst. Man Cybern. Part C Appl. Rev. **29**, 422–439 (1999)
20. Durfee, E., Lesser, V.: Negotiating task decomposition and allocation using partial global planning. Distrib. Artif. Intell. **2**, 229–244 (1989)
21. ECSS Secretariat: Space engineering—software—part 2: Document requirements definitions (DRDs). Technical report, ESA-ESTEC, Requirements & Standards Division, Noordwijk, The Netherlands (2005)
22. ESA Board for Software Standardization and Control (BSSC): Guide to the Software Detailed Design and Production Phase. ESA, Paris CEDEX, France (1995)

23. ESA: Automatic code and test generation. esa.int (2007). http://www.esa.int/TEC/Software_engineering_and_standardisation/TECOQAUXBQE_2.html
24. ESA: Verification models for advanced human—automation interaction in safety critical flight operations (statement of work). Technical report, ESA (2011)
25. Fickas, S., Feather, M.: Requirements monitoring in dynamic environments. In: Proceedings of the IEEE International Symposium on Requirements Engineering (RE 1995), pp. 140–147. IEEE Computer Society, Washington (1995)
26. Foner, L.N.: Entertaining agents: A sociological case study. In: Proceedings of the 1st International Conference on Autonomous Agents, pp. 122–129 (1997)
27. Gamma, E., Helm, R., Johnson, R., Vlissides, J.: Design Patterns. Addison-Wesley, Boston (1994)
28. Gerlich, R., Kerep, M.: Distributed and parallel systems and HOOD4. In: Ada in Europe. Lecture Notes in Computer Science, pp. 228–243. No. 103. Springer, Berlin (1996)
29. Ghosh, D., Sharman, R., Rao, H.R., Upadhyaya, S.: Self-healing systems—survey and synthesis. Decis. Support Syst. **42**(4), 2164–2185 (2007)
30. Gilbert, D., Aparicio, M., Atkinson, B., Brady, S., Ciccarino, J., Grosof, B., O'Connor, P., Osisek, D., Pritko, S., Spagna, R., Wilson, L.: IBM Intelligent Agent Strategy—White Paper. IBM Corporation, New York (1995)
31. Gilbert, D.: IBM Intelligent Agent Strategy. IBM Corporation, New York (1995)
32. Gillespie, T., West, R.: Requirements for autonomous unmanned air systems set by legal issues. Int. C2 J. **4**(2), 11–13 (2010)
33. Goldsby, H., Sawyer, P., Bencomo, N., Hughes, D., Cheng, B.: Goal-based modeling of dynamically adaptive system requirements. In: Proceedings of the 15th Annual IEEE International Conference on the Engineering of Computer Based Systems (ECBS). IEEE Computer Society (2008)
34. Halbwachs, N.: Synchronous Programming of Reactive Systems. Kluwer Academic Publishers, Boston (1993)
35. Hayes-Roth, B.: An architecture for adaptive intelligent systems. Artif. Intell. **72**(1–2), 329–365 (1995)
36. Hellstern, G., Wilson, R., Harris, F.: Adaptive motion planning approaches for small UAV flight. In: Proceedings of Infotech@Aerospace Conference 2012. AIAA, Garden Grove, California, USA, AIAA 2012-2477 (2012)
37. Herrmann, D.: Software Safety and Reliability. IEEE CS Press, Los Alamitos 1999)
38. Hess, A.: Prognostics and health management—a thirty-year retrospective. Joint Strike Fighter Program Office (2010). http://ti.arc.nasa.gov/projects/ishem/papers_pres.php
39. Hierons, R.M., Bogdanov, K., Bowen, J.P., Cleaveland, R., Derrick, J., Dick, J., Gheorghe, M., Harman, M., Kapoor, K., Krause, P., Luettgen, G., Simons, A.J.H., Vilkomir, S., Woodward, M.R., Zedan, H.: Using formal specification to support testing. ACM Comput. Surv. **41**(2), 1–76 (2009)
40. IBM Corporation: An architectural blueprint for autonomic computing, 4th edn. IBM Corporation, Technical report (2006)
41. IBM Corporation: Policy management for autonomic computing—version 1.2. Technical report, IBM Tivoli (2005)
42. IEEE Computer Society: IEEE Standard IEEE-Std-830-1998: IEEE recommended practice for software requirements specification (1998)
43. Kephart, J.O., Chess, D.M.: The vision of autonomic computing. IEEE Computer **36**(1), 41–50 (2003)
44. Lapouchnian, A., Yu, Y., Liaskos, S., Mylopoulos, J.: Requirements-driven design of autonomic application software. In: Proceedings of the 2006 Conference of the Center for Advanced Studies on Collaborative Research (CASCON 2006), p. 7. ACM (2006)
45. Life Cycle Management Working Group (LCMWG): INCOSE. incose.org (2010). http://www.incose.org/practice/techactivities/wg/lcmwg/
46. Madni, A.: Agiletecting: A principled approach to introducing agility in systems engineering and product development enterprises. J. Integr. Des. Process Sci. **12**(4), 1–7 (2008)

47. Maes, P.: Artificial life meets entertainment: lifelike autonomous agents. Commun. ACM **38**(11), 108–114 (1995)
48. Muscettola, N., Nayak, P., Pell, B., Williams, B.: Remote agent: to boldly go where no AI system has gone before. Artif. Intell. **103**(1–2), 5–48 (1998)
49. Musgrave, G., Larsen, A., Sgoba, T. (eds.): Safety Design for Space Systems. Elsevier, Oxford (2009)
50. Mylopoulos, J., Chung, L., Nixon, B.: Representing and using non-functional requirements: a process-oriented approach. IEEE Trans. Softw. Eng. **18**(6), 483–497 (1992)
51. NASA: Software Safety: NASA Technical Standard NASA-STD-8719.13A. NASA (1997)
52. NASA, Goddard Space Flight Center: GMSEC mission statement. gmsec.gsfc.nasa.gov (2008). http://gmsec.gsfc.nasa.gov/
53. National Aeronautics and Space Administration: Design, development, test and evaluation(DDT&E) considerations for safe and reliability human rated spacecraft systems. Technical report, NASA TechnicalReport RP-06-208. National Aeronautics and Space Administration, Langley Research Center, Hampton (2006)
54. National Aeronautics and Space Administration: NASA Systems Engineering Handbook: NASA/SP-2007-6105 Rev. 1. NASA Headquarters, Washington, D.C. (2007)
55. Pecheur, C., Simmons, R., Engrand, P.: Formal verification of autonomy models. In: Rouff, C., et al. [62] (eds.) Agent Technology from a Formal Perspective (2006)
56. Philippe, C.: Validation, and certification challenges for control systems. In: The Impact of Control Technology. IEEE Control Systems Society (2011)
57. Robinson, P.J.: HOOD: Hierarchical Object-Oriented Design. Prentice Hall, London (1992)
58. Rodriguez, Y., Madni, A.: Adaptability in engineering resilient systems (ERS). In: Infotech@Aerospace Conference 2012. AIAA, Garden Grove, California, VA, USA, AIAA 2012–2410 (2012)
59. Rouff, C., Hinchey, M., Rash, J., Truszkowski, W., Gordon-Spears, D. (eds.): Agent Technology from a Formal Perspective. Springer, London (2006)
60. Rouff, C., Rash, J., Hinchey, M., Truszkowski, W.: Formal methods at NASA goddard space flight center. In: Rouff, C., et al. (eds.) Agent Technology from a Formal Perspective (2006)
61. Royce, W.W.: Managing the development of large software systems. In: Proceedings of the 9th International Conference of Software Engineering, pp. 328–338. IEEE Computer Society (1987)
62. Russell, S., Norvig, P.: Artificial Intelligence: A Modern Approach. Prentice-Hall, Egnlewood Cliff (2009)
63. Savor, T., Seviora, R.: An approach to automatic detection of software failures in real-time systems. In: Proceedings of the IEEE Real-Time Technology and Applications Symposium, pp. 136–147. IEEE Computer Society, Los Alamitos, California (1997)
64. Scerri, P., Pynadath, D., Tambe, M.: Towards adjustable autonomy for the real-world. J. AI Res. **17**, 171–228 (2002)
65. Sierhuis, M., Clancey, W., von Hoof, R., Seah, C., Scott, M., Nado, R., Blumenberg, S., Shafto, M., Anderson, B., Bruins, A., Buckley, C., Diegelman, T., Hall, T., Hood, D., Reynolds, F., Toschlog, J., Tucker, T.: NASA's OCA mirroring system: An application of multiagent systems in mission control. In: Proceedings of Autonomous Agents and Multi Agent Conference (Industry Track), Budapest, Hungary (2009)
66. Simmons, R., Goodwin, R., Haigh, K., Koenig, S., O'Sullivan, J., Velosso, M.: Experience with a layered robot architecture. ACM SIGART Bull. **8**, 1–4 (1997)
67. Software Engineering and Standardization, ESA: Design. esa.int (2007). http://www.esa.int/TEC/Software_engineering_and_standardisation/TECELAUXBQE_0.html
68. Software Engineering and Standardization, ESA: Overview of software life cycle related activities. esa.int (2007). http://www.esa.int/TEC/Software_engineering_and_standardisation/TEC0CEUXBQE_0.html
69. Software Engineering and Standardization, ESA: Requirement engineering and modelling. esa.int (2007). http://www.esa.int/TEC/Software_engineering_and_standardisation/TECLCAUXBQE_0.html

70. Software Engineering and Standardization, ESA: Software engineering and standard-
    ization. esa.int (2009). http://www.esa.int/TEC/Software_engineering_and_standardisation/
    TECP5EUXBQE_0.html
71. Software Engineering and Standardization, ESA: System-software co-engineering - avion-
    ics systems modelling. esa.int (2011). http://www.esa.int/TEC/Software_engineering_and_
    standardisation/TECRE9UXBQE_0.html
72. Spitzer, C.: Honeywell primus epic aircraft diagnostic maintenance system. In: Digital Avionics
    Handbook, 2nd edn. Health Management Systems, pp. 22–23. CRC (2007)
73. Sutcliffe, A., Fickas, S., Sohlberg, M.: PC-RE a method for personal and context requirements
    engineering with some experience. Requir. Eng. J. **11**, 1–17 (2006)
74. Sycara, K.: Multiagent systems. AI Mag. **19**(2), 79–92 (1998)
75. SYST—System & Software Technology Group: DOBERTSEE—dependant on-board embed-
    ded real-time software engineering environment. syst.eui.upm.es Madrid, Spain (2012). https://
    syst.eui.upm.es/node/125
76. The Future of Aerospace Standardization Working Group, Aerospace Industries Association of
    America Inc: The future of aerospace standardization. aia-aerospace.org (2005). http://www.
    aia-aerospace.org/assets/aerospace_standardization0105.pdf
77. Thoms, J.: Understanding the impact of machine technologies on human team cognition. In:
    Proceedings of the 4th SEAS DTC Technical Conference, Paper B7 (2009)
78. Truszkowski, W., Hinchey, M., Rash, J., Rouff, C.: NASA's swarm missions: the challenge of
    building autonomous software. IT Prof. **6**(5), 47–52 (2004)
79. Truszkowski, W., Hallock, L., Rouff, C., Karlin, J., Rash, J., Hinchey, M., Sterritt, R.:
    Autonomous and Autonomic Systems—with Applications to NASA Intelligent Spacecraft
    Operations and Exploration Systems. Springer, Berlin (2009)
80. UK Systems Engineering and Autonomous Systems Defence Technology Centre (SEAS DTC).
    seasdtc.com (2010). http://www.seasdtc.com/
81. van Lamsweerde, A.: Requirements engineering in the Year 00: A research perspective. In:
    Proceedings of the 22nd IEEE International Conference on Software Engineering (ICSE-2000),
    pp. 5–19. ACM (2000)
82. Vassev, E., Hinchey, M., Balasubramaniam, D., Dobson, S.: An ASSL approach to handling
    uncertainty in self-adaptive systems. In: Proceedings of the 34th annual IEEE Software Engi-
    neering Workshop (SEW 34), pp. 11–18. IEEE Computer Society (2011)
83. Vassev, E., Hinchey, M., Paquet, J.: Towards an ASSL specification model for NASA swarm-
    based exploration missions. In: Proceedings of the 23rd Annual ACM Symposium on Applied
    Computing (SAC 2008)—AC Track, pp. 1652–1657. ACM (2008)
84. Vassev, E., Hinchey, M.: Modeling the image-processing behavior of the NASA Voyager Mis-
    sion with ASSL. In: Proceedings of the 3rd IEEE International Conference on Space Mission
    Challenges for Information Technology (SMC-IT'09), pp. 246–253. IEEE Computer Society
    (2009)
85. Vassev, E.: Towards a framework for specification and code generation of autonomic systems.
    Ph.D. thesis, Computer Science and Software Engineering Department, Concordia University,
    Quebec, Canada (2008)
86. Vassev, E.: ASSL: Autonomic System Specification Language—A Framework for Specifica-
    tion and Code Generation of Autonomic Systems. LAP Lambert Academic Publishing, Saar-
    brucken (2009)
87. Vassev, E., Hinchey, M.: ASSL: A software engineering approach to autonomic computing.
    IEEE Comput. **42**(6), 106–109 (2009)
88. Vassev, E., Hinchey, M.: The challenge of developing autonomic systems. IEEE Comput.
    43(12), 93–96 (2010)
89. Vassev, E., Sterritt, R., Rouff, C., Hinchey, M.: Swarm technology at NASA: building resilient
    systems. IT Prof. **14**(2), 36–42 (2012)
90. W3C Working Group: Web services architecture. w3c.org (2004). http://www.w3.org/TR/
    ws-arch

91. Waslander, S.L.: Multi-agent systems design for aerospace applications. Ph.D. thesis, Department of Aeronautics and Astronautics, Stanford University (2007)
92. Web ProForum tutorials. iec.org (2005). http://www.iec.org
93. Williams, B., Nayak, P.: A model-based approach to reactive self-configuring systems. Proc. AAAI/IAAI **2**, 971–978 (1996)
94. Wooldridge, M.: Intelligent agents. In: Multi-Agent Systems, pp. 3–51. MIT Press, Cambridge (1999)
95. Wooldridge, M., Jennings, N.R.: Intelligent agents: theory and practice. Knowl. Eng. Rev. **10**(2), 115–152 (1995)

Chapter 2
Handling Autonomy Requirements for ESA Systems

Abstract Contemporary software-intensive systems, such as modern spacecraft and unmanned exploration platforms (e.g., ExoMars) generally exhibit a number of autonomic features resulting in complex behavior and complex interactions with the operational environment, often leading to a need for self-adaptation. To properly develop such systems, it is very important to properly handle the autonomy requirements. This chapter discusses the notion of autonomy in the context of ESA Missions, and outlines aspects of requirements engineering along with specification models and formal methods for aerospace. The chapter goes in-depth about special *generic autonomy requirements* for space missions along with controller architectures for robotic systems controlling such missions. In detail are discussed formal methods and approaches that cope with both generic autonomy requirements and controller architectures, and as such can lay the foundations of a new Autonomy Requirements Engineering Model dedicated to autonomic features of space missions.

2.1 Introduction

Appropriate formal methods help ESA developers express and understand autonomy requirements to some extent. Formal methods assist in the construction of the Autonomy Requirements Engineering Model (AREM) suitable for the development of autonomous components for ESA systems. AREM takes into account all the aspects of an autonomic system as shown in Chap. 1 and emphasizes the so-called *self-* requirements* (Sects. 1.2.3 and 1.3) by taking into consideration the traditional *functional* and *non-functional* requirements of spacecraft systems (e.g., safety requirements). However, we can ask the question: *Why formal methods?* Traditionally, formal methods have had the necessary potential for modeling and validating the control behavior of software-intensive systems[1] and they may help in expressing autonomy requirements and modeling autonomic and self-adaptive behavior. It is our understanding that the application of formal methods will help ESA developers *unambiguously express autonomy requirements*, which are currently expressed in

---

[1] Modern spacecraft and autonomous robotics systems are considered to be software-intensive.

© Springer International Publishing Switzerland 2014   47
E. Vassev and M. Hinchey, *Autonomy Requirements Engineering for Space Missions*,
NASA Monographs in Systems and Software Engineering,
DOI 10.1007/978-3-319-09816-6_2

natural language. We expect that appropriate formal methods will improve the software development cycle of autonomic features for ESA's software-intensive systems in terms of:

- rigorous and unambiguous specification of autonomy requirements;
- autonomy requirements traceability, verification and validation;
- derivation of test cases and automatic test case generation based on requirements specification.

Moreover, a successful AREM should consider so-called *controller architectures for robotic systems* (Sect. 2.3) to eventually derive successor architectures for controllers for autonomous spacecraft.

Autonomy Requirements Engineering (ARE) should be considered as a software engineering process of (1) determining what *autonomic features* are to be developed for a particular software-intensive system or subsystems and (2) the software artifacts generated by that process. Note that the outcome of ARE (requirements specifications, models, etc.) is a precursor of design of autonomic features. The ARE process should involve all of the following:

- autonomy requirements elicitation;
- autonomy requirements analysis;
- autonomy requirements representation;
- autonomy requirements communication;
- development of acceptance criteria and procedures for autonomy requirements.

Note that the targeted AREM approach is a framework incorporating formal methods dedicated to autonomic features of software-intensive systems. The AREM framework allows for specification and modeling of autonomy requirements and it provides for validation and traceability of specified autonomy requirements. Thus, AREM is a requirements engineering approach helping to create reliable software that maximizes the probability of satisfying user expectations. This is possible because the framework toolset is going to provide verification mechanisms for *automatic reasoning* about specified autonomy requirements. A basic validation approach could be *consistency checking* where autonomy requirements are verified by performing exhaustive traversal to check for both syntax and consistency errors and to check whether requirements conform to predefined autonomy correctness properties, defined by ESA engineers. For example, correctness properties can be set to target the requirements feasibility.

Moreover, to handle *logical errors* (specification flaws) and to be able to assert safety (e.g., freedom from deadlock) and liveness (nice-to-have) properties, AREM can eventually provide for both model-checking and test-case generation mechanisms. Finally, AREM can be supplied with code generation mechanisms to facilitate the implementation of autonomic features.

2.1.1 Autonomy and Automation

Recall that automated processes replace routine manual processes with software/hardware ones that follow a step-by-step sequence that may still include human participation. *Autonomous processes*, on the other hand, emulate human processes rather than simply replacing them.

Complete autonomy may not be desirable or possible for some systems. In such cases, *adjustable* and *mixed autonomy* may need to be used [36]. In adjustable autonomy, the level of autonomy of the system (e.g., spacecraft) can vary depending on the circumstances or the needed interaction and control. The autonomy can be adjusted to be either *complete*, *partial*, or no *autonomy*. In these cases the adjustment may be done automatically by the system depending on the situation (e.g., an autonomous spacecraft may ask for help from mission control) or may be requested by the human control. Challenges in adjustable autonomy include knowing when it needs to be adjusted, as well as how much and how to make the transition between levels of autonomy. In mixed autonomy, autonomous agents and people work together to accomplish a goal or perform a task. Often agents perform the low level details of the task (e.g., analogous to the craft's preparation for landing) while the human performs the higher-level functions (e.g., analogous to the actual landing).

2.1.2 Levels of Autonomy for ESA Missions

ESA considers four *autonomy levels* for the execution of nominal mission operations [14]:

- execution mainly under real-time ground control;
- execution of pre-planned mission operations onboard;
- execution of adaptive mission operations onboard;
- execution of goal-oriented mission operations onboard.

These autonomy levels are summarized in Table 2.1. As shown in that table, ESA approaches the *autonomicity problem* very carefully in a stepwise manner. In this approach the highest-possible autonomy is the goal-oriented autonomy (level E4) where goals are determined by human operators and autonomous spacecraft decide what to do to autonomously achieve the desired goals. Still, this autonomy level hasn't been achieved yet. The current level of spacecraft autonomy is level E2 and ExoMars is expected to operate at level E3.

Table 2.1 ESA's Mission-execution autonomy levels [14]

Autonomy level	Description	Functions
E1	Mission execution under ground control	Real-time control from ground for nominal operations
	Limited onboard capability for safety issues	Execution of time-tagged commands for safety issues
E2	Execution of pre-planned, ground-defined, mission operations onboard	Capability to store time-based commands in an onboard scheduler
E3	Execution of adaptive mission operations onboard	Event-based autonomous operations
		Execution of onboard operations control procedures
E4	Execution of goal-oriented mission operations onboard	Goal-oriented mission replanning

2.2 Requirements Engineering, Specification Models and Formal Methods for Aerospace

Requirements engineering is currently identified as one of the weak points of the software development process used in aerospace projects. Many space project reviews identify weakness in the software requirements in the early development [17]. Requirements solicitation, analysis, and management are key elements of a successful and safe development process for any system. Many costly and critical system failures can ultimately be traced back to missing, incorrect, misunderstood, or incompatible requirements. This leads to incomplete development and difficulties in system integration and software re-engineering and a very high price.

In Sect. 2.3.1, we discuss the characteristics of the Space Missions Requirements Analysis activity helping to identify classes of requirements for space missions.

2.2.1 Requirements Specification and Modeling

The importance of having consolidated software requirements makes the use of special *specification and modeling techniques* that help software engineers to achieve complete and consistent requirements desirable. Models at software level are called specifications (e.g., technical specification) and they may assists with the verification of the requirements and eventually with further design, implementation, and testing. For example, specification models may help software engineers with automatic code and test-case generation [16]. Of course, this approach requires a good definition of the system/software process, a deep knowledge of the code generator, and a strong control of the software architecture.

For more on requirements engineering (e.g., requirements metrics and character-istics of requirements), please refer to Chap. 1.

2.2.2 Requirements Engineering for Autonomous Systems

An autonomous system is able to monitor its behavior and eventually modify the same according to changes in the operational environment, thus being considered as self-adaptation (Sect. 2.2.3 and for more details Chap. 1). As such, autonomous systems must continuously monitor changes in its context and react accordingly. But what aspects of the environment should such a system monitor? Clearly, the system cannot monitor everything. And exactly what should the system do if it detects less than optimal conditions in the environment? Presumably, the system still needs to maintain a set of high-level goals that should be satisfied regardless of the environmental conditions, e.g., mission goals of unmanned spacecraft used for space exploration. But non-critical goals could be not that strict [47], thus allowing the system a degree of flexibility during operation. These questions (and others) form the core considerations for building autonomous systems.

Traditionally, requirements engineering is concerned with *what a system should do and within which constraints it must do it* (Sect. 2.2). Requirements engineering for autonomous systems (and self-adaptive systems), therefore, must address what adaptations are possible and under what constrains, and how those adaptations are realized. In particular, questions to be addressed include: (1) *What aspects of the environment are relevant for adaptation?* and (2) *Which requirements are allowed to vary or evolve at run-time, and which must always be maintained?*. Requirements engineering for autonomous systems must deal with uncertainty, because the exe-cution environment often is dynamic and the information about future execution environments is incomplete, and therefore the requirements for the behavior of the system may need to change (at run-time) in response to the changing environment.

Requirements engineering for autonomous systems appears to be a wide open research area with only a limited number of approaches yet considered. In this chapter, we present a few formal methods that eventually can be successful in capturing autonomy requirements.

2.2.3 Generic Autonomy Requirements

The first step towards development of a new software-intensive system is to deter-mine the system's requirements, which includes both elicitation and specification (or modeling) of the same. In general, requirements fall into two categories: *func-tional* and *non-functional*. Whereas the former define the system's functionality the latter emphasize system's qualities (e.g. performance) and constraints under which a system is required to operate. Like any computer system, *autonomic systems*[2] (ASs) also need to fulfill specific requirements from these two categories. However, unlike the other systems, the development of an AS is driven by the so called *self-management objectives* (also could be considered as *self-adaptive objectives*) and *attributes* (Chap. 1), which introduce special requirements termed self-* requirements [57]. Despite their differences in terms of application domain and functionality, all ASs are capable of self-management and are driven by one or more self-management objectives. Note that this requirement automatically involves (1) self-diagnosis (to analyze a problem situation and to determine a diagnosis) and (2) self-adaptation (to repair the discovered faults). The ability to perform adequate self-diagnosis depends largely on the quality and quantity of its knowledge of its current state, i.e., on the system awareness.

The following is a list of generic autonomy requirements [57] stemming from the self-* requirements:

2.2.3.1 Self-* Requirements (Autonomicity)

Autonomicity is one of the essential characteristics of ASs. Autonomicity aims at freeing human operators from complex tasks, which typically require a lot of decision making without human intervention. Autonomicity, however, is not only intelligent behavior but also an organizational manner. Adaptability is not possible without a certain degree of autonomy. A rule engine obeying a predefined set of conditional statements (e.g., if-then-else) put in an endless loop is the simplest form of autonomicity implementation. In many cases though, such a simple rule-based mechanism may not be sufficient and the rule engine should force feedback learning and learning by observation to refine the decisions concerning the priority of services and their granted objectives and quality of service, respectively.

2.2.3.2 Knowledge

Knowledge is a large complex aggregation composed of constituent parts representing knowledge of different kind. Every kind of knowledge may be used to derive knowledge models of specific domains of interest. For example, the following kinds of knowledge may be considered [13]:

- *domain knowledge*—refers to the application domain facts, theories, and heuristics;
- *control knowledge*—describes problem-solving strategies, functional models, etc.;
- *explanatory knowledge*—defines rules and explanations of the system's reasoning process, as well as the way they are generated;

---

[2] The term "autonomic systems" is often used in the scientific literature as a synonym of self-adaptive and autonomous systems.

- *system knowledge*—describes data contents and structure, pointers to the implementation of useful algorithms needed to process both data and knowledge, etc. System knowledge also may define user models and strategies for communication with users.

Moreover, being considered as essential system and environment information, knowledge may be classified as (1) internal knowledge—knowledge about the system itself and (2) external knowledge—knowledge about the system environment. Another knowledge classification could consider a priori knowledge (knowledge initially given to a system) and experience knowledge (knowledge gained from analysis of tasks performed during the lifetime of a system). Therefore, it depends on the problem domain what kinds of knowledge may be considered and what knowledge models may be derived from those kinds. For example, we may consider knowledge specific to:

- internal component structure and behavior;
- system-level structure and behavior;
- environment structure and behavior;
- different situations where an AS component or the system itself might end up in;
- components' and system's capabilities of communication and integration with other systems.

2.2.3.3 Awareness

An aware system is able to notice a change and understand the implications of that change. Conceptually, awareness is a product of *knowledge representation*, *knowledge processing*, and *monitoring*. In general, we address two types of awareness in ASs:

- *self-awareness*—a system (or a system's component) has detailed knowledge about its own entities, current states, capacity and capabilities, physical connections and ownership relations with other systems in its environment;
- *context-awareness*—a system (or a system's component) knows how to negotiate, communicate and interact with its environment and how to anticipate environmental states, situations and changes.

2.2.3.4 Monitoring

Monitoring is the process of obtaining knowledge through a collection of sensors instrumented within the system itself. Note that monitoring is not responsible for diagnostic reasoning or adaptation tasks. One of the main challenges of monitoring is to determine which information is most crucial for analysis of the system's behavior, and when. The notion of monitoring is closely related to the notion of awareness because it is a matter of awareness, which information indicates a situation in which a certain adaptation is necessary.

2.2.3.5 Adaptability

Adaptability may result in changes to some functionality, algorithms or system parameters as well as the system's structure or any other aspect of the system. Note that self-adaptation requires a model of the system's environment. Adaptability is conceptualized as a concept to achieve change. It is in sharp contrast to creating new builds. A key research gap in this area is how to measure "adaptability".

2.2.3.6 Dynamicity

Dynamicity shows the system's ability to change at runtime. Dynamicity may also include a system's ability to exchange certain (defective or obsolete) components without changing the observable behavior. Conceptually, dynamicity deals with concerns like preserving states during functionality change, starting, stopping and restarting system functions, etc.

2.2.3.7 Robustness

ASs should benefit from robustness since this may facilitate the design of system parts that deal with the self-* requirements. Beside a special focus on error avoidance, several requirements aiming at correcting errors should also be enforced. Robustness can often be achieved by decoupling and asynchronous communication, e.g., between interacting AS components. Error avoidance, error prevention, and fault tolerance are proven techniques in software engineering, which help us in preventing error propagation when designing ASs.

2.2.3.8 Resilience

Adaptability might be considered as a quality attribute that is a prerequisite for resilience and system agility [28]. Closely related to safety, resilience enables aerospace systems to bounce back from unanticipated disruptions as well as to equip aging systems with the ability to respond to changing operational requirements.

2.2.3.9 Mobility

Mobility enfolds all parts of the system: from mobility of code on the lowest granularity level via mobility of services or components up to mobility of devices or even mobility of the overall system. Mobility enables dynamic discovery and usage of new resources, recovery of crucial functionalities, etc. For example, ASs may rely on mobility of code to transfer some functionality relevant for security updates or other self-management issues.

2.3 Generic Autonomy Requirements for Space Missions

In this section, along with the Space Mission Requirements Analysis we elaborate on different classes of space missions and derive generic autonomy requirements per class of missions. Thus, we put in the context of space missions the generic autonomy requirements presented in Sect. 2.2.3.

2.3.1 Space Mission Requirements Analysis

Space Mission Analysis is an activity that takes aspects such as payload operational requirements and spacecraft system constraints as inputs, and generates as an output a mission specification. A key aspect of this process is the selection of the orbital parameters (or trajectory parameters) of the final mission orbit as well as the intermediate orbits during the early orbit acquisition phase. Note that the mission specification leads to design requirements on the spacecraft systems and subsystems. The Space Mission Analysis and Design (SMAD) Process consists of the following steps [20, 61]:

- Define Objectives:

  - Define broad objectives and constraints.
  - Estimate quantitative mission needs and requirements.

- Characterize the Mission:

  - Define alternative mission concepts.
  - Define alternative mission architectures.
  - Identify system drivers for each architecture.
  - Characterize mission concepts and architectures.

- Evaluate the Mission:

  - Identify critical requirements.
  - Evaluate mission utility.
  - Define baseline mission concept.

- Define Requirements:

  - Define system requirements.
  - Allocate requirements to system elements.

Typical Functional requirements are related to:

- *performance*: factors impacting this requirement include the primary mission objective, payload size, orbit, pointing;
- *coverage*: impacting factors include orbit, number of satellites, scheduling;
- *responsiveness*: impacting factors include communications architecture, processing delays, operations;
- *secondary mission* (if applicable).

Typical Operational requirements are:

- *duration*: factors impacting this requirement include nature of the mission (experimental or operational), level of redundancy, orbit (e.g., altitude);
- *availability*: impacting factors include level of redundancy;
- *survivability*: impacting factors include orbit, hardening, electronics;
- *data distribution*: impacting factors include communications architecture;
- *data content, form and format*: impacting factors include user needs, level and place of processing, payload.
- *ground station visibility*;
- *eclipse duration*: consider the eclipse period for spacecraft in an Earth orbit;
- *launch windows*: the time of launch of a spacecraft is often constrained by dynamic aspects related to reaching the mission orbit, or by system requirements;
- *communication windows*.

Typical Constraints are:

- *cost*: factors impacting this constraint include number of spacecraft, size and complexity, orbit;
- *schedule*: impacting factors include technical readiness, program size;
- *political*: impacting factors include Sponsoring organization (customer), whether international program;
- *interfaces*: impacting factors include level of user and operator infrastructure;
- *development constraints*: impacting factors include Sponsoring organization.

In general, space missions can be classified into two main groups: *Earth-orbiting missions* and *interplanetary missions* [20]. In the following sections, classes and subclasses of space missions are presented together with *generic autonomy requirements* for each one of these classes and subclasses. Note that the autonomy requirements presented here are currently not all realistic. Autonomy in space missions is about delegating control from the ground base to spacecraft, and due to security and cost reasons, neither ESA nor NASA is currently considering autonomy to take place in the processes of establishing missions' orbits or trajectories. Although not being realistic at the moment, we elaborate on such autonomy requirements, for the reason of completeness.

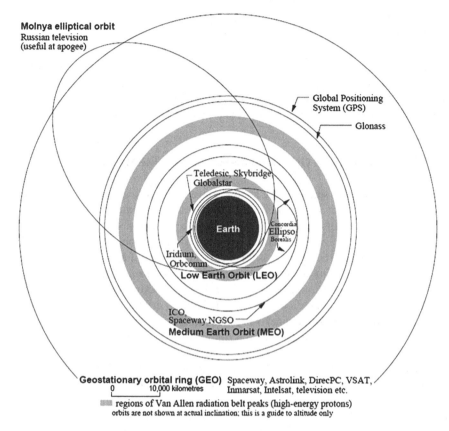

Fig. 2.1 Common earth orbits, figure courtesy of Wood [62]

2.3.2 Earth-Orbiting Missions

The Earth-Orbiting Missions is a class of missions that represents artificial satellites placed into Earth orbit and used for a large number of purposes. Different orbits give satellites different vantage points for viewing Earth, i.e., different Earth orbits give satellites varying perspectives, each valuable for different reasons. Some satellites hover over a single spot, providing a constant view of one face of the Earth, while others circle the planet. Figure 2.1 depicts common Earth satellite orbits [62].

Common Challenge: Orbital Perturbations

There are a variety of effects that will cause orbital perturbations during the lifetime of a satellite [5]:

- *third body perturbations*: dominated by the gravitational forces of the Sun and the Moon;
- *perturbations due to a non-spherical Earth*;

- *atmospheric drag*: principal non-gravitational force acting on a satellite and it only affects satellites in low-Earth orbit. Drag acts in the direction of opposite of the satellite's velocity resulting in a removal of energy from the orbit. This loss of energy results in the size of the orbit decreasing, which then leads to a further increase in drag;
- *solar radiation*: solar radiation pressure is an effect that is strongest on satellites with large area to mass ratios. It results in periodic variations in all orbital elements.

2.3.2.1 Polar Low Earth Orbit/Remote-Sensing Satellite Missions

These missions involve satellites that fly low orbit and use different earth-observation instruments that gather information about the Earth (land, water, ice and atmosphere) using a variety of measurement principles. The choice of orbit for a Low Earth Orbit (LEO) remote sensing spacecraft is governed by mission objectives and payload operational requirements. A LEO orbit is below an altitude of approximately 2,000 km (1,200 mi). Spacecraft in LEO encounter *atmospheric drag* in the form of gases in the thermosphere (approximately 80–500 km up) or exosphere (approximately 500 km and up), depending on orbit height. LEO is an orbit around Earth between the atmosphere and below the inner Van Allen radiation belt. The altitude is usually not less than 300 km because that would be impractical due to the larger atmospheric drag.

Equatorial low Earth orbits (ELEO) are a subset of LEO. These orbits, with low inclination to the Equator, allow rapid revisit times and have the lowest ΔV (a measure of the amount of "effort" that is needed to change from one trajectory to another by making an orbital maneuver) requirement of any orbit. Orbits with a high inclination angle are usually called polar orbits. Higher orbits include Medium Earth Orbit (MEO), sometimes called intermediate circular orbit (ICO), and further above, Geostationary Orbit (GEO).

Mission Challenges and Generic Autonomy Requirements

The common challenge in Polar LEO and Remote-Sensing Satellite Missions is to determine the right orbit altitude. The orbit altitude is principally established by a trade-off between instrument resolution and the fuel required to maintain the orbit in the presence of aerodynamic drag. Orbits higher than low orbit can lead to early failure of electronic components due to intense radiation and charge accumulation.

Considering these issues, we determine the following *autonomy requirements*:

- *self-* requirements* (autonomicity):
    - *self-orbit* (autonomously acquire the target orbit; adapt to orbit perturbations);
    - *self-protection* (autonomously detect the presence of radiation and move to escape);
    - *self-scheduling* (based on operational goals and knowledge of the system and its environment, autonomously determine what task to perform next);

– *self-reparation* (implies operations re-planning based on performance degradation or failures);

- *knowledge*: mission objectives, payload operational requirements, instruments onboard together with their characteristics (e.g., instruments resolution), the Van Allen radiation belt, ground stations, communication links, data transmission format, orbit planes, eclipse period, spacecraft altitude, communication mechanisms onboard, Earth gravity;
- *awareness*: orbit awareness, radiation awareness, altitude awareness, position awareness, instrument awareness, neighboring satellites, sensitive to thermal stimuli, Earth gravitational force, data-transfer awareness, ground station visibility awareness, Earth rotation awareness, speed awareness, communication awareness, altitude awareness, air resistance awareness;
- *monitoring*: electronic components, surrounding environment (e.g., radiation level), atmospheric drags, ground station, altitude and orbit;
- *adaptability*: adaptable mission parameters, adapt to loss of energy, adapt to high radiation, adapt to weak satellite-ground station communication link, adapt to low energy;
- *dynamicity*: dynamic communication links;
- *robustness*: robust to temperature changes, robust to orbital perturbations, robust to communication losses;
- *resilience*: loss of energy is recoverable, resilient to radiation;
- *mobility*: information goes in and out, changing position within the orbit plane.

2.3.2.2 Satellite Constellation Missions

These missions are presented by multi-satellite systems where a group of satellites called a "constellation" work together. Such a constellation can be considered to be a number of satellites with coordinated ground coverage, operating together under shared control, synchronized so that they overlap well in coverage and complement rather than interfere with other satellites' important coverage [20]. For a constellation to operate, it may be necessary to use more than a single ground station, especially when the space segment consists of a large number of satellites (Fig. 2.2). Intersatellite links (ISL) are bidirectional communication links between satellites in LEO or MEO orbits.

Mission Challenges and Generic Autonomy Requirements

There are a few important challenges in Satellite Constellation Missions. Such missions rely on high distributiveness: a distributed system in space and a distributed system on ground are combined in a distributed space mission. One of the major issues is that the topology of the distributed space mission changes over time, which places stringent requirements on communication. The topology change is on the one side caused from the orbit dynamics, on the other side may be manually controlled to switch to a desired formation or constellation. Moreover, due to the movement of

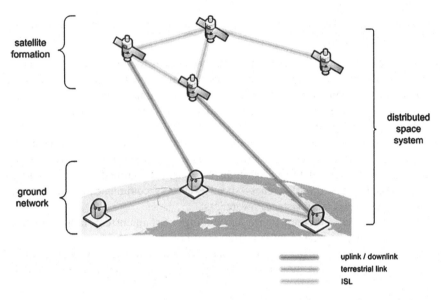

Fig. 2.2 Satellite constellation mission [37]

the satellites in their orbits, the communication links between ground stations and satellites change frequently and data flow in the satellite network has to be coordinated. A considerable challenge is also the invariance of the constellation geometry when subject to orbital perturbations (there could be a large number of possible constellation configurations that may satisfy a particular mission requirement).

Considering these issues, we determine the following *autonomy requirements* (also add the requirements of Polar LEO/Remote-Sensing Satellite Missions):

- *self-* requirements* (autonomicity):

  - *self-formation* (autonomously determine the right satellite configuration and perform it);
  - *self-reparation* (broken communication links must be restored autonomously);
  - *self-scheduling* (autonomously determine which satellites operate when; payload);
  - *self-coordination* (autonomously coordinate operations where several spacecraft may coordinate their operations on achieving a common goal: (1) Earth observation of a specific region performed by several spacecraft: at different times or with different instruments for sensor-fusion purposes and (2) coordination of scientific experiments);
  - *self-organization* (to distribute data in a space network a high degree of self-organization is required, i.e., autonomous routing capabilities due to changing topology);
  - *self-geometry* (autonomously adapt the constellation geometry to orbit perturbations);

- *knowledge*: constellation satellites (or neighboring satellites), inter-satellite communication links, group payload, constellation orbit planes, constellation geometry (e.g., Walker Delta pattern constellation), total number of satellites;
- *awareness*: formation awareness, satellites synchronization awareness;
- *monitoring*: constellation configuration;
- *adaptability*: adapt to new formations, adapt to weak inter-satellite communication links, adapt constellation geometry to orbital perturbations;
- *dynamicity*: dynamic formation (dynamic topology), dynamic inter-satellites communication links (change affects communication);
- *robustness*: robust to inter-satellite communication losses, robust to a single satellite loss;
- *resilience*: resilient satellite formations;
- *mobility*: inter-constellation mobility (information and satellites), moving satellites within an orbit plane, moving satellites from one orbit plane to another.

2.3.2.3 Geostationary Earth Orbit Missions

This class of missions involves satellites orbiting at Geostationary Earth Orbit (GEO) usually for providing global communications [20]. Satellites in such an orbit have an orbital period equal to one sidereal day (the Earth's rotational period or 23 h 56 min). The 24-h geostationary orbit clearly offers unique advantages, providing almost complete global coverage from merely three satellites, and with no need for the ground antenna to switch between the satellites. Several transfer orbit revolutions occur before injection of the satellite into near-circular, near-GEO orbit.

Mission Challenges and Generic Autonomy Requirements

A geostationary orbit can only be achieved at an altitude very close to 35,786 km (22,236 mi), and directly above the Equator.

Considering these issues, we determine the following *autonomy requirements* (also add the requirements of Polar LEO/Remote-Sensing Satellite Missions):

- *self-* requirements* (autonomicity):

  - *self-GEO-keeping* (use thrusters to autonomously maintain the geostationary orbit—position, altitude and speed, by adapting to perturbations such as the solar wind, radiation pressure, variations in the Earth's gravitational field, and the gravitational effect of the Moon and Sun);

- *knowledge*: GEO coordinates, perturbation factors, GEO altitude, solar wind, Moon's gravitational field, Sun's gravitational field;
- *awareness*: orbit perturbation awareness, solar wind awareness, radiation pressure awareness, Moon's gravitational effect awareness, Sun's gravitational effect awareness;
- *monitoring*: GEO position, other GEO satellites, Moon position, Sun position;

- *adaptability*: adapt to communication latency (geostationary orbits are far enough away from Earth that communication latency becomes significant—about a quarter of a second), adapt to perturbations (such as the solar wind, radiation pressure, variations in the Earth's gravitational field, and the gravitational effect of the Moon and Sun);
- *dynamicity*: dynamic GEO positioning and altitude;
- *robustness*: robust to communication latency;
- *resilience*: resilient GEO positioning;
- *mobility*: moving the satellite within the GEO plane.

2.3.2.4 Highly Elliptic Orbit Missions

In this class of missions, spacecraft in elliptic orbits move more rapidly at perigee than at apogee. This offers the prospect of a pass of increased duration over a ground station if the apogee is situated above it. Two mission subclasses are derived [20]: *Space-born Observatories* and *Communication Spacecraft*.

Space-borne Observatories

Spacecraft are used in observatory mode, which means the spacecraft instruments are operated as if they were located in a room adjacent to the astronomer's workstation. To achieve extended periods of time, the payload can be pointed to desired astrophysical targets whilst uninterrupted contact with a ground station is maintained. In general, there will be an interruption of observational time while the spacecraft passes through the perigee region.

Mission Challenges and Generic Autonomy Requirements

There are a few important challenges to consider in Space-borne Observatories. The first one is the orbit optimization, i.e., the spacecraft's orbit period must be optimized with respect to the ground station coverage. In addition, the radiation environment may preclude the operation of certain types of payload.

Considering these issues, we determine the following *autonomy requirements* (also add the requirements of Polar LEO/Remote-Sensing Satellite Missions):

- *self-* requirements* (autonomicity):

  - *self-optimization* (autonomously maintain the optimum spacecraft's orbit period with respect to the ground station coverage and keep up with it);
  - *self-protection* (autonomously detect high radiation and cover sensitive instruments);
  - *self-reparation* (autonomously detect problems in instruments and repair; broken communication links must be restored autonomously);
  - *self-command* (autonomously evaluate the effect of executing remote commands before perform those to guarantee that the spacecraft will not fall in a dangerous situation due to a command execution);
  - *self-scheduling* (autonomously determine which instruments operate when);

- *self-coordination* (autonomously coordinate data flow gathered by different instruments onboard);
- *self-tuning* (autonomously tune the instruments onboard);

- *knowledge*: instruments onboard, inter-instrument communication links, objects/phenomena to observe, Moon's gravitational field, Sun's gravitational field;
- *awareness*: operation awareness, instruments synchronization awareness, Moon's gravitational force awareness, Sun's gravitational force awareness;
- *monitoring*: instruments operation, Moon position, Sun position;
- *adaptability*: adapt to new tasks, adapt to instrument losses, adapt to instrument performance degradation;
- *dynamicity*: dynamic instrument configuration and tuning;
- *robustness*: robust to inter-instrument communication losses, robust to a single instrument loss;
- *resilience*: resilient instruments: (1) implies possible mitigations for the performance degradation and (2) autonomous recalibration to maintain the measurement data quality;
- *mobility*: inter-instrument mobility of information, moving observatory within an orbit plane, moving observatory from one orbit plane to another.

Communication Spacecraft

In this mission subclass, orbiting communication spacecraft fly highly ecliptic orbits and are used to transfer data on Earth. With regard to the ecliptic orbit, there two possible orbits [20]:

- *Molniya Orbit*—highly elliptic with a 12-h period where the spacecraft moves relatively slowly in the apogee region; to provide 24-h regional service, at least three Molniya spacecraft are needed.
- *Tundra Orbit*—elliptical orbit with a period one sidereal day (23 h 56 min). It can provide 24 h coverage with a minimum of only two spacecraft; the orbital parameters can be chosen so that the spacecraft does not traverse the Earth's radiation belts.

Mission Challenges and Generic Autonomy Requirements

There are a few important challenges to consider in Communication Spacecraft. The first one is the orbit perturbations, i.e., third-body forces may perturb the perigee height, causing atmosphere reentry. In addition, the radiation environment, e.g., a passage through Van Allen radiation belts, may cause accelerated degradation of power and electronic systems. Another challange is stemming from the variation in satellite range and range-rate, which may have a number of impacts upon the communication payload design:

- variation in time propagation;
- frequency variation due to Doppler effect;
- variation in received signal power;

- change of ground coverage pattern during each orbit.

Considering these issues, we determine the following *autonomy requirements* (also add the requirements of Polar LEO/Remote-Sensing Satellite Missions):

- *self-* requirements* (autonomicity):
  - *self-protection* (autonomously detect when the spacecraft is passing through the Van Allen radiation belts to cover the electronic systems and minimize the power usage);
  - *self-optimization* (autonomously optimize the communication payload by taking into consideration the impact caused by: variation in time propagation, frequency variation due to Doppler effect, variation in received signal power, and change of ground coverage pattern during each orbit);
  - *self-reparation* (autonomously detect problems in the communication system and repair);
  - *self-scheduling* (autonomously determine when to emit transmissions);

- *knowledge*: Van Allen radiation belts, Doppler effect, ground coverage pattern, Moon gravity, Sun gravity, Molniya Orbit/Tundra Orbit;
- *awareness*: signal power awareness, Moon's gravitational force awareness, Sun's gravitational force awareness;
- *monitoring*: Van Allen radiation belts, Moon position, Sun position;
- *adaptability*: adapt to changes in the ground coverage pattern, adapt to changes in time propagation, adapt to changes in communication frequency;
- *dynamicity*: dynamic communication frequency, dynamic ground coverage pattern, avoid radiation belts;
- *robustness*: robust to radiation;
- *resilience*: resilient communication payload;
- *mobility*: moving satellite within the orbit plane.

2.3.3 Interplanetary Missions

Interplanetary missions involve more than one planet or planet satellite. General trajectory information needs to be developed and understood for each mission. Interplanetary trajectories are influenced by perturbations caused by the gravitational influence of the Sun and planetary bodies within the solar system. Software tools are used to compute a large number of trajectories. Figure 2.3 presents possible trajectories for current Mars missions' opportunities [21].

Mission Challenges and Generic Autonomy Requirements

The major challenges to consider in Interplanetary Missions are communication propagation delays, communication bandwidth limitations, and hazardous environment. Communication propagation delays imply little or no possibility for real-time control by the ground station on Earth. The hazardous environment introduces risks such as surface interactions, thermal conditions, power availability, and radiation.

Considering these issues, we determine the following *autonomy requirements*:

- *self-* requirements* (autonomicity):

  - *self-trajectory* (autonomously acquire the most optimal trajectory; adapt to trajectory perturbations);
  - *self-protection* (autonomously detect the presence of radiation);
  - *self-scheduling* (autonomously determine what task to perform next—equipment onboard should support the tasks execution);
  - *self-reparation* (broken communication links must be restored autonomously; when malfunctioning, component should be fixed autonomously where possible);

- *knowledge*: mission objectives, payload operational requirements, instruments onboard together with their characteristics (e.g., instruments resolution), Van Allen radiation belt, ground stations, communication links, data transmission format,

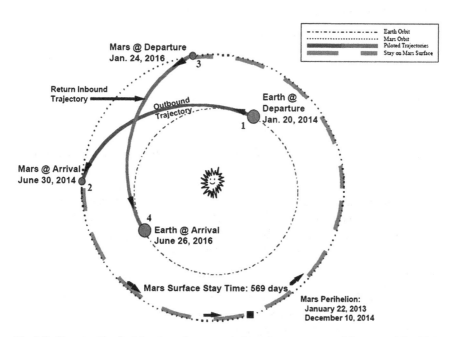

Fig. 2.3 Opportunities for Mars interplanetary missions, figure courtesy of George and Kos [21]

eclipse period, altitude, communication mechanisms onboard, Earth gravity, Moon gravity, Sun gravity, solar system, target planet characteristics;

- *awareness*: trajectory awareness, radiation awareness, air resistance awareness, instrument awareness, sensitive to thermal stimuli, gravitational forces awareness, data-transfer awareness, speed awareness, communication awareness;
- *monitoring*: electronic components onboard, surrounding environment (e.g., radiation level, space objects), planned operations (status, progress, feasibility, etc.);
- *adaptability*: adaptable mission parameters, possibility for re-planning (adaptation) of operations, adapt to loss of energy, adapt to high radiation, adapt to weak a satellite-ground station communication link, adapt to low energy;
- *dynamicity*: dynamic communication links;
- *robustness*: robust to temperature changes, robust to trajectory perturbations, robust to communication losses;
- *resilience*: loss of energy is recoverable, resilient to radiation;
- *mobility*: information goes in and out, changing trajectory;

2.3.3.1 Small Object Missions: "To Orbit" and "To Land" Missions

The objective of such missions is to investigate the properties of minor bodies in the solar system, mainly asteroids, comets and the satellites of the major planets [20]. Particular interest lies in the hypothesis that these small objects might help us understand the genesis and evolution of the solar system.

Mission Challenges and Generic Autonomy Requirements

Asteroids and cometary bodies are often characterized by an irregular shape, which poses some challenges to the mission designers:

- *monitor the environment around small objects*—often not known a priori and self-adaptation must be considered where a range of environments need to be accommodated in the mission design:

  - the near-body environment might not be clean, i.e., presence of dust and debris; a near-body environment exhibiting dust and debris will cause orbit and altitude perturbations;
  - cometary bodies can have a very dynamic near-body environment, particularly when closer than 3 AU to the Sun; comets may exhibit visible coma, hydrogen cloud and dust and plasma tails;
  - the gravity field does not approximate to that of a sphere;

- *motion around small, irregularly shaped bodies*:

  - find the sufficient distance to approximate to the Keplerian Orbits; for close orbits where the orbit radius is of the same order as the body's size the trajectory shape no longer approximates to a conic section;
  - determine the gravitational field of the body; payload imagery can provide quantitative information regarding the size, shape and rotational state of the body;

 – determine the overall mass and density of the body—can use the so-called "mascon" method that builds the body's shape via a collection of spherical masses of uniform size and density;

- *landing on small, irregularly shaped bodies*:

 – physical properties of the comet and its environment are generally unknown prior to the mission; we need to build generic models of the target body (e.g., a comet), which encompass a range of properties expected; key factors to determine: orbital speed, orbital period, escape velocity and impact speed;
 – landing takes long time and requires trajectory manoeuvers and it is important not to exceed escape velocity; the lander needs to have knowledge and control of its altitude.

Considering these issues, we determine the following *autonomy requirements* (also add the generic requirements for Interplanetary Missions):

- *self-* requirements* (autonomicity):

 – *self-orbiting* (autonomously acquire the most optimal orbit; adapt to orbit perturbations due to possible dust and derbies);
 – *self-protection* (autonomously detect the presence of dust and derbies and move to escape or cover instruments);
 – *self-landing* (autonomously adapt the landing procedure to landing goals);
 – *self-gravity* (autonomously compute the gravitational field of the object—mass, density and shape of the object);
 – *self-escape* (autonomously acquire the escape procedures and use it to leave the object);

- *knowledge*: physics of minor space bodies, physics of cometary bodies, Keplerian Orbits;
- *awareness*: awareness of dust and debris in the object surrounding environment, object shape awareness, object gravitational force, object spin awareness, object speed awareness, surface distance awareness, spacecraft's orbital speed awareness, spacecraft's orbital period awareness, escape velocity awareness, body's magnetic fields awareness;
- *monitoring*: the environment around the target object, the landing surface, comet's characteristics (such as: visible coma, hydrogen cloud and dust and plasma tails);
- *adaptability*: adapt the system operations to the goals to be achieved, adapt to the environment around the target object (landing and orbiting operations must take into consideration both orbit and altitude perturbations), adapt to the shape of the orbited object, adapt to the landing surface;
- *dynamicity*: dynamic near-body environment, dynamic landing procedure (may require trajectory maneuvers);
- *robustness*: robust to dust and debris;
- *resilience*: resilient to magnetic fields changes;
- *mobility*: trajectory maneuvers for landing and orbiting.

2.3.3.2 Missions Using Low-Thrust Trajectories

Such missions use spacecraft for orbit control activities in GEO (Geostationary Earth Orbit), drag compensation in LEO, Lunar orbit missions and missions to comets and asteroids. These missions often have a complex mission profile utilizing ion propulsion in combination with multiple *gravity-assist manoeuvers* (e.g., ESA's BepiColombo mission).

Mission Challenges and Generic Autonomy Requirements

Major challenges to consider in Missions Using Low-thrust Trajectories are:

- low-thrust trajectories in a central force field—the motion of an orbiting spacecraft is influenced by a continuous low-thrust: a challenging task is to determine a steering law for the thrust vector, so that a particular objective can be achieved; direct trajectory cannot be implemented using such low thrust, and so a spiraling transfer trajectory must be used.
- steering laws: secular rates of the orbit elements, maximum rate of change of orbital energy, maximum rate of change of orbital inclination;
- interplanetary missions using low-thrust:

  - low-thrust Earth escape;
  - low-thrust planetary capture—achieve capture around the destination planet;
  - sun-centered transfer;

Considering these issues, we determine the following *autonomy requirements* (also add the generic requirements for Interplanetary Missions):

- *self-* requirements* (autonomicity):

  - *self-low-thrust-trajectory* (autonomously determine a steering law for a thrust vector);
  - *self-capture* (autonomously determine a steering law and use low thrust to achieve capture around a destination planet);
  - *self-escape* (autonomously determine a steering law and use low thrust to achieve escape from a planet);

- *knowledge*: central force field physics, steering law models, secular rates of the orbit elements, maximum rate of change of orbital energy, maximum rate of change of orbital inclination;
- *awareness*: planetary capture awareness, planetary escape awareness, trajectory velocity awareness, planet's magnetic fields awareness, awareness of the spacecraft's position on the projected trajectory;
- *monitoring*: the environment around the planet;
- *adaptability*: adapt the low thrust trajectory to orbit and/or altitude perturbations;
- *dynamicity*: dynamic near-body environment, dynamic trajectory following procedure (may require trajectory maneuvers);
- *robustness*: robust to dust and debris;

- *resilience*: resilient to magnetic fields changes;
- *mobility*: trajectory maneuvers for avoiding orbit and/or altitude perturbations.

2.3.3.3 Planetary Atmospheric Entry and Aeromaneuvering Missions

Such missions require entering the atmosphere of a planet to take probes or land [20]. Principle effect of an atmosphere on a satellite trajectory is to reduce the energy of the orbit. These missions include some degree of aeromaneuvering, with a "mass penalty"—additional propellant mass is required to protect the vehicle from the dynamic pressure and thermal effects of aeromaneuvering.

Mission Challenges and Generic Autonomy Requirements

Major challenges to consider in Missions Using Low-thrust Trajectories are:

- along-track effects: associated with aerobraking and reduce the translational energy of a spacecraft:
  - direct atmospheric entry—aeroforces are used to reduce the vehicle's speed to facilitate soft landing;
  - orbital aerocapture—aeroforces are used to transfer a vehicle's orbital state from hyperbolic to elliptical;
  - aero-assisted orbit transfer—an atmospheric pass is used to modify the orbit (e.g., transferring a vehicle from high orbit to low orbit by using an aerobraking maneuver);
- across-track effects: produce out-of-plan accelerations and can be used to modify the orbit plane inclination;
- atmospheric entry: a space vehicle experiences approximate exponentially increasing atmospheric density; provides a changing aerodynamic environment. As the vehicle progresses into the atmosphere tick shock waves are formed about the vehicle. Eventually, if the vehicle penetrates sufficiently low into the atmosphere, a continuum flow region is encountered where velocity remains hypersonic. Particular challenges here are:
  - the process is difficult to describe analytically and often bridging functions are used to describe the aerodynamic properties of the vehicle;
  - high temperature is generated at the contact surface that must be absorbed by the heat shield and vehicle surface. The high temperature leads to chemical reactions in the atmospheric gas and excitation of internal energy models such as vibration, together dissociation and ionization;
- principle constraints: peak dynamic load and peak thermal load, together with how long these loads persist;

Considering these issues, we determine the following *autonomy requirements* (also add the autonomy requirements for Small Object Missions—"to orbit" and "to land" Missions):

- *self-* requirements* (autonomicity):

  - *self-orbital-aerocapture* (autonomously use the aeroforces to transfer a vehicle's orbital state from hyperbolic to elliptical);
  - *self-aero-assisted-orbit-transfer* (autonomously use atmospheric passes to modify the orbit);
  - *self-soft-landing* (autonomously use aeroforces to reduce the vehicle's speed and perform soft landing);
  - *self-orbit-inclination* (autonomously use out-of-plan accelerations to modify the orbit plane inclination);

- *knowledge*: aerodynamic properties of the spacecraft, spacecraft's heat shield, across-track effects, atmospheric shock waves, gas chemical reactions, peak dynamic load, peak thermal load;
- *awareness*: atmospheric density awareness, temperature awareness, across-track effect awareness, shock waves awareness, vibration awareness, gas dissociation awareness, gas ionization awareness, chemical reactions awareness;
- *monitoring*: atmospheric density, temperature at the contact surface of the spacecraft, atmospheric chemical reactions;
- *adaptability*: adapt to out-of-plan accelerations;
- *dynamicity*: changing aerodynamic environment, dynamic velocity (depends on the atmospheric density);
- *robustness*: robust to high temperatures and steering forces;
- *resilience*: resilient to changes in the atmospheric density;
- *mobility*: trajectory aeromaneuvering for landing and orbiting.

2.4 Controller Architectures for Robotic Systems

In this section we elaborate on the so-called controller architectures for robotic systems to conclude the possible platforms for autonomous behavior controllers. This will add on to the generic autonomy requirements for space missions and will help us to conclude the characteristics of possible platforms (e.g., formal methods) for ARE.

2.4.1 Architectural Issues Related to Autonomy

By introducing (or increasing) autonomy to space missions, we imply changes to both the *control architecture* and the *commanding protocol*. This is mainly due to the fact that most of the operational conditions are not fully known in advance and we often need to deal with parameterized behaviors. Thus, we do not precisely know at design time the sequence of low-level commands that will be executed when a high-level command is issued. In situations when the system operates with performance and resource uncertainties as well as other constraints stemming from the partially unknown environment, "the use of event-driven sequence execution is a much better approach than the traditional time-triggered command execution because commands executed at a precise time will fail under unexpected circumstances" [32]. Recall that systems following event-driven sequence execution are classified as having E3 level of autonomy according to ESA's autonomy classification (Sect. 2.1.2). The occurrence of events is non-deterministic and so the sequence of low-level actions that are executed by the system (and even the result). Actually, this is what makes autonomous systems difficult to verify and test.

The highest level of autonomy is goal-oriented operation (E4 level) (Sect. 2.1.2). From the autonomy-design and -implementation perspective, this level provides for the highest level of abstraction because goals have the advantage of *being easier to specify than the actions that are necessary to reach them* and the responsibility of deciding how to best achieve these goals is transferred to the *onboard controllers*. This level of autonomy has been tested successfully in missions such as Deep Space 1 [30] and Earth Observing Mission-1 (EO-1) [31] and is based on *automated reasoning*.

2.4.2 Controller Architectures for Robotic Systems

Architectures for *autonomous control* in robotic systems require concurrent embedded real-time performance, and are typically too complex to be developed and operated using conventional programming techniques. The complexity demands of such systems require frameworks and tools that are based on well-defined concepts that enable the effective realization of systems to meet high-level goals. Experience shows that layering is a powerful means for structuring functionalities and control, being therefore a powerful tool for system design, increasing modularity, robustness, ease of debugging, computational capability, reactivity and use of information to make decisions, therefore the need of these systems to contain several sub-systems with different levels of abstraction.

The core of an autonomous controller is a subsystem, known variously as the *execution system*, *virtual machine*, or *sequence engine*, that executes commands and monitors the environment [32]. Execution systems vary in sophistication, from those that execute linear sequences of commands at fixed times, to those that can plan and schedule in reaction to unexpected changes in the environment. Every robotic system requires some sort of execution system, although the level of autonomy and complexity of the controller varies greatly.

Three main architecture classes for autonomous control in robotic systems are in use: *deliberative architectures*, *reactive architectures*, and *hybrid architectures*.

2.4.2.1 Deliberative Architectures

The so-called *deliberative architecture controllers* are based on a particular type of *knowledge-based system* that contains an explicitly represented *symbolic model of the world*. Deliberation is the explicit consideration of alternative behaviors (courses of actions)—i.e., generating alternatives and choosing one of the possible alternatives. Decisions are made via *logical and statistical reasoning* based on pattern matching and symbolic manipulation. The approach suggests that intelligent behavior can be generated by providing a system with a symbolic representation of its environment and its desired behavior and by syntactically manipulating this representation and the decision-making is viewed as a logic deduction. Deliberative architectures are goal-oriented and thus, they are suitable for building the highest possible level of autonomy (E4 level).

2.4.2.2 Reactive Architectures

The so-called *reactive architecture controllers* differ from deliberative controllers in that they have a very limited set of beliefs and instead of *explicitly defined goals*; their actions are determined by a set of behaviors which are triggered by events within the environment. In reactive architectures, there are no central functional modules, such as perception reasoning, learning, etc. Instead an agent consists of a completely distributed decentralized set of competence modules, more often called behaviors. The best known reactive architecture is the so-called *Subsumption Architecture*. It is created to expose a number of behaviors (each behavior may be thought of as an individual action function) which are implemented as Finite State Machines (FSM). Reactive architectures are event-oriented and are suitable for building the E3 level of autonomy.

2.4.2.3 Hybrid (Layered) Architecture

The so-called *layered architectures* put together both deliberative and reactive architectures by breaking down the different proactive and reactive elements of an agent into different layers. This way of abstraction allows complex agents to be modeled more easily and is flexible enough for use in many agent systems. Each function required of the agent is decomposed into a different layer. The reactive components are responsible for relatively simple, low-level, robust behaviors, while the deliberative components are responsible for organizing and sequencing complex behaviors. The key issue is in the *integration of the reactive and deliberative layers*. The favored option is to use a *three-tiered approach* in which a planning component mediates between low-level behaviors and high-level goal-oriented modeling [32].

Figure 2.4 presents a three-tiered architecture. As shown there are three main layers [32]:

- a Decision Layer is a mechanism for performing time-consuming deliberative computations, with goal-driven planning and scheduling facilities;
- an Executive Layer is a reactive plan execution mechanism, with execution sequencing facilities;
- a Control (Functional) Layer is a reactive feedback control mechanism, with reactive execution facilities.

In three-layer architectures the three components run as separate computational processes. Reactive layers typically use very simple representations of the current or previous state of the environment and work over very short timescales in tight sensor-driven feedback loops, while deliberative layers use complex counterfactual representations and work on much longer timescales, from minutes to hours and more [32].

In regard to layer dependency and positioning, there are a variety of hybrid architectures, some of which are presented below.

Horizontal and Vertical Layering

In horizontal layering the controller consists of behaviors that take input from the environment and create some sort of output. In vertical layering the environmental input triggers a low layer which then passes information to the layer above it and so on allowing for considerable complexity. The great advantage of horizontally layered architectures is their conceptual simplicity: if we need a controller to exhibit *different types of behavior we implement* different layers.

One-pass and Two-pass Vertical Layered Architectures

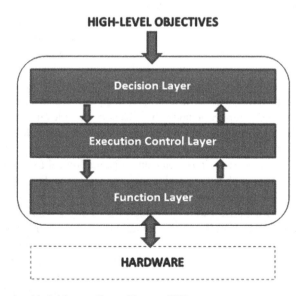

Fig. 2.4 Three-tiered hybrid controller architecture [32]

In the first, control flows sequentially through each layer, until the final layer generates an action output. In the second, information flows up the architecture and control flows back down. In decentralized control, the layers operate concurrently and independently, processing sensor data and generating actions. In hierarchical control the layers operate serially with higher level deliberative layers controlling the execution of low-level reactive layers. In concurrent control the layers operate simultaneously and can modify the behavior of adjacent layers.

2.5 Formal Methods for ARE

Formal methods originate from formal logic and refer to a plethora of mathematically-based activities where both notations and tools with mathematical basis are used. Formal notations (also known as formal languages) are used to precisely and unambiguously specify system requirements or to model system design. Formal tools provide the needed formal support to prove correctness of specified system properties and eventually correctness of their implementation.

Formal methods provide a vast family of formal notations in the form of formal specification languages (sometimes called modeling languages). In general, we use these to precisely describe with the logical underpinning of mathematics features of the system under consideration at a higher level of abstraction than the one provided by implementation. Thus, formal languages are used to provide a formal and neutral, i.e., implementation-independent, representation (often called formal specification) of systems. In avionics, formal methods are used for requirements specification, system modeling and code generation, and validation.

Formal languages have been used to develop deliberative robot controllers (Sect. 2.4.2). In [60] an agent programming language called Goal is used to program a cognitive robot control architecture that combines low-level sub-symbolic control with high-level symbolic control. The Goal language helps to realize a cognitive layer whereas low-level execution control and processing of sensor data are delegated to components in other layers. Goal supports a goal-oriented behavior and decomposition of complex behavior by means of modules that can focus their attention on relevant sub-goals. In [39] the high-level language Golog is used for robot programming. Golog supports writing control programs in a high-level logical language, and provides an interpreter that, given a logical axiomatization of a domain, will determine a plan. Golog also supports actions and situations (actually the language incorporates Situation Calculus [7]).

Autonomic System Specification Language (ASSL) is a declarative specification language for ASs with well-defined semantics [54–56]. It implements modern programming language concepts and constructs like inheritance, modularity, type system, and high abstract expressiveness. Conceptually, ASSL is defined through formalization tiers. Over these tiers, ASSL provides a multi-tier specification model that is designed to be scalable and exposes a judicious selection and configuration of

infrastructure elements and mechanisms needed by an AS. ASSL has been successfully used for the specification of autonomic features of a variety of ASs.

KnowLang [49, 50] is an approach to knowledge representation model for self-
adaptive behavior and awareness. The ultimate goal is to allow for awareness and
self-awareness capabilities (Sect. 2.5.2) of autonomous systems. The KnowLang
framework strives to solve complex problems where the operational environment is
non-deterministic and a system needs to reason at runtime to find missing answers.
In comparison to Goal and Golog described above, KnowLang is far more expressive
especially at the level of modeling self-adaptive behavior, which is supported neither
by Goal nor by Golog. KnowLang supports integration of situations, goals, policies,
and actions with Bayesian network probability distributions which allows for self-
adaptation based on both *logical* and *statistical reasoning*.

In the following subsections, we present in detail the goal-oriented requirements engineering approach along with two successful formal methods: ASSL and
KnowLang, which we consider as the most promising approaches to ARE for space
missions. Note that these methods cope well with both the generic autonomy requirements for space missions (Sect. 2.3) and controller architectures for robotic systems
(Sect. 2.4).

2.5.1 *Goal-Oriented Requirements Engineering*

The *goal-oriented approach* to Software Requirements Engineering is about capturing and analyzing stakeholder intentions to derive functional and non-functional
(hereafter quality) requirements [12, 29]. In essence, this approach extends upstream
the software development process by adding a new phase called *Early Requirements
Analysis*. The fundamental concepts used to drive the goal-oriented form of analysis are those of *goal* and *actor*. To fulfill a stakeholder goal, the Goal-Oriented
Requirements Engineering (GORE) [46] approach provides for *analyzing the space
of alternatives*, For more details on GORE, please, refer to Sect. 1.5.1 in Chap. 1

2.5.1.1 GORE for Autonomy Requirements

There has been interest in trying to apply GORE to tackle requirements for ASs
[27]. The basic idea is to build *goal models* that can help us to consecutively design
autonomous systems in several ways:

1. A goal model might provide the starting point for the development of an AS
   by analyzing the environment for the system-to-be and by identifying the problems that exist in this environment as well as the needs that the system under
   development has to address:

(a) GORE might assist the Space Mission Requirements Analysis Process (Sect. 2.3.1) in defining mission objectives and constraints and in estimating quantitative mission needs and requirements.
(b) With GORE mission goals can be identified along with the mission actors (mission spacecraft, spacecraft components, environmental elements, base station, etc.).
(c) Requirements goal models can be used as a *baseline for validating the system*.

2. Goal models provide a means to represent *alternative ways* in which the objectives of the system can be met and analyze and rank these alternatives with respect to *quality concerns* and other constraints:

(a) This allows for exploration and analysis of alternative system behaviors at design time, which leads to more predictable and trusted ASs.
(b) If the alternatives that are initially delivered with the system perform well, there is no need for complex interactions on autonomy behavior among autonomy components.
(c) Of course, not all alternatives can be identified at design time. In an open and dynamic environment, new and better alternatives may present themselves and some of the identified and implemented alternatives may become impractical.
d) In certain situations, new alternatives will have to be discovered and implemented by the system at runtime. However, the process of discovery, analysis, and implementation of new alternatives at runtime is complex and error-prone. By exploring the space of alternative process specifications at design time, we are minimizing the need for that difficult task.

3. Goal models provide the traceability mechanism from AS designs to requirements. When a change in requirements is detected at runtime (e.g., a major change in the global mission goal), goal models can be used to re-evaluate the system behavior alternatives with respect to the new requirements and to determine if system reconfiguration is needed:

(a) If a change in requirements affected a particular goal in the model, it is possible to see how this goal is decomposed and which autonomy components (autonomic elements) implementing the goal are in turn affected.
(b) By analyzing the goal model, it is possible to identify how a failure to achieve some particular goal affects the overall objective of the system.
(c) Highly variable goal models can be used to visualize the currently selected system configuration along with its alternatives and to communicate suggested configuration changes to users in high-level terms.

4. Goal models provide a unifying intentional view of the system by relating goals assigned to individual autonomy components (autonomic elements) to high-level system objectives and quality concerns:

(a) High-level objectives or quality concerns serve as the common knowledge shared among the autonomy components to achieve the global system optimization. This way, the system can avoid the pitfalls of missing the globally optimal configuration due to only relying on local optimizations.

(b) Goal models might be used to identify part of the knowledge requirements of the system (Sects. 2.2.3 and 2.3).

5. GORE might be used to manage conflicts among multiple goals including self-* objectives (autonomicity requirements) (Sects. 2.2.3 and 2.3). Goals have been recognized to provide the roots for detecting conflicts among requirements and for resolving them eventually [34, 45]. Note that by resolving conflicts among goals or obstacles to goal achievement, new goals (or self-* objectives) may emerge.

6. Resilience and robustness autonomy requirements might be handled by GORE as soft-constraints. For example, such requirements for GEO Missions (Sect. 2.3.2.3) are defined as *robustness: robust to communication latency* and *resilience: resilient GEO positioning*. These requirements can be specified as soft-goals leading the system towards *reducing and copying with communication latency* and *keeping GEO positioning optimal*. Note that specifying soft goals is not an easy task. The problem is that there is no clear-cut satisfaction condition for a soft-goal. Soft-goals are related to the notion of satisfaction [38]. Unlike regular goals, soft-goals can seldom be accomplished or satisfied. For soft-goals, eventually, we need to find solutions that are *"good enough"* where soft-goals are satisfied to a sufficient degree. Thus, when specifying robustness and resilience autonomy requirements we need to set the desired degree of satisfaction, e.g., by using probabilities.

7. Monitoring, mobility, dynamicity and adaptability might also be specified as soft-goals, but with relatively high degree of satisfaction. These three types of autonomy requirements represent important quality requirements that the system in question need to meet to provide conditions making autonomicity possible. Thus, their degree of satisfaction should be relatively high. Eventually, adaptability requirements might be treated as hard goals because they determine what parts of the system in question can be adapted (not how).

2.5.1.2 Goal Modeling

The benefit of goal modeling is to support heuristic, qualitative or formal reasoning schemes during requirements engineering. Goals are generally modelled by intrinsic features such as their type and attributes, and by their links to other goals and to other elements of a requirements model. Goals can be hierarchically organized and prioritized where high-level goals (e.g., mission objectives) might comprise related, low-level, sub-goals that can be organized to provide different alternatives of achieving the high-level goals. For example, KnowLang specifies goals either as a *transition from a state to a desired state* or simply as *a transition to a desired state* (Sect. 2.5.4.2). In this approach, a state presents particular conditions that must be met involving the system, environment or both, and a goal can be achieved via multiple inter-state-transitions with alternatives.

Goals are modeled with ASSL as *service-level objectives* (SLO) (Sect. 2.5.3) that can be correlated with events. SLO events can be fired when objectives get degraded or normalized, which allows the system react to changes in goals realization.

Goal modeling with languages like KnowLang, can be used to develop deliberative controllers for autonomous spacecraft. For example, KnowLang helps to realize a cognitive layer whereas system goals are pursued and low-level execution control and processing of sensor data are delegated to different components. Goal modeling supports a goal-oriented behavior and decomposition of complex behavior by means of policies that can focus on relevant sub-goals (Sect. 2.5.4.2).

2.5.2 Awareness Modeling

Awareness generally is classified into two major areas: *self-awareness*, pertaining to the internal world, and *context-awareness*, pertaining to the external world (Sect. 2.2.3). Autonomic computing research defines these two classes [25] as following:

- A self-aware system has detailed knowledge about its own entities, current states, capacity and capabilities, physical connections, and ownership relations with other systems in its environment.
- A context-aware system knows how to sense, negotiate, communicate, and interact with environmental systems and how to anticipate environmental system states, situations, and changes.

Perhaps a third class could be *situational awareness*, which is self-explanatory. Other classes could draw attention to specific problems, such as operational conditions and performance (operational awareness), control processes (control awareness), interaction processes (interaction awareness), and navigation processes (navigation awareness). Although classes of awareness can differ by subject, they all require a subjective perception of events and data "within a volume of time and space, the comprehension of their meaning, and the projection of their status in the near future" [15].

To better understand the idea of awareness in space missions, consider an exploration robot. Its navigation awareness mechanism could build a map on the fly, with landmarks represented as part of the environment knowledge, so that navigation becomes simply a matter of reading sensor data from cameras and plotting the robot's position at the time of observation. Via repeated position plots, the robot's course and land-reference speed can be established.

Recent research efforts have focused on awareness implementations in software-intensive systems. For example, commercially available server-monitoring platforms, such as Nimbus [44] and Cittio's Watch Tower [43], offer robust, lightweight sensing and reporting capabilities across large server farms. Such solutions are oriented toward massive data collection and performance reporting, so they leave much of the final analysis and decision making to a human administrator. Other approaches achieve awareness through model-based detection and response based on offline training and models constructed to represent different scenarios that the system can recognize at runtime.

To function, the mechanism implementing the awareness must be structured to take into consideration different stages—for example, it might be built over a complex chain of functions such as *raw data gathering*, *data passing*, *filtering*, *conversion*, *assessment*, *projection*, and *learning* [58]. As Fig. 2.5 shows, ideally, all the awareness functions could be structured as an awareness pyramid, forming the mechanism that converts raw data into conclusions, problem prediction, and eventually learning. As shown in Fig. 2.5, the first three levels include monitoring tasks; the fourth, recognition tasks; the fifth and sixth, assessment tasks; and the last, learning tasks. The pyramid levels in Fig. 2.5 represent awareness functions that can be grouped into four specific tasks:

- *monitoring*—collects, aggregates, filters, manages, and reports internal and external details such as metrics and topologies gathered from the system's internal entities and its context;
- *recognition*—uses knowledge structures and data patterns to aggregate and convert raw data into knowledge symbols;
- *assessment*—tracks changes and determines points of interest, generates hypotheses about situations involving these points, and recognizes situational patterns;
- *learning*—generates new situational patterns and maintains a history of property changes.

Aggregation can be included as a subtask at any function level; it's intended to improve overall awareness performance. For example, it can pull together large amounts of sensory data during the filtering stage or recognition tasks can apply it to improve classification.

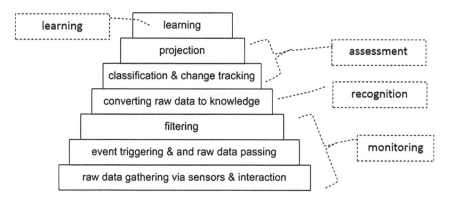

Fig. 2.5 The awareness pyramid [58]

The awareness process isn't as straightforward as it might seem- rather, it's cyclic, with several iterations over the various awareness functions. Closing the chain of awareness functions can form an awareness control loop in which different awareness classes can emerge [57]. The process's cyclic nature is why awareness itself is so complex, with several levels of exhibition and degrees of perception. The levels can be related to data readability and reliability—that is, they might include noisy data that must be cleaned up and eventually interpreted with some degree of probability. Other levels might include early awareness, which is a product of one or two passes of the awareness control loop, and late awareness, which should be more mature in terms of conclusions and projections.

2.5.3 ASSL

ASSL [54–56] is a model-oriented specification language for autonomic systems (ASs) (Chap. 1). ASSL considers ASs, as composed of *autonomic elements* (AEs) (Chap. 1) interacting over special *interaction protocols*.

To specify ASs, ASSL uses a multi-tier specification model. By their nature, the ASSL tiers are levels of abstraction of different aspects of the AS under consideration. These provide domain-specific constructs (specific to the autonomic computing domain) such as self-management policies, communication interfaces, execution semantics, actions, etc. There are three major tiers (three major abstraction perspectives), each composed of sub-tiers.

- *AS Tier*—forms a general and global AS perspective, where we define the general system rules in terms of service-level objectives (SLO) and self-management policies, architecture topology, and global actions, events, and metrics applied in these rules.
- *AS Interaction Protocol (ASIP) Tier*—forms a communication protocol perspective, where we define the means of communication between the so-called autonomic elements (system components).
- *AE Tier*—forms a unit-level perspective, where we define interacting sets of AEs with their own behavior.

Figure 2.6 represents the tiers in ASSL. As we can see, the ASSL specification model decomposes an AS in two directions: first into levels of functional abstraction, and second into functionally related sub-tiers. This decomposition fits naturally to the needs of the ASs builders, i.e., to build an AS:

1. We need a plan, i.e., a global picture of the entire system, which is specified at the AS tier.
2. We need the building blocks to construct that system—we specify our "bricks" at the AE tier.
3. We need the glue to put the bricks together and build the system. Our glue is the communication protocol, which we specify at the ASIP tier.

```
        I. Autonomic System (AS)
         * AS Service-level Objectives
         * AS Self-managing Policies
         * AS Architecture
         * AS Actions
         * AS Events
         * AS Metrics
       II. AS Interaction Protocol (ASIP)
         * AS Messages
         * AS Communication Channels
         * AS Communication Functions
      III. Autonomic Element (AE)
         * AE Service-level Objectives
         * AE Self-managing Policies
         * AE Friends
         * AE Interaction Protocol (AEIP)
           - AE Messages
           - AE Communication Channels
           - AE Communication Functions
           - AE Managed Elements
         * AE Recovery Protocol
         * AE Behavior Models
         * AE Outcomes
         * AE Actions
         * AE Events
         * AE Metrics
```

Fig. 2.6 ASSL multi-tier specification model

ASSL is designed to tackle the so-called *self-* requirements* (Sect. 2.2.3). To do so, the framework imposers a requirements engineering approach where self-* requirements are specified as special *policy models* [54, 55]. Note that the ASSL policy models specify special self-* policies (e.g., self-healing) driving the system in critical situations. To specify ASSL policy models, we need to come up with self-adapting scenarios where we may consider important events, actions, SLOs, etc. Note that the ASSL SLOs are actually high-order goal models where the GORE approach (Sect. 2.5.1) can be successfully applied to elicit goals and connect those goals with the proper policies. ASSL has been used in a variety of projects targeting functional prototypes of autonomous NASA space exploration missions [48, 52].

2.5.3.1 Specifying and Generating Prototypes with ASSL

The ASSL tiers are intended to specify different aspects of the AS in question, but it is not necessary to employ all of those in order to model an AS. Usually, an ASSL specification is built around self-management policies, which make that specification AC-driven. The ASSL formal model addresses policy specification at both AS and AE tiers. Policies are specified with special constructs called *fluents* and *mappings*:

- *Fluents* are states with duration and when the system gets into a specific fluent, a policy may be activated.
- *Mappings* map particular fluents to particular actions to be undertaken by the specified AS.

ASSL expresses fluents with *fluent-activating* and *fluent-terminating events*, i.e., the self-management policies are driven by events. In order to express mappings, conditions and actions are considered, where the former determine the latter in a deterministic manner.

The following ASSL code presents an example specification of a self-healing policy. Please refer to [54, 55] for more details on the ASSL specification model and grammar.

```
ASSELF_MANAGEMENT {
 SELF_HEALING {
  FLUENT inLosingSpacecraft {
   INITIATED_BY { EVENTS.spaceCraftLost }
   TERMINATED_BY { EVENTS.earthNotified }
  }
  MAPPING {
   CONDITIONS { inLosingSpacecraft }
   DO_ACTIONS { ACTIONS.notifyEarth }
  }
 }
} // ASSELF_MANAGEMENT
```

Once a specification is complete, it can be validated with the ASSL built-in consistency checking mechanism and a functional prototype can be generated automatically. The prototypes generated with the ASSL framework are fully-operational multithreaded event-driven applications with embedded messaging.

2.5.3.2 Handling Event-Based Autonomy with ASSL

ASSL is designed to tackle the *self-* requirements* (Sect. 2.2.3). In addition, ASSL could be extremely powerful when handling the ESA's L3 event-based autonomy (Sect. 2.1.2). ASSL aims at event-driven autonomic behavior. Recall that to specify self-management policies, we need to specify appropriate events (Sect. 2.5.3.1). Here, we rely on the reach set of event types exposed by ASSL [54, 55]. For example, to specify ASSL events, one may use logical expressions over SLOs, or may relate events with metrics, other events, actions, time, and messages. Moreover, ASSL allows for the specification of special conditions that must be stated before an event is prompted. Therefore, events can be constrained by adding such conditions to their specification.

Finally, ASSL appears to be very well suited for developing autonomous controllers for reactive architectures (Sect. 2.4.2.2). It is event-driven (exposes a rich set of possible events raised in the environment and the system itself). Special competence models can be built by using the self-adaptive policy and relying on ASSL fluents and actions to provide for desired behaviors. Note that ASSL implies layering (Fig. 2.6) for structuring functionalities in event-driven autonomy and provides computational structures that can be possibly effective when handling *layered controller architectures* (Sect. 2.4.2.3).

2.5.4 KnowLang

KnowLang is a framework for Knowledge Representation and Reasoning (KR&R) that aims at efficient and comprehensive *knowledge structuring and awareness* based on logical and statistical reasoning. It helps software engineers to tackle requirements via (1) explicit representation of domain concepts and relationships; (2) explicit representation of particular and general factual knowledge, in terms of predicates, names, connectives, quantifiers and identity; and (3) uncertain knowledge in which additive probabilities are used to represent degrees of belief.

A key feature of KnowLang is a *multi-tier specification model* [49, 50] allowing for integration of ontologies together with rules and Bayesian networks. At its very core, KnowLang is a formal specification language providing a comprehensive specification model aiming at addressing the knowledge representation problem for intelligent systems including engineering autonomy requirements. The complexity of the problem necessitated the use of a specification model where knowledge (consider also knowledge requirements) can be presented at different levels of abstraction and grouped by following both hierarchical and functional patterns. KnowLang imposes a multi-tier specification model (Fig. 2.6) where we specify a special knowledge base (KB) composed of layers dedicated to knowledge corpuses, KB (knowledge base) operators and inference primitives [49, 50].

The tier of knowledge corpuses is used to specify KR structures. The tier of KB operators provides access to knowledge corpuses via special class of *ASK* and *TELL operators* where ASK operators are dedicated to knowledge querying and retrieval and TELL operators allow for knowledge update. Moreover, this tier provides for special inter-ontology operators intended to work on one or more ontologies specified within the knowledge corpuses. Note that all the KB operators may imply the use of *inference primitives*, i.e., new knowledge might be inferred and eventually stored in the KB. The tier of inference primitives is intended to specify algorithms for reasoning and knowledge inference.

For more details on the KnowLang's multi-tier specification model, please refer to [49, 50].

2.5.4.1 Requirements Engineering with KnowLang

KnowLang can be successfully used to capture both functional (behavior requirements) and non-functional requirements (data requirements, constraints, etc.). Exclusively dedicated to knowledge modeling, KnowLang provides a rich set of constructs that helps us specify data requirements and functional requirements following a goal-oriented and/or behavior-oriented approach. When we specify knowledge with KnowLang, we build a KB with a variety of knowledge structures such as *ontologies*, *facts*, *rules*, and *constraints* where we need to specify the ontologies first in order to provide the *"vocabulary"* for the other knowledge structures.

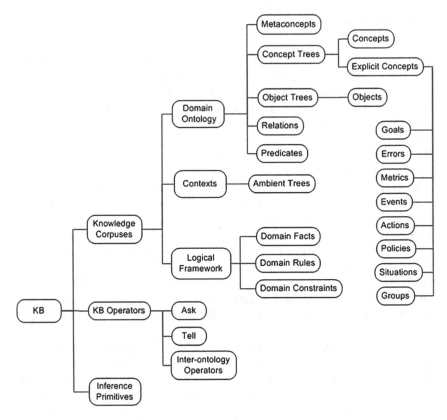

Fig. 2.7 KnowLang specification model

A KnowLang ontology is specified over *concept trees* (data classes, similar to classes in a domain model), *object trees*, *relations*, and *predicates* (Fig. 2.7). Each concept is specified with special properties and functionalities and is hierarchically linked to other concepts through *PARENTS* and *CHILDREN* relationships. In addition, for reasoning purposes every concept specified with KnowLang has an intrinsic *STATES* attribute that may be associated with a set of possible state values the concept instances might be in [49, 50]. The concept instances are considered as objects and are structured in object trees. The latter are a conceptualization of how objects existing in the world of interest are related to each other. The relationships in an *object tree* are based on the principle that objects have properties, where the value of a property is another object, which in turn also has properties.

Figure 2.8 depicts the graphical representation of a concept tree specified with KnowLang. In KnowLang, concepts and objects might be connected via *relations* expressing *relation requirements*. Relations connect two concepts, two objects, or an object with a concept and may have probability-distribution attribute (e.g., over time, over situations, over concepts' properties, etc.). Probability distribution is provided

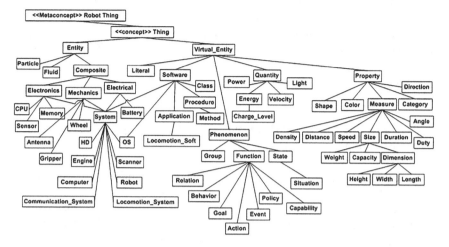

Fig. 2.8 KnowLang ontology specification sample

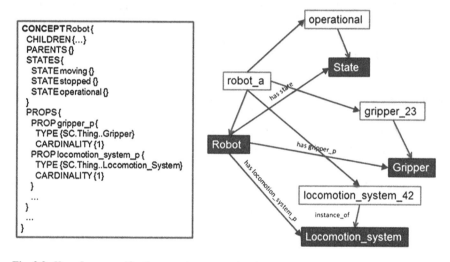

Fig. 2.9 KnowLang specification sample—concept and concept map

to support probabilistic reasoning and by specifying relations with *probability distributions* we actually specify Bayesian networks connecting the concepts and objects of an ontology. Figure 2.9 shows a KnowLang specification sample demonstrating both the language syntax [53] and its visual counterpart—a concept map based on inter-relations with no probability distributions. In general, modeling knowledge with KnowLang goes over a few phases:

1. Initial knowledge requirements gathering—involves domain experts to determine the basic notions, relations and functions (operations) of the domain of interest.

2. Behavior definition—identifies situations and behavior policies as "control data" helping to identify important self-adaptive scenarios.
3. Knowledge structuring—encapsulates domain entities, situations and behavior policies into KnowLang structures like concepts, properties, functionalities, objects, relations, facts and rules.

2.5.4.2 Capturing Autonomy Requirements with KnowLang: Modeling Self-Adaptive Behavior

KnowLang employs special knowledge structures for capturing self-* autonomy requirements (Sects. 2.2.3 and 2.3) by modeling *autonomic self-adaptive behavior* [51]. Such a behavior can be expressed via KnowLang policies, events, actions, situations and relations between policies and situations (Definitions 2.1–2.8). Policies (Π) are at the core of autonomic behavior (autonomic behavior can be associated with autonomy requirements). A policy π has a goal (g), policy situations (Si_π), policy-situation relations (R_π), and policy conditions (N_π) mapped to policy actions (A_π) where the evaluation of N_π may eventually (with some degree of probability) imply the evaluation of actions (denoted with $N_\pi \overset{[Z]}{\to} A_\pi$ (Definition 2.2). A condition is a Boolean function over ontology (Definition 2.4), e.g., the occurrence of a certain event.

Definition 2.1 $\Pi := \{\pi_1, \pi_2, ..., \pi_n\}, n \geq 0$ (Policies)

Definition 2.2 $\pi :=< g, Si_\pi, [R_\pi], N_\pi, A_\pi, map(N_\pi, A_\pi, [Z]) >$
$\quad A_\pi \subset A, N_\pi \overset{[Z]}{\to} A_\pi \quad (A_\pi$—Policy Actions)
$\quad Si_\pi \subset Si, Si_\pi := \{si_{\pi_1}, si_{\pi_2}, ..., si_{\pi_n}\}, n \geq 0$
$\quad R_\pi \subset R, R_\pi := \{r_{\pi_1}, r_{\pi_2}, ..., r_{\pi_n}\}, n \geq 0$
$\quad \forall r_\pi \in R_\pi \bullet (r_\pi :=< si_\pi, [rn], [Z], \pi >), si_\pi \in Si_\pi$
$\quad Si_\pi \overset{[R_\pi]}{\to} \pi \to N_\pi$

Definition 2.3 $N_\pi := \{n_1, n_2, ..., n_k\}, k \geq 0$ (Conditions)

Definition 2.4 $n := be(O)$ (Condition—Boolean Expression)

Definition 2.5 $g := \langle \Rightarrow s' \rangle | \langle s \Rightarrow s' \rangle$ (Goal)

Definition 2.6 $s := be(O)$ (State)

Definition 2.7 $Si := \{si_1, si_2, ..., si_n\}, n \geq 0$ (Situations)

Definition 2.8 $si :=< s, A \overset{\leftarrow}{si}, [E \overset{\leftarrow}{si}], A_{si} >$ (Situation)
$\quad A \overset{\leftarrow}{si} \subset A \quad (A \overset{\leftarrow}{si}$—Executed Actions)
$\quad A_{si} \subset A \quad (A_{si}$—Possible Actions)
$\quad E \overset{\leftarrow}{si} \subset E \quad (E \overset{\leftarrow}{si}$—Situation Events)

Policy situations (Si_π) are situations that may trigger (or imply) a policy π, in compliance with the policy-situations relations R_π (denoted with $Si_\pi \overset{[R_\pi]}{\rightarrow} \pi$), thus implying the evaluation of the policy conditions N_π (denoted with $\pi \rightarrow N_\pi$) (Definition 2.2). Therefore, the optional policy-situation relations (R_π) justify the relationships between a policy and the associated situations (Definition 2.2). In addition, the self-adaptive behavior requires relations to be specified to connect policies with situations over an optional probability distribution (Z) where a policy might be related to multiple situations and vice versa. Probability distribution is provided to support *probabilistic reasoning* and to help the KnowLang Reasoner choose the most probable situation-policy "pair". Thus, we may specify a few relations connecting a specific situation to different policies to be undertaken when the system is in that particular situation and the probability distribution over these relations (involving the same situation) should help the KnowLang Reasoner decide which policy to choose (denoted with $Si_\pi \overset{[R_\pi]}{\rightarrow} \pi$—Definition 2.2).

A goal g is a desirable transition to a state or from a specific state to another state (denoted with $s \Rightarrow s'$) (Definition 2.5). A state s is a Boolean expression over ontology ($be(O)$) (Definition 2.6), e.g., "a specific property of an object must hold a specific value". A situation is expressed with a state (s), a history of actions ($A \overset{\leftarrow}{si}$) (actions executed to get to state s), actions A_{si} that can be performed from state s and an optional history of events $E \overset{\leftarrow}{si}$ that eventually occurred to get to state s (Definition 2.8).

Ideally, policies are specified to handle specific situations, which may trigger the application of policies. A policy exhibits a behavior via actions generated in the environment or in the system itself. Specific conditions determine, which specific actions (among the actions associated with that policy—Definition 2.2) shall be executed. These conditions are often generic and may differ from the situations triggering the policy. Thus, the behavior not only depends on the specific situations a policy is specified to handle, but also depends on additional conditions. Such conditions might be organized in a way allowing for synchronization of different situations on the same policy. When a policy is applied, it checks what particular conditions are met and performs the mapped actions (see $map(N_\pi, A_\pi, [Z])$)—Definition 2.2). An optional probability distribution can additionally restrict the action execution. Although initially specified, the probability distribution at both mapping and relation levels is recomputed after the execution of any involved action. The re-computation is based on the consequences of the action execution, which allows for reinforcement learning.

2.5.4.3 Probability Assessment

The KnowLang approach to modeling self-adaptive behavior requires computation of probability values for ending in possible states when particular actions are executed. In this subsection, we present a *model for assessing probability* applicable to the computation of such probability values. In our approach, the probability assessment is an indicator of the number of possible execution paths an AS (e.g., ExoMars) may take, meaning the amount of certainty (excess entropy) in the autonomic behavior. To assess that behavior prior to implementation, it is important to understand the interactions among the system components and also the complex interactions with the surrounding environment (space). This can be achieved by modeling the behavior of the *individual reactive components* and the behavior of the *environment factors* (e.g., solar storm, gravity of a planet, etc.), together with the global system behavior as Discrete Time Markov Chains [18], and by assessing the level of probability through calculating the probabilities of the state transitions in the corresponding models. We assume that the component interactions and the environment-system interaction are stochastic processes where the events are not controlled by the AS and thus, their probabilities are considered equal.

The theoretical foundation for our Probability Assessment Model is the property of Markov chains, which states that, given the current state of the whole spacecraft system, its future evolution is independent of its history, which is also the main characteristic of a reactive and autonomic spacecraft [57, 59].

An algebraic representation of a Markov chain is a matrix (called transition matrix) (Table 2.2) where the rows and columns correspond to the states, and the entry p_{ij} in the ith row, jth column is the transition probability of being in state s_j at the stage following state s_i. We need to build such a transition matrix taking into account both the system components and environment factors influencing the system behavior. The following property holds for the calculated probabilities:

$$\sum_j z_{ij} = 1$$

We contend that probability should be calculated from the steady state of the Markov chain. A *steady state* (or equilibrium state) is one in which the probability of being in a state before and after a transition is the same as time progresses. Here, we define probability for a spacecraft system composed of k components and taking into account x environment factors as the level of certainty quantified by the source excess entropy, as follows:

Table 2.2 Transition matrix Z

	s_1	s_2	...	s_i	...	s_n
s_1	p_{11}	p_{12}	...	p_{1j}	...	p_{1n}
s_2	p_{21}	p_{22}	...	p_{2j}	...	p_{2n}
...	...	...	...	...	...	...
s_i	p_{i1}	p_{i2}	...	p_{ij}	...	p_{in}
...	...	...	...	...	...	...
s_n	p_{n1}	p_{n2}	...	p_{nj}	...	p_{nn}

$$P_{SCE} = \sum_{i=1,k} H_i + \sum_{e=1,x} H_e - H$$

$$H_i = -\sum_j p_{ij} \log_2(p_{ij})$$

$$H_e = -\sum_j p_{ej} \log_2(p_{ej})$$

$$H = -\left(\sum_i v_i \sum_j p_{ij} \log_2(p_{ij}) + \sum_e v_e \sum_j p_{ej} \log_2(p_{ej})\right)$$

Here,

- H is an entropy that quantifies the level of uncertainty in the Markov chain corresponding to the entire AS system;
- H_i is a level of uncertainty in a Markov chain corresponding to an autonomic system component;
- H_e is a level of uncertainty in a Markov chain corresponding to an environmental factor, e.g., distance to ground base, solar storm, gravity force of a planet, etc.;
- v is a steady state distribution vector for the corresponding Markov chain;
- p_{ij} values are transition probabilities in the extended state machines modeling the behavior of the i-th component;
- p_{ej} values are transition probabilities in the extended state machines modeling the behavior of the eth environmental factor.

Note that for a transition matrix P, the steady state distribution vector v satisfies the property $v * P = v$, and the sum of its components v_i is equal to 1.

2.5.4.4 Building Deliberative Controllers with KnowLang

KnowLang provides both the specification structures and runtime mechanism (reasoner) for the development of *deliberative controllers* (Sect. 2.4.2.1). It provides for a comprehensive knowledge representation mechanism and support to both logical and statistical reasoning based on integrated Bayesian networks. Moreover, similar to ASSL, KnowLang also implies layering (i.e., it might be used to handle *layered controller architectures*—Sect. 2.4.2.3) for structuring functionalities and computational structures used for reasoning purposes in goal-oriented autonomy. KnowLang provides a deliberative architecture controller through its KnowLang Reasoner. The reasoner is supplied as a component hosted by the autonomous system and thus, it runs in the system's Operational Context as any other system's component. However, it operates in the Knowledge Representation Context (KR Context) and on the KR symbols (represented knowledge). The system talks to the reasoner via special *ASK* and *TELL* Operators allowing for knowledge queries and knowledge updates (Fig. 2.10). Upon demand, the KnowLang Reasoner can also build up and return a self-adaptive behavior model—a chain of actions to be realized in the environment or in the system.

KnowLang provides for a predefined set of *ASK* and *TELL* Operators allowing for communication with the KB. *TELL* Operators feed the KR Context with

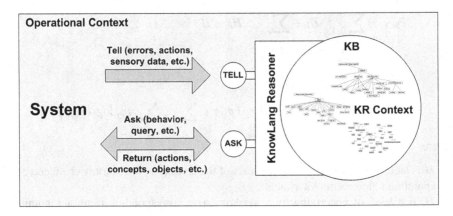

Fig. 2.10 KnowLang reasoner

important information driven by errors, executed actions, new sensory data, etc., thus helping the KnowLang Reasoner update the KR with recent changes in both the system and execution environment. The system uses ASK Operators to receive recommended behavior where knowledge is used against the perception of the world to generate appropriate actions in compliance to some goals and beliefs. In addition, ASK Operators may provide the system with awareness-based conclusions about the current state of the system or the environment and ideally with behavior models for self-adaptation.

2.6 Case Studies: Specifying Autonomy Requirements

In this section, we present three case studies where KnowLang and ASSL have been used to capture autonomy requirements. The first two examples are theoretical models of E4-level autonomic behavior developed with KnowLang and the third one is a concrete example where ASSL has been used to handle E3-level autonomy.

2.6.1 Handling Autonomy Requirements with KnowLang

KnowLang can be used as a *goal-oriented* approach to handling autonomy requirements. By specifying with KnowLang goals and policies handling those goals, actually, we express autonomy requirements (Sect. 2.5.4.2). Note that KnowLang can be successfully used to handle autonomy requirements for all four levels of autonomy recognized by ESA, including the E4 level, which is considered to represent *goal-oriented autonomy* (Sect. 2.1.2).

Fig. 2.11 Elements of the ExoMars program 2016–2018, picture courtesy of ESA

2.6.1.1 Case Study: Autonomy Requirements for ExoMars

To illustrate autonomic self-adaptive behavior based on this approach, we are going to elaborate on the ExoMars (Fig. 2.11) case study by assuming that the robotized rover discovers an interesting rock and it receives a command from the Earth to go and take samples from it.

Eventually, after receiving that command, the rover lost communication with the base on Earth and subsequently starts operating in autonomous mode following requirements for autonomy behavior expressed with KnowLang.

Let us assume that we have used KnowLang to specify autonomy requirements for ExoMars where in addition to another explicit knowledge, we have also specified policy $p1$ (see the KnowLang code below). Although we are missing the basic specification of the involved actions, goal, situation and relation, we can conclude that the current situation $si1$: *a massive rock has been discovered* will trigger a policy $p1$: *go to the rock location* if the relation $r1(si1, p1)$ has the higher probabilistic belief rate.

```
CONCEPT_POLICY p1 { //go to rock
  CHILDREN {} PARENTS {SC.Thing..Policy}
  SPEC {
    POLICY_GOAL {Goal.g1} //get to the rock location
    POLICY_SITUATIONS {Situation.si1} //rock is discovered
    POLICY_RELATIONS {Relation.r1} //relates p1 and si1
    POLICY_ACCTIONS {Action.Turn, Action.Move}
```

```
POLICY_MAPPINGS {
  MAPPING {
    CONDITIONS {ExoMars.Battery.level >= 0.5 AND Action.GetPriorityTasks (ExoMars) = 0}
    DO_ACTIONS { Action.Turn(Action.GetObjectAngle), Action.Move}
    PROBABILITY {1}
  }
 }
}
}

CONCEPT_POLICY p2 { //avoid obstacle
  CHILDREN {}
  PARENTS {SC.Thing..Policy}
  SPEC {
    POLICY_GOAL {Goal.g2} //free road
    POLICY_SITUATIONS {Situation.si2} //road is blocked
    POLICY_RELATIONS {Relation.r1} //relates p2 and si2
    POLICY_ACCTIONS {Action.TurnRight, Action.TurnLeft, Action.Move}
    POLICY_MAPPINGS {
      MAPPING {
        DO_ACTIONS {Action.TurnRight, Action.Move}
        PROBABILITY {0.6}
      }
      MAPPING {
        DO_ACTIONS {Action.TurnLeft, Action.Move}
        PROBABILITY {0.4}
      }
    }
  }
}
```

The $p1$ policy will realize actions *Turn* and *Move* iff the rover's battery is charged at least 50 % and there is no another higher priority task to finish up first (currently ongoing or scheduled). Ideally, the autonomic behavior will be produced by a sequence of actions, e.g., $\{Action.Turn(Action.GetSignalAngle), Action.Move\}$.

ExoMars will perform the generated actions and will start moving towards the rock. Let us assume that while moving, at certain point, the rover will hit a crack in the terrain and get into a situation $si2$: *road is blocked*, which by specification is related to policy $p2$: *avoid obstacle* (see KnowLang code above). Policy $p2$ will force the rover to turn right and move, because of the initial probability distribution in the *MAPPING* sections (see KnowLang code above). Eventually, the rover will reach a bridge in the crack and thus, will accomplish the $p2$'s goal $g2$: *free road*. Then it will go back to the initial situation $si1$: *a massive rock has been discovered*, which will trigger the policy $p1$: *go to the rock location* and the robot will start moving again towards the located rock.

Let us suppose that there are more cracks on the route to the located rock and any time when ExoMars gets into situation $si2$: "*road is blocked*" it will continue applying the $p2$ policy by avoiding the crack from the right side until it hits a very long crack on the right side and gets into a situation $si3$: "*tracked object is lost*". This new situation shall trigger another policy $p3$: "*go back until object appears*", which will move the robot back to a point where the rock can be located again and then, the robot will get back to situation $si2$ and policy $p2$. Following $p2$, the robot can fall again into $si3$ and then back to $si2$. However, every time when policy $p2$ fails to accomplish its goal $g2$: "*free road*", the KnowLang Reasoner re-computes the probability distribution in the *MAPPING* sections (see KnowLang code above), which eventually may lead to a point where by applying policy $p2$ the robot will turn left and move, i.e., it will self-adapt to the current situation and will try to avoid the crack from the left side.

Note that in this case study, we presented adaptation at the level of conditional mapping within a policy as presented in the formal KnowLang model for self-adaptive behavior (Sect. 2.5.4.2).

2.6.1.2 Case Study: Autonomy Requirements for a Transportation Robot

In this case study, we demonstrate how KnowLang can be used to handle autonomy requirements for a transportation robot carrying items from point A to point B by using two possible routes—route one and route two (Fig. 2.12).

Similar to the previous case study (Sect. 2.6.1.1), we specify autonomy requirements to handle autonomous behavior by specifying with KnowLang policies, goals, and situations, together with the accompanying actions, events, etc. Let's assume

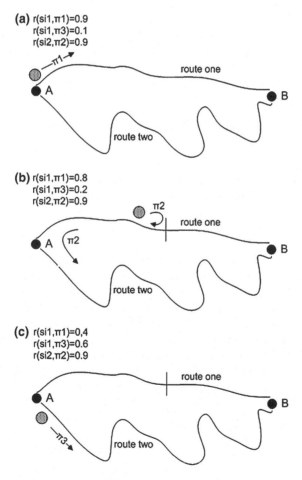

Fig. 2.12 Transportation robot case study

that we specified a situation $si1$: "*robot is in point A and loaded with items*", which will trigger a policy $\pi1$:"*go to point B via route one*" if the relation $r(si1, \pi1)$ has the higher probabilistic belief rate (let's assume that such a rate has been initially given to this relation because route one is shorter—Fig. 2.12a).

Any time when the robot gets into situation $si1$ it will continue applying the $\pi1$ policy until it gets into a situation $si2$: "*route one is blocked*" while applying that policy. The $si2$ situation will trigger a policy $\pi2$: "*go back to $si1$ and then apply policy $\pi3$*" (Fig. 2.12b). Policy $\pi3$ is defined as $\pi3$: "*go to point B via route two*". The unsuccessful application of policy $\pi1$ will decrease the probabilistic belief rate of relation $r(si1, \pi1)$ and the eventual successful application of policy $\pi3$ will increase the probabilistic belief rate of relation $r(si1, \pi3)$ (Fig. 2.12b). Thus, if route one continues to be blocked in the future, the relation $r(si1, \pi3)$ will get to have a higher probabilistic belief rate than the relation $r(si1, \pi1)$ and the robot will change its behavior by choosing route two as a primary route (Fig. 2.12c). Similarly, this situation can change in response to external stimuli, e.g., route two got blocked or a "*route one is obstacle-free*" message is received by the robot.

Note that in this case study, we presented adaptation at the level of situation-policy relations as presented in the formal KnowLang model for self-adaptive behavior (Sect. 2.5.4.2).

2.6.2 Specifying Autonomy Requirements for Voyager with ASSL

In this subsection, we demonstrate how the ASSL framework can be used to specify *self-* requirements* for an unmanned mission. In this exercise, we explore the image-processing system implemented onboard the Voyager spacecraft [41]. In order to take pictures, Voyager II carries two television cameras onboard—one for wide-angle images and one for narrow-angle images, where each camera records images with a resolution of 800×800 pixels. Both cameras can record images in black-and-white only, but each camera is equipped with a set of color filters, which helps in the reconstruction of images be as fully-colored ones. To transmit pictures to Earth, Voyager II uses its 12-foot dish antenna [41] to send streams of pixels. It uses the same microwave frequencies used for radar. However, due to the long distance and to fundamental laws of physics, the strength of the radio signal is diminished proportionally and it reaches antennas on Earth with a strength 20 billion times weaker [8]. To counter this, the signals are received by a network of enormous antennas located in Australia, Japan, California, and Spain. Next, all the faint signals received from Voyager II are combined and processed by the Voyager Mission base on Earth to reduce electronic noise, blend, and filter the composed pictures.

2.6.2.1 Voyager Image-Processing Behavior Algorithm

An autonomous-specific behavior is observed in the Voyager spacecraft when a picture must be taken and sent to Earth. The following elements describe the algorithm we apply to specify the image-processing behavior observed in the Voyager mission with ASSL.

1. The Voyager II spacecraft:

   (a) uses its cameras to monitor space objects and decide when it is time to take a picture;
   (b) takes a picture with its wide-image camera or with its narrow-image camera;
   (c) notifies the antennas on Earth with "image session start" messages that an image transmission is about to start;
   (d) applies each color filter and sends the stream of pixels for each filter to Earth;
   (e) notifies antennas on Earth for the end of each session with "image session end" messages.

2. The antennas on Earth:

   (a) are prompted to receive the image by the "image session start" messages (one per applied filter);
   (b) receive image pixels;
   (c) are prompted to terminate the image sessions by "image session end" messages;
   (d) send the collected images to the Voyager Mission base on Earth.

3. The Voyager Mission base on Earth receives the image messages from the antennas.

2.6.2.2 Specifying Voyager Mission with ASSL

In order to specify the algorithm described in Sect. 2.4.2.1, we apply the ASSL multi-tier specification model (Sect. 2.5.3) and specified the Voyager II Mission at the three main ASSL tiers—AS (autonomic system) tier, $ASIP$ (autonomic system specification protocol) tier, and AE (autonomic element) tier. Hence, in our specification, we specify the Voyager II spacecraft and the antennas on Earth as AEs (autonomic elements) that follow their encoded autonomic behavior and exchange predefined ASSL messages over predefined ASSL communication channels. The Voyager mission's autonomic behavior is specified at both AS and AE tiers as a *self-management policy* called $IMAGE\_PROCESSING$. Thus, the global autonomic behavior of the Voyager II Mission is determined by the specification of that policy at each AE and at the global AS tier. The full specification is presented in Appendix A.

AS Tier Specification

At this tier, we specify the global AS-level autonomic behavior of the Voyager Mission. This behavior is encoded in the specification of an $IMAGE\_PROCESSING$

self-management policy. At this tier, that policy specifies an image-receiving process taking place at the four antennas on Earth (located in Australia, Japan, California, and Spain). In fact, as specified at the AS Tier, this policy forms the autonomic image-processing behavior of the Voyager Mission base on Earth. Here, we specified four *"inProcessingImage_"* fluents (one per antenna), which are initiated by events prompted when an image has been received, and terminated by events prompted when the received image has been processed. Further, all the four fluents are mapped to a *processImage* action. The following specification sample shows a fluent specification together with its mapping:

```
FLUENT inProcessingImage_AntSpain {
 INITIATED_BY { EVENTS.imageAntSpainReceived }
 TERMINATED_BY { EVENTS.imageAntSpainProcessed }
}
MAPPING {
 CONDITIONS { inProcessingImage_AntAustralia }
 DO_ACTIONS { ACTIONS.processImage(''Antenna_Australia'') }
}
```

Here, the specification of the events that initiate and terminate that fluent is the following:

```
EVENT imageAntSpainReceived {
 ACTIVATION { RECEIVED { ASIP.MESSAGES.msgImageAntSpain }
 }
}
EVENT imageAntSpainProcessed { }
```

Note that the *processImage* action is an *IMPL* action [54, 55], i.e., it is a kind of abstract action that does not specify any statements to be performed. The ASSL framework considers the *IMPL* actions as *"to be manually implemented"* after code generation. The following is a partial specification of that action:

```
ACTION IMPL processImage {
 PARAMETERS { string antennaName }
 GUARDS {
  ASSELF_MANAGEMENT.OTHER_POLICIES.IMAGE_PROCESSING.inProcessingImage_AntAustralia
   OR
  ASSELF_MANAGEMENT.OTHER_POLICIES.IMAGE_PROCESSING.inProcessingImage_AntJapan
  ....
 }
 TRIGGERS {
  IF antennaName = ''Antenna_Australia'' THEN
   EVENTS.imageAntAustraliaProcessed
  END
  ELSE ....
 }
}
```

Here, the *processImage* action is specified to accept a single parameter. The latter allows that action to process images from all four antennas. Moreover, there is a special *GUARDS* clause that is specified to prevent execution of the action when none of the four fluents is initiated. The action triggers an *imageAnt*[antenna name]*Processed* event if the action is performed with no exceptions.

ASIP Tier Specification

At this tier, we specify the AS-level communication protocol—the autonomic system interaction protocol (ASIP) (Sect. 2.5.3). This communication protocol is specified to be used by the four antennas when these communicate with the Voyager Mission base on Earth. Here, at this tier we specify four image messages (one per antenna), a communication channel that is used to communicate these messages, and communication functions (e.g., *sendImageMsg* and *receiveImageMsg*) to send and receive these messages over that communication channel. Note that the communication functions accept a parameter that allows same communication functions to send or receive messages to and from different antennas. Please refer to Appendix A for the ASSL specification of the Voyager ASIP.

AE Tier Specification

At this tier, we specified five AEs. The Voyager II spacecraft and all four antennas on Earth (the antennas located in Australia, Japan, California, and Spain), are specify as AEs. Note that here, we specify the *IMAGE_PROCESSING* self-management policy at the level of single AE and thus, this policy is realized over all AEs specified for the Voyager Mission. The following elements present important details of this specification. Please, refer to Appendix A for the complete specification.

AE Voyager

The most complex AE is the one specified for the Voyager II spacecraft. To express the *IMAGE_PROCESSING* self-management policy for this AE, we specified two fluents: *inTakingPicture* and *inProcessingPicturePixels*. The following ASSL code presents that self-management policy with both fluents and mapping sections.

```
AESELF_MANAGEMENT {
 OTHER_POLICIES {
  POLICY IMAGE_PROCESSING {
   FLUENT inTakingPicture {
    INITIATED_BY { EVENTS.timeToTakePicture }
    TERMINATED_BY { EVENTS.pictureTaken }
   }
   FLUENT inProcessingPicturePixels {
    INITIATED_BY { EVENTS.pictureTaken }
    TERMINATED_BY { EVENTS.pictureProcessed }
   }
   MAPPING {
    CONDITIONS { inTakingPicture }
    DO_ACTIONS { ACTIONS.takePicture }
   }
   MAPPING {
    CONDITIONS { inProcessingPicturePixels }
    DO_ACTIONS { ACTIONS.processPicture }
   }
  }
 }
} // AESELF_MANAGEMENT
```

Here, the *inTakingPicture* fluent is initiated by a *timeToTakePicture* event and terminated by a *pictureTaken* event. This event also initiates the *inProcessing Pic-turePixels* fluent, which is terminated by the *pictureProcessed* event. Both fluents are mapped to the actions *takePicture* and *processPicture* respectively.

In addition, we specified an *AEIP* (autonomic element interaction protocol) (Sect. 2.5.3), which is used by the Voyager AE to communicate with the four antenna AEs and to monitor and control the two cameras (wide-image camera and narrow-image camera) on board. Thus, with this AEIP we specified:

- ASSL messages needed to send an image pixel and messages that notify the antenna AEs that an image-receiving session is about to begin or end.
- A private communication channel.

- Three communication functions that send the AEIP messages over the AEIP communication channel.
- Two special managed elements (termed *wideAngleCamera* and *narrowAngle-Camera*) to specify interface functions needed by the Voyager AE to monitor and control both cameras. Through their interface functions, both managed elements are used by the actions mapped to the fluents *inTakingPicture* and *inProcessingPicturePixels* to take pictures, apply filters, and detect interesting space objects.

The following specification sample shows a partial specification of one of these managed elements.

```
MANAGED_ELEMENT wideAngleCamera {
 INTERFACE_FUNCTION takePicture { }
 ....
 INTERFACE_FUNCTION countInterestingObjects {
  RETURNS { integer }
 }
}
```

Moreover, an *interestingObjects* metric is specified to count all detected interesting objects, which the Voyager AE takes pictures of. The source of this metric is specified as one of the managed element interface functions (*countInteresting-Objects*), i.e., the metric gets updated by that interface function.

```
METRIC interestingObjects {
 METRIC_TYPE { RESOURCE }
 METRIC_SOURCE { AEIP.MANAGED_ELEMENTS.wideAngleCamera.countInterestingObjects }
 THRESHOLD_CLASS { integer [ 0~ ) }
}
```

Note that the *timeToTakePicture* event (it activates the *inTakingPicture* fluent) is prompted by a change in this metric's value. Here, in order to simulate this condition, we also activate this event every 60s on a periodic basis.

```
EVENT timeToTakePicture {
 ACTIVATION { CHANGED { METRICS.interestingObjects } OR PERIOD { 60 SEC } }
}
```

The four antenna AEs are specified as friends (at the *FRIENDS* sub-tier) of the Voyager AE. According to the ASSL semantics [54, 55] friends can share private interaction protocols. Thus, the antenna AEs can use the messages and channels specified by the AEIP of the Voyager AE.

Antenna AEs

We specify the four antennas receiving signals from the Voyager II spacecraft as AEs, i.e., we specified AEs termed *Antenna_Australia*, *Antenna_Japan*, *Antenna_California*, and *Antenna_Spain*. Here, the *IMAGE_PROCESSING* self-management policy for these AEs is specified with a few pairs of *inStartingImageSession - inCollectingImagePixels* fluents. A pair of such fluents is specified per image filter and determines states of the antenna AE when an image-receiving session is starting and when the antenna AE is collecting the image pixels.

Because the Voyager AE processes the images by applying different filters and sends each filtered image separately, we specified for each applied filter different fluents in the antenna AEs [52] (see Appendix A for the complete $IMAGE\_PROCE$-$SSING$ specification at the antenna AEs). This allows an antenna AE to process a collection of multiple filtered images simultaneously. Note that according to the ASSL formal semantics, a fluent cannot be re-initiated while it is initiated, thus preventing the same fluent be initiated simultaneously twice or more times [54, 55]. Here, these fluents are initiated and terminated by AE events specified to be prompted by the Voyager AE's messages notifying that an image-receiving session begins or ends. The following partial specification shows two of the $IMAGE\_PROCESSING$ fluents. These fluents are mapped to AE actions that collect the image pixels per filtered image.

```
FLUENT inStartingGreenImageSession {
 INITIATED_BY { EVENTS.greenImageSessionIsAboutToStart }
 TERMINATED_BY { EVENTS.imageSessionStartedGreen }
}
FLUENT inCollectingImagePixelsBlue {
 INITIATED_BY { EVENTS.imageSessionStartedBlue }
 TERMINATED_BY { EVENTS.imageSessionEndedBlue }
}
```

In addition, an $inSendingImage$ fluent is specified. This fluent activates when the antenna AE is done with the image collection work, i.e., all the filtered images (for all the applied filters) have been collected. The fluent is mapped to a sendImage action that sends the filtered images as one image to the Voyager Mission base on Earth. The following listing presents two of the events used to initiate those fluents.

```
EVENT greenImageSessionIsAboutToStart {
 ACTIVATION { SENT { AES.Voyager.AEIP.MESSAGES.msgGreenSessionBeginAus } }
}
EVENT imageSessionStartedBlue {
 ACTIVATION { RECEIVED { AES.Voyager.AEIP.MESSAGES.msgBlueSessionBeginAus } }
}
```

Note that the $greenImageSessionIsAboutToStart$ event is prompted when the Voyager's $msgGreenSessionBeginSpn$ message has been sent, and the $imageSession$-$StartedBlue$ event is prompted when the Voyager AE's $msgBlueSessionBeginSpn$ message has been received by the antenna. Moreover, each antenna AE specifies communication functions which allows the AE to receive the Voyager AE's messages (Appendix A). These communication functions are called by the AE actions.

2.7 Summary

Contemporary software-intensive systems, such as modern spacecraft and unmanned exploration platforms (e.g., ExoMars) generally exhibit a number of autonomic features resulting in complex behavior and complex interactions with the operational environment, often leading to a need of self-adaptation. To properly develop such systems, it is very important to handle the autonomy requirements properly. However, requirements engineering for ASs appears to be a wide open research area with only a limited number of approaches yet considered. It is our understanding that formal methods can eventually be successful in capturing autonomy requirements. An AS-dedicated formalism might help developers with a well-defined formal semantics that makes the specification of autonomy requirements a base from which developers can design, implement, and verify ASs.

In this chapter, we have presented *generic autonomy requirements* for space missions along with *controller architectures* for robotic systems. Further, we have presented formal methods that cope with both generic autonomy requirements and controller architectures, and as such can lay the foundations of a new AREM (Autonomy Requirements Engineering Model) framework dedicated to autonomic features of software-intensive systems including autonomous space missions. As presented, the targeted AREM approach shall be eventually goal-oriented and based on both KnowLang and ASSL formal methods. As a proof of concept and to demonstrate the expressiveness of the specification languages, we have presented three case studies where KnowLang and ASSL were used to capture to some extend autonomy requirements for both L4 and L3 levels of autonomy.

References

1. Amey, P.: Correctness by construction: better can also be cheaper. CrossTalk Mag. J. Def. Softw. Eng. **2**, 24–28 (2002)
2. Andrei, O., Kirchner, H.: A higher-order graph calculus for autonomic computing. In: Graph Theory, Computational Intelligence and Thought. No. 5420 in Lecture Notes in Computer Science, pp. 15–26. Springer, Heidelberg (2008)
3. Assurance Process for Complex Electronics, NASA: Requirements engineering (2009). http://www.hq.nasa.gov/office/codeq/software/ComplexElectronics/l_requirements2.htm
4. Banâtre, J.P., Fradet, P., Radenac, Y.: Programming self-organizing systems with the higher-order chemical language. Int. J. Unconv. Comput. **3**(3), 161–177 (2007)
5. Beaudette, S.: Satellite Mission Analysis, FDR-SAT-2004-3.2.A. Technical report, Carleton University (2004)
6. Benveniste, A., Caspi, P., Edwards, S., Halbwachs, N., Guernic, P.L., Simone, R.D.: The synchronous languages twelve years later. Proc. IEEE **91**(1), 64–83 (2003)
7. Brachman, R.J., Levesque, H.J.: Knowledge Representation and Reasoning. Elsevier, San Francisco (2004)
8. Browne, W.M.: Technical "Magic" Converts a Puny Signal into Pictures. NY Times (1989)
9. Cheng, B., Atlee, J.: Research directions in requirements engineering. In: Proceedings of the 2007 Conference on Future of Software Engineering (FOSE 2007), pp. 285–303. IEEE Computer Society, Los Alamitos (2007)
10. Cheng, S.W., Garlan, D., Schmerl, B.: Architecture-based self-adaptation in the presence of multiple objectives. In: Proceedings of the 2006 International Workshop on Self-Adaptation and Self-Managing Systems (SEAMS'06), pp. 2–8 (2006)
11. Cortim: LEXIOR: LEXIcal analysis for improvement of requirements. www.cortim.com
12. Dardenne, A., van Lamsweerde, A., Fickas, S.: Goal-directed requirements acquisitions. Sci. Comput. Program. **20**, 3–50 (1993)
13. Devedzic, V., Radovic, D.: A framework for building intelligent manufacturing systems. IEEE Trans. Syst. Man Cybern. C Appl. Rev. **29**, 422–439 (1999)
14. ECSS Secretariat: Space engineering: space segment operability. Technical report, ESA-ESTEC, Requirements and Standards Division, ECSS-E-ST-70-11C, Noordwijk, The Netherlands (2008)

15. Endsley, M.: Toward a theory of situation awareness in dynamic systems. Hum. Factors **37**(1), 32–64 (1995)
16. ESA: Automatic code and test generation (2007). http://www.esa.int/TEC/Software_engineering_and_standardisation/TECOQAUXBQE_2.html
17. ESA: Requirement engineering and modeling, software engineering and standardization (2007). http://www.esa.int/TEC/Software_engineering_and_standardisation/TECLCAUXBQE_0.html
18. Ewens, W.J., Grant, G.R.: Stochastic processes (i): Poison processes and Markov chains. In: Statistical Methods in Bioinformatics, 2nd edn. Springer, New York (2005)
19. Fickas, S., Feather, M.: Requirements monitoring in dynamic environments. In: Proceedings of the IEEE International Symposium on Requirements Engineering (RE 1995), pp. 140–147. IEEE Computer Society, Los Alamitos (1995)
20. Fortescue, P., Swinerd, G., Stark, J. (eds.): Spacecraft Systems Engineering, 4th edn. Wiley, New York (2011)
21. George, L., Kos, L.: Interplanetary Mission Design Handbook: Earth-to-Mars Mission Opportunities and Mars-to-Earth Return Opportunities 2009–2024. NASA,Marshall Space Flight Center. Springfield, Huntsville (1998)
22. Goldsby, H., Sawyer, P., Bencomo, N., Hughes, D., Cheng, B.: Goal-based modeling of dynamically adaptive system requirements. In: Proceedings of the 15th Annual IEEE International Conference on the Engineering of Computer Based Systems (ECBS). IEEE Computer Society, Los Alamitos (2008)
23. Halbwachs, N.: Synchronous Programming of Reactive Systems. Kluwer Academic Publishers, Boston (1993)
24. IBM Corporation: Policy management for autonomic computing—version 1.2. Technical report, IBM Tivoli (2005)
25. IBM: Autonomic computing: IBM's perspective on the state of information technology, IBM autonomic computing manifesto (2001). http://www.research.ibm.com/autonomic/manifesto/autonomic_computing.pdf
26. IEEE Computer Society: IEEE Standard IEEE-Std-830-1998: IEEE Recommended Practice for Software Requirements Specification (1998)
27. Lapouchnian, A., Yu, Y., Liaskos, S., Mylopoulos, J.: Requirements-driven design of autonomic application software. In: Proceedings of the 2006 Conference of the Center for Advanced Studies on Collaborative Research (CASCON 2006), p. 7. ACM, Boston (2006)
28. Madni, A.: Agiletecting: a principled approach to introducing agility in systems engineering and product development enterprises. J. Integr. Des. Process Sci. **12**(4), 1–7 (2008)
29. Mylopoulos, J., Chung, L., Nixon, B.: Representing and using non-functional requirements: a process-oriented approach. IEEE Trans. Softw. Eng. **18**(6), 483–497 (1992)
30. NASA: Deep Space 1 (2010). http://nmp.jpl.nasa.gov/ds1/
31. NASA, Goddard Space Flight Center: The extended mission Earth Observing-1 (2008). http://eo1.gsfc.nasa.gov/
32. Ocón, J. et al.: Autonomous controller—survey of the state of the art, Version 1.3, GOAC, GMV-GOAC-TN01. Technical report, ESTEC/Contract No. 22361/09/NL/RA (2011)
33. ProForum, W.: Web ProForum tutorials. http://www.iec.org
34. Robinson, W.N.: Integrating multiple specifications using domain goals. In: Proceedings of the 5th International Workshop on Software Specification and Design (IWSSD-5), pp. 219–225. IEEE, New York (1989)
35. Savor, T., Seviora, R.: An approach to automatic detection of software failures in real-time systems. In: Proceedings of the IEEE Real-Time Technology and Applications Symposium, pp. 136–147. IEEE Computer Society, Los Alamitos (1997)
36. Scerri, P., Pynadath, D., Tambe, M.: Towards adjustable autonomy for the real-world. J. Artif. Intell. Res. **17**(1), 171–228 (2002)
37. Schmidt, M., Schilling, K.: Satellite constellations and ground networks—a new perspective on distributed space missions. In: Proceedings of 2nd Nano-Satellite Symposium, Tokyo, Japan (2011)

38. Simon, H.: The Sciences of the Artificial, 2nd edn. MIT Press, Cambridge (1981)
39. Soutchanski, M.: High-level robot programming and program execution. In: Proceedings of the ICAPS'03 Workshop on Plan Execution. AAAI Press, Cambridge (2003)
40. Sutcliffe, A., Fickas, S., Sohlberg, M.: PC-RE a method for personal and context requirements engineering with some experience. Requir. Eng. J. **11**, 1–17 (2006)
41. The Planetary Society: Space topics: Voyager—the story of the mission (2010). http://planetary.org/explore/topics/space_missions/voyager/objectives.html
42. Truszkowski, W., Hallock, L., Rouff, C., Karlin, J., Rash, J., Hinchey, M., Sterritt, R.: Autonomous and Autonomic Systems—with Applications to NASA Intelligent Spacecraft Operations and Exploration Systems. Springer, Berlin (2009)
43. UBM Tech: Cittio's WatchTower 3.0 (2014). http://www.networkcomputing.com/careers-and-certifications/cittios-watchtower-30/d/d-id/1218255?
44. University of Chicago: Nimbus (2014). http://www.nimbusproject.org
45. van Lamsweerde, A., Darimont, R., Letier, E.: Managing conflicts in goal-driven requirements engineering. In: IEEE Transactions on Software Engineering, Special Issue on Inconsistency Management in Software Development (1998)
46. van Lamsweerde, A.: Requirements engineering in the year 00: a research perspective. In: Proceedings of the 22nd IEEE International Conference on Software Engineering (ICSE-2000), pp. 5–19. ACM, Boston (2000)
47. Vassev, E., Hinchey, M., Balasubramaniam, D., Dobson, S.: An ASSL approach to handling uncertainty in self-adaptive systems. In: Proceedings of the 34th annual IEEE Software Engineering Workshop (SEW34), pp. 11–18. IEEE Computer Society, Los Alamitos (2011)
48. Vassev, E., Hinchey, M., Paquet, J.: Towards an ASSL specification model for NASA swarm-based exploration missions. In: Proceedings of the 23rd Annual ACM Symposium on Applied Computing (SAC 2008)—AC Track, pp. 1652–1657. ACM, Boston (2008)
49. Vassev, E., Hinchey, M.: Knowledge representation and awareness in autonomic service-component ensembles—state of the art. In: Proceedings of the 14th IEEE International Symposium on Object/Component/ Service-Oriented Real-time Distributed Computing Workshops, pp. 110–119. IEEE Computer Society, Los Alamitos (2011)
50. Vassev, E., Hinchey, M.: Knowledge representation for cognitive robotic systems. In: Proceedings of the 15th IEEE International Symposium on Object/Component/Service-Oriented Real-time Distributed Computing Workshops (ISCORCW 2012), pp. 156–163. IEEE Computer Society, Los Alamitos (2012)
51. Vassev, E., Hinchey, M.: Knowledge-based self-adaptation. In: Proceedings of the 6th Latin-American Symposium on Dependable Computing (LADC 2013), Rio de Janeiro, Brazil, pp. 11–18. SBC - Brazilian Computer Society Press, Rio de Janeiro (2013)
52. Vassev, E., Hinchey, M.: Modeling the image-processing behavior of the NASA Voyager Mission with ASSL. In: Proceedings of the 3rd IEEE International Conference on Space Mission Challenges for Information Technology (SMC-IT'09), pp. 246–253. IEEE Computer Society, Los Alamitos (2009)
53. Vassev, E.: KnowLang grammar in BNF, lero-tr-2012-04. Technical report, Lero, University of Limerick (2012)
54. Vassev, E.: Towards a framework for specification and code generation of autonomic systems. Ph.D. thesis, Computer Science and Software Engineering Department, Concordia University, Quebec, Canada (2008)
55. Vassev, E. (ed.): ASSL: Autonomic System Specification Language—A Framework for Specification and Code Generation of Autonomic Systems. LAP Lambert Academic Publishing, Saarbrucken (2009)
56. Vassev, E., Hinchey, M.: ASSL: a software engineering approach to autonomic computing. IEEE Comput. **42**(6), 106–109 (2009)
57. Vassev, E., Hinchey, M.: The challenge of developing autonomic systems. IEEE Comput. **43**(12), 93–96 (2010)
58. Vassev, E., Hinchey, M.: Awareness in software-intensive systems. IEEE Comput. **45**(12), 84–87 (2012)

59. Vassev, E., Sterritt, R., Rouff, C., Hinchey, M.: Swarm technology at NASA: building resilient systems. IT Prof. **14**(2), 36–42 (2012)
60. Wei, C., Hindriks, K.V.: An agent-based cognitive robot architecture. In: Proceedings of Programming Multi-Agent Systems (ProMAS) Workshop Affiliated with AAMAS 2012, Valencia, Spain, pp. 55–68 (2012)
61. Wertz, J., Larson, W. (eds.): Space Mission Analysis and Design, 3rd edn. Microcosm Press, Dordrecht (1999)
62. Wood, L.: Satellite constellation networks. In: Yongguang Zhang (ed.) Internetworking and Computing Over Satellite Networks, pp. 13–34. Kluwer Academic Publishers, Dordrecht (2003)

Chapter 3
Autonomy Requirements Engineering

Abstract This chapter draws upon the discussion and results presented in the previous two chapters to define and outline an Autonomy Requirements Engineering (ARE) method. ARE targets the integration and promotion of autonomy in unmanned space missions by providing a mechanism and methodology for elicitation and expression of autonomy requirements. ARE relies on *goal-oriented requirements engineering* to elicit and define the system goals, and uses the *generic autonomy requirements* model to derive and define assistive and eventually alternative objectives. The system may pursue these "*self-* objectives*" in the presence of factors threatening the achievement of the initial system goals. Once identified, the autonomy requirements are specified with the KnowLang language. A proof-of-concept case study demonstrating the ARE's ability to handle autonomy requirements is presented and discussed in detail. The presented case study is a requirements engineering case study on the discovery and expression of autonomy requirements for ESA's BepiColombo Mission.

3.1 Introduction

The integration and promotion of autonomy in unmanned space missions is an extremely challenging task. Among the many challenges engineers must overcome are those related to the elicitation and expression of autonomy requirements. This chapter draws upon the discussion and results presented in the previous two chapters to define and outline an Autonomy Requirements Engineering (ARE) method along with a proof-of-concept case study demonstrating ARE's ability to handle autonomy requirements. The presented case study is a requirements engineering case study on the discovery and expression of autonomy requirements for the ESA's BepiColombo Mission [11, 12, 16, 23, 26, 39]. Note that the case study outlines both the ARE approach and generates a proof-of-concept outcome in the form of special goals models and autonomy requirements that can be further used to design and develop autonomy features for BepiColombo.

BepiColombo is an ESA cornerstone mission to Mercury [32] (Fig. 3.1) scheduled for launch in 2015. Among several investigations, BepiColombo will make a complete map of Mercury at different wavelengths. It will chart the planet's mineralogy

© Springer International Publishing Switzerland 2014   105
E. Vassev and M. Hinchey, *Autonomy Requirements Engineering for Space Missions*,
NASA Monographs in Systems and Software Engineering,
DOI 10.1007/978-3-319-09816-6_3

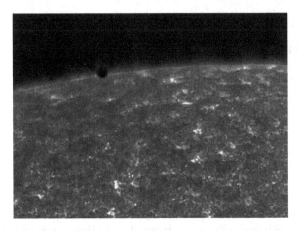

Fig. 3.1 Transit of Mercury seen by the TRACE satellite, photo courtesy of NASA

and elemental composition, determine whether the interior of the planet is molten or not, and investigate the extent and origin of Mercury's magnetic field. The mission involves two components: the Mercury Planetary Orbiter (MPO) and the Mercury Magnetospheric Orbiter (MMO). The spacecraft will have a 6 year interplanetary cruise to Mercury using solar-electric propulsion and Moon, Venus, and Mercury gravity assists. On arrival in January 2022, the MPO and MMO will be captured into polar orbits. During the voyage to Mercury, the *two orbiters* grouped into a *composite module* and a *transfer module* (consisting of *electric propulsion* and traditional *chemical rockets*) will form one single carrier spacecraft. When approaching Mercury in 2022, the transfer module will be separated and the composite module will use rocket engines and a technique called *weak stability boundary capture* to bring itself into polar orbit around the planet. When the MMO orbit is reached, the MPO will separate and lower its altitude to its own *operational orbit*. Observations from orbit will be taken for at least one Earth year.

3.2 ARE: Autonomy Requirements Engineering

As explained in Chap. 2, a comprehensive and efficient ARE approach should take into account all the autonomy aspects of the targeted system and emphasize the so-called *self-* requirements* by taking into consideration the traditional functional and non-functional requirements of spacecraft systems (e.g., safety requirements).

In our approach, ARE: (1) relies on Goal-Oriented Requirements Engineering (GORE) to elicit and define the system goals and then (2) uses the Generic Autonomy Requirements (GAR) model, put in the context of space missions (Chap. 2) to derive and define assistive and eventually *alternative goals* (or objectives) the system may pursue in the presence of factors threatening the achievement of the initial system goals. Once identified, the autonomy requirements including the self-* objectives might be further specified with languages complying with GAR (e.g., ASSL [37] or KnowLang [36]).

The proposed ARE method is a software engineering process helping to (1) determine what autonomic features are to be developed for a particular space mission and (2) generate autonomy requirements supporting those features. Note that the outcome of ARE (goals models, requirements specifications, etc.) is a precursor of design of autonomic features.

3.2.1 GAR: Generic Autonomy Requirements

Despite their differences in terms of application domain and functionality, all autonomous systems are capable of autonomous behavior (or autonomicity) driven by one or more self-management objectives. Thus, the development of autonomous systems is driven by the self-management objectives (also could be considered as self-adaptive objectives) and attributes, which introduce special requirements termed self-* requirements. Note that this requirement automatically involves (1) *self-diagnosis* to analyze a problem situation and to determine a diagnosis and (2) *self-adaptation* to repair discovered faults. The ability to perform adequate self-diagnosis depends largely on the quality and quantity of the system's knowledge of its current state, i.e., on the system awareness. Based on the self-* requirements, GAR defines a set of generic autonomy requirements (Chap. 2):

- *autonomicity* (self-* objectives)—Autonomicity is one of the essential characteristics of autonomous systems. The self-* objectives provide for autonomous behavior (e.g., self-configuring, self-healing, self-optimizing, and self-protecting).
- *knowledge*—An autonomous system is intended to possess awareness capabilities based on well-structured knowledge and algorithms operating over the same.
- *awareness*—A product of knowledge representation, reasoning, and monitoring.
- *monitoring*—The process of obtaining raw data through a collection of sensors or events.
- *adaptability*—The ability to achieve change in observable behavior and/or structure. Adaptability may require changes in functionality, algorithms, system parameters, or structure. The property is amplified by self-adaptation.
- *dynamicity*—The technical ability to perform a change at runtime. For example, a technical ability to remove, add or exchange services and components.
- *robustness*—The ability to cope with errors during execution.
- *resilience*—A quality attribute prerequisite for resilience and system agility. Closely related to safety, resilience enables systems to bounce back from unanticipated disruptions.

- *mobility*—A property demonstrating what moves in the system at both design time and runtime.

In addition, GAR defines important considerations for building autonomous systems:

- Autonomous systems must continuously monitor changes in its context and react accordingly.
- What aspects of the environment should such a system monitor?—clearly, the system cannot monitor everything.
- Exactly what should the system do if it detects less than optimal conditions in the environment?
- The system needs to maintain a set of high-level goals that should be satisfied regardless of the environmental conditions.
- Eventually, non-critical goals could be not that strict, thus allowing the system a degree of flexibility during operation.

In Chap. 2, we presented GAR put in the context of space missions. This helped us derive GAR for Space Missions (GAR-SM) used in our ARE model.

3.2.2 GORE for ARE

The Goal-Oriented Requirements Engineering (GORE) [35] has extended upstream the software development process by adding a new phase called Early Requirements Analysis. The fundamental concepts used to drive the goal-oriented form of analysis are those of goal and actor. To fulfill a stakeholder goal, GORE helps engineers analyze the space of alternatives, which makes the process of generating functional and non-functional (quality) requirements more systematic in the sense that the designer is exploring an explicitly represented space of alternatives. GORE produces goals models that represent system objectives and their inter-relationships. Goals are generally modeled with intrinsic features such as their type, actors and targets, and with links to other goals and to other elements of the requirements model (e.g., constraints). Goals can be hierarchically organized and prioritized where high-level goals (e.g., mission objectives) might comprise related, low-level, sub-goals that can be organized to provide different alternatives to achieving the high-level goals.

GORE was extensively explained in Chaps. 1 and 2 we demonstrated how GORE can cope with GAR. In our ARE model, we merge GORE with GAR-SM to arrive at goals models where system goals are supported by self-* objectives promoting autonomicity in system behavior.

3.2.3 Understanding ARE

The ARE approach combines *generic autonomy requirements* (GAR) with *goal-oriented requirements engineering* (GORE). Using this approach, software engineers can determine what autonomic features to develop for a particular space mission as well as what artifacts that process might generate (e.g., goals models and requirements specification). The inputs required by this approach are the *mission goals* and the *domain-specific GAR* reflecting specifics of the mission class (e.g., interplanetary missions).

The first step in developing any new software-intensive system is to determine the system's functional and non-functional requirements. The former requirements define what the system will actually do, while the latter requirements refer to its qualities, such as performance, along with any constraints under which the system must operate. Despite differences in application domain and functionality, all autonomous systems extend upstream the regular software-intensive systems with special *self-managing objectives* (self-* objectives). Basically, the self-* objectives provide the system's ability to automatically discover, diagnose, and cope with various problems. This ability depends on the system's degree of autonomicity, quality and quantity of knowledge, awareness and monitoring capabilities, and quality characteristics such as adaptability, dynamicity, robustness, resilience, and mobility. Basically, this is the basis of the ARE approach: autonomy requirements are detected as self-objectives backed up by different capabilities and quality characteristics outlined by the GAR model.

Currently, this approach is the only complete and comprehensive solution to the problem of autonomy requirements elicitation and specification. Note that the approach targets exclusively the *self-* objectives* as the only means to explicitly determine and define autonomy requirements. Thus, it is not meant to handle the regular functional and non-functional requirements of the systems, presuming that those might by tackled by the traditional requirements engineering approaches, e.g., use case modeling, domain modeling, constraints modeling (OCL), etc. Functional and non-functional requirements might be captured by our ARE approach only as part of the self-* objectives elicitation, i.e., some of the GAR's requirements might be considered as functional and non-functional requirements.

The ARE approach starts with the creation of a *goals model* that represents system objectives and their interrelationships for the mission in question. For this, we use GORE where ARE goals are generally modeled with intrinsic features such as *type*, *actor*, and *target*, with links to other goals and constraints in the requirements model. Goals models might be organized in different ways copying with the mission specifics and engineers' understanding about the mission goals. Thus we may have (1) hierarchical structures where goals reside different level of granularity; (2) concurrent structures where goals are considered as concurrent; etc. The goals models are not formal and we use natural language along with UML-like diagrams to record them.

The next step in the ARE approach is to work on each one of the system goals along with the elicited environmental constraints to come up with the self-* objectives providing the autonomy requirements for this particular system's behavior. In this phase, we apply our GAR model to a mission goal to derive autonomy requirements in the form of goal's supportive and alternative self-* objectives along with the necessary capabilities and quality characteristics. In the first part of this phase, we record the GAR model in natural language. In the second part though, we use a formal notation to express this model in a more precise way. Note that, this model carries more details about the autonomy requirements, and can be further used for different analysis activities, including requirements validation and verification. However, the formal model is not mandatory in this approach and we can simply write the requirements details in natural language instead. Of course, a formal model has significant advantages over natural language, which lay mainly in the ambiguity of the natural language and the mathematical precision provided by the formal notation's semantics.

ARE can be used at several stages in the work flow from initiating a mission concept through to building and launching a spacecraft:

- As has been demonstrated in the case study for the BepiColombo mission (Sects. 3.3–3.5), the high level mission goals can be used in conjunction with a fairly general GAR model to generate a high level model incorporating the autonomy requirements (self-* objectives). This model could be combined with a reasoning engine to establish whether or not all the requirements are mutually compatible. It could also be used to communicate the requirements as long as the engineers can see what alternative behavior is required when the mission is following a particular goal and under what circumstances.
- The model can be used to assist in the compilation of the Autonomy Requirements (AR) section of the system requirements specification document. The goals model along with the autonomy requirements elicited per goal will form such a section. This eventually, will help to easily derive some of the functional and non-functional requirements—related to the monitoring activities, knowledge, and AR quality attributes. As mentioned above, the formal part can be omitted and instead we may write down the detailed ARs in natural language.
- The process of writing the ARs can also be used to add further details to the ARE model.
- If the formal model is required, with the necessary tool support it should be possible to formally validate and verify the ARs. It should be also possible with appropriate tools to derive from the formal model ARs written in natural language
- Eventually, if both the ARs written in a natural language and the formal model are made available together to the software design engineers, it should help to ensure more accurate implementation of the software with fewer bugs.

3.2.4 From Goals to Self-* Objectives

3.2.4.1 System Goals and Goals Models

Goals have long been recognized to be essential components involved in the requirements engineering (RE) process. As Ross and Schoman stated in their seminal paper, *requirements definition must say why a system is needed, based on current or foreseen conditions, which may be internal operations or an external market. It must say what system features will serve and satisfy this context. And it must say how the system is to be constructed* [31]. To elicit the system goals, typically, the current system (along with the mission where the system is going to be used) under consideration is analyzed in its organizational, operational and technical settings; problems are pointed out and opportunities are identified; high-level goals are then identified and refined to address such problems and meet the opportunities; requirements are then elaborated to meet those goals. Such natural practice has led requirements documentation standards to require a specific document section devoted to the objectives the system should meet (see, e.g., the IEEE-Std-830/1993 standards).

Goal identification is not necessarily an easy task [2, 17, 30, 34]. Sometimes goals can be explicitly stated by stakeholders or in preliminary material available to requirements engineers, e.g., mission description. Often though, they are implicit so that goal elicitation has to be undertaken. The *preliminary analysis* of the current system (and the mission to be accomplished by that system) is an important source for goal identification. Such analysis usually results in a list of problems and deficiencies that can be formulated precisely. Negating those formulations yields a first list of goals to be achieved by the system-to-be. In our experience, goals can also be identified systematically by searching for intentional keywords in the preliminary documents provided, e.g., mission description. Once a preliminary set of goals and goal-related constraints is obtained and validated with stakeholders, many other goals can be identified by *refinement* and *abstraction*, just by asking HOW and WHY questions about the goals/constraints already available [35]. Other goals are identified by resolving conflicts among goals or obstacles to goal achievement. Further, such goals might be eventually defined as self-* objectives.

Goals are generally modeled by *intrinsic features* such as their type and attributes, and by their links to other goals and to other elements of a requirements model. Goals can be hierarchically organized and prioritized where high-level goals (e.g., mission objectives) might comprise related, low-level, sub-goals that can be organized to provide different alternatives of achieving the high-level goals. In ARE, goals are registered in plain text with characteristics like *actors*, *targets*, and *rationale*. Moreover, inter-goal relationships are captured by goals models putting together all goals along with associated constraints. ARE's *goals models* are presented in UML-like diagrams. Goals models can help us to consecutively assist in capturing autonomy requirements in several ways:

1. An ARE goals model may provide the starting point for capturing autonomy requirements by analyzing the environment for the system-to-be and by identifying the problems that exist in this environment as well as the needs that the system under development has to address to accomplish its goals.
2. ARE goals models may be used to provide a means to represent alternative ways where the objectives of the system can be met and analyze and rank these alternatives with respect to *quality concerns* and other *constraints*, e.g., environmental constraints:

    a. This allows for exploration and analysis of alternative system behaviors at design time.

    b. If the alternatives that are initially delivered with the system perform well, there is no need for complex interactions on autonomy behavior among autonomy components.

    c. Not all the alternatives can be identified at design time. In an open and dynamic environment, new and better alternatives may present themselves and some of the identified and implemented alternatives may become impractical.

    d. In certain situations, new alternatives will have to be discovered and implemented by the system at runtime. However, the process of discovery, analysis, and implementation of new alternatives at runtime is complex and error-prone. By exploring the space of alternatives at design time, we are minimizing the need for that difficult task.

3. ARE goals models may provide the traceability mechanism from design to requirements. When a change in requirements is detected at runtime (e.g., a major change in the global mission goal), goals models can be used to re-evaluate the system behavior alternatives with respect to the new requirements and to determine if system reconfiguration is needed:

    a. If a change in requirements affects a particular goal in the model, it is possible to see how this goal is decomposed and which parts of the system implementing the functionality needed to achieve that goal are in turn affected.

    b. By analyzing a goals model, it is possible to identify how a failure to achieve some particular goal affects the overall objective of the system.

    c. Highly variable goals models can be used to visualize the currently selected system configuration along with its alternatives and to suggest configuration changes to users in high-level terms.

4. ARE goals models provide a unifying intentional view of the system by relating goals assigned to individual parts of the system (usually expressed as actors and targets of a goal) to high-level system objectives and quality concerns:

    a. High-level objectives or quality concerns serve as the common knowledge shared among the autonomous system's parts (or components) to achieve the global system optimization. In this way, the system can avoid the pitfalls of missing the globally optimal configuration due to only relying on local optimizations.

    b. Goals models might be used to identify part of the knowledge requirements, e.g., actors or targets.

Moreover, goals models might be used to manage conflicts among multiple goals including self-* objectives. Goals have been recognized to provide the roots for detecting conflicts among requirements and for resolving them eventually [29, 33]. Note that by resolving conflicts among goals or obstacles to goal achievement, new goals (or self-* objectives) may emerge.

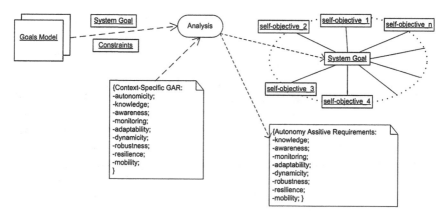

Fig. 3.2 The ARE process of deriving self-* objectives per system goal

3.2.4.2 Self-* Objectives and Autonomy-Assistive Requirements

ARE uses goals models as a basis helping to derive *self-* objectives* per a system (mission) goal by applying a model for *generic autonomy requirements* (GAR) to any system goal. The self-* objectives represent assistive and eventually *alternative goals* (or objectives) the system may pursue in the presence of factors threatening the achievement of the initial system goals. The diagram presented in Fig. 3.2 depicts the process of deriving the *self-* objectives* from a goals model of the system-to-be. Basically, a context-specific GAR model provides some initial self-* objectives, which should be further analyzed and refined in the context of the specific system goal to see their applicability. For example, the context-specific GAR models for the different classes of space missions (Sect. 2.3) define a predefined set of self-* objectives for each class of space missions. These self-* objectives cope with both constraints and challenges spacecraft must overcome while performing a mission of specific class. For example, GAR defines the following self-* objectives for the class of Polar Low Earth Orbit (LEO)/Remote-Sensing Satellite Missions (Sect. 2.3.2.1):

- *self-orbit*—autonomously acquire the target orbit; adapt to orbit perturbations;
- *self-protection*—autonomously detect the presence of radiation and move to escape;
- *self-scheduling*—based on operational goals and knowledge of the system and its environment, autonomously determine what task to perform next;
- *self-reparation*—implies operations re-planning based on performance degradation or failures;

As shown in Fig. 3.2, in addition to the derived *self-* objectives*, the ARE Process of Deriving Self-* Objectives produces *autonomy assistive requirements*. These requirements (also defined as adaptation-assistive attributes) are initially defined by the GAR model (Sect. 2.3) and are intended to support the achievements of the self-* objectives. The autonomy assistive requirements might be defined as following:

- *knowledge*—Basically, data requirements that need to be structured to allow efficient reasoning.
- *awareness*—A sort of functional requirements where knowledge is used as an input along with events and/or sensor signals to derive particular system states.
- *resilience and robustness*—A sort of soft goals. For example, such requirements for Geostationary Earth Orbit (GEO) Missions (Sect. 2.3.2.3) are defined as *robustness: robust to communication latency* and *resilience: resilient GEO positioning*. These requirements can be specified as soft goals leading the system towards *reducing and copying with communication latency* and *keeping GEO positioning optimal*. A soft goal is satisfied rather than achieved. Note that specifying soft goals is not an easy task. The problem is that there is no clear-cut satisfaction condition for a soft goal. Soft goals are related to the notion of satisfaction. Unlike regular goals, soft goals can seldom be accomplished or satisfied. For soft goals, eventually, we need to find solutions that are *good enough* where soft goals are satisfied to a sufficient degree. Thus, when specifying robustness and resilience autonomy requirements we need to set the desired degree of satisfaction, e.g., by using probabilities.
- *monitoring, mobility, dynamicity, and adaptability*—These also might be defined as soft goals, but with relatively high degree of satisfaction. These three types of autonomy requirements represent important quality requirements that the system in question needs to meet to provide conditions making autonomicity possible. Thus, their degree of satisfaction should be relatively high. Eventually, adaptability requirements might be treated as hard goals because they determine what parts of the system in question can be adapted (not how).

3.2.4.3 Constraints and Self-* Objectives

In addition to the self-* objectives derived from the context-specific GAR model, more self-* objectives might be derived from the constraints associated with the targeted system goal. Note that the Analysis step in Fig. 3.2 uses the context-specific GAR model and elaborates on both system goal and constraints associated with that goal. Often environmental constraints introduce factors that may violate the system goals and self-* objectives will be required to overcome those constraints. Actually, constraints represent obstacles to the achievement of a goal. Constructing self-* objectives from goal constraints can be regarded as a form of *constraint programming*, in which a very abstract logic sentence describing a goal with its actors and targets (it may be written in a natural language as well) is extended to include concepts from *constraint satisfaction* and *system capabilities* that enable the achievement of the goal. *Task Analysis* [20] is proposed as a good methodology for identify system capabilities. Task analysis can be defined as the study of what a system is required to do, in terms of actions and/or cognitive processes in order to achieve a given goal. Hierarchical task analysis, specifically, is a method of decomposing a high level capability down to its lowest levels in order to enumerate every capability required of a system. In ARE, the capabilities are actually abstractions of system operations that need to be performed to maintain the goal fulfillment along with constraint satisfaction. In this approach, we need to query the provability of the targeted goal, which contains constraints, and then if the system goal cannot be fulfilled due to constraint satisfaction, a self-* objective is derived as an assistive system goal preserving both the original system's goal targets and constraint satisfaction. A good example from the BepiColombo case study demonstrating this process is presented in Sect. 3.5. In this example, both high temperature and irradiation are environmental constraints that helped to determine variants of the self-protection objective assisting the scientific objectives of BepiColombo.

Note that constraints influence the definition of policies and scenarios when specifying or recording in natural language self-* objectives (Sect. 3.2.5.2).

3.2.4.4 Space Mission Analysis and Self-* Objectives

Considering the Space Missions domain, the analysis performed to determine self-* objectives might be part of the Space Mission Analysis, which is an activity that takes aspects such as *payload operational requirements* and *spacecraft system constraints* as inputs, and generates as an output a mission specification. A key aspect of this process is the selection of *mission parameters*, e.g., trajectory parameters. Note that the mission specification leads to design requirements on the spacecraft systems and subsystems. The Space Mission Analysis and Design (SMAD) Process consists of the following steps [15, 38]:

- Define Objectives:

  - Define broad objectives and constraints;
  - Estimate quantitative mission needs and requirements.

- Characterize the Mission:

  - Define alternative mission concepts;
  - Define alternative mission architectures;
  - Identify system drivers for each architecture;
  - Characterize mission concepts and architectures.

- Evaluate the Mission:

  - Identify critical requirements;
  - Evaluate mission utility;
  - Define baseline mission concept.

- Define Requirements:

  - Define system requirements;
  - Allocate requirements to system elements.

Typical Functional requirements are related to:

- *performance*: factors impacting this requirement include the primary mission objective, payload size, orbit, pointing;

- *coverage*: impacting factors include orbit, number of satellites, scheduling;
- *responsiveness*: impacting factors include communications architecture, processing delays, operations;
- *secondary mission* (if applicable).

Typical Operational requirements are:

- *duration*: factors impacting this requirement include nature of the mission (experimental or operational), level of redundancy, orbit (e.g., altitude);
- *availability*: impacting factors include level of redundancy;
- *survivability*: impacting factors include orbit, hardening, electronics;
- *data distribution*: impacting factors include communications architecture;
- *data content, form, and format*: impacting factors include user needs, level and place of processing, payload;
- *ground station visibility*;
- *eclipse duration*: consider the eclipse period for spacecraft in an Earth orbit;
- *launch windows*: the time of launch of a spacecraft is often constrained by dynamic aspects related to reaching the mission orbit, or by system requirements.

Typical Constraints are:

- *cost*: factors impacting this constraint include number of spacecraft, size and complexity, orbit;
- *schedule*: impacting factors include technical readiness, program size;
- *political*: impacting factors include Sponsoring organization (customer), whether international program;
- *interfaces*: impacting factors include level of user and operator infrastructure;
- *development constraints*: impacting factors include Sponsoring organization.

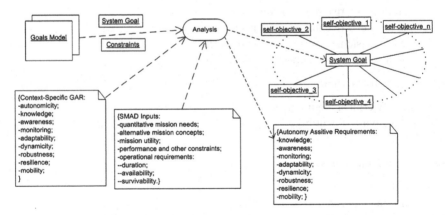

Fig. 3.3 The ARE process of "deriving self-* objectives per system goal" as part of SMAD

Ideally, SMAD might integrate the ARE Process of Deriving Self-* Objectives per System Goal as long as SMAD helps to identify the system goals, functionality and constraints. In this approach, the Analysis Step of that process (Fig. 3.3) might also use other inputs such as: quantitative mission needs, alternative mission concepts, mission utility, performance and other constraints, and operational requirements (e.g., duration, availability, survivability). Note that despite the different input parameters, the global invariant driving the Analysis Step is always defined as:

> What the system (spacecraft on a mission) should do when the system goals (or mission objectives) cannot be achieved by simply following the operational instructions?

Along with the SMAD input provided to the Analysis Step (Fig. 3.3), SMAD also can be used to provide information for deriving additional self-* objectives related to:

- *Accuracy goals*—non-functional goals requiring the state of the system components and environmental objects to accurately reflect the state of the corresponding monitored/controlled objects in both the system and environment. Note that such goals are often overlooked in the RE process and their violation may be responsible for major failures [21].
- *Performance goals*—specialized into time and space performance goals, the former being specialized into response time and throughput goals [25].
- *Security goals*—specialized into confidentiality, integrity and availability goals [1]. Note that the latter can be specialized in turn until reaching domain-specific security goals.
- *Satisfaction goals*—concerned with satisfying agent requests (human operators or system components.
- *Information goals*—concerned with keeping specific agents informed about other objects' states [8].
- *Achieve (resp. cease) goals*—concerned with system behavior related to certain required properties that should be eventually satisfied in some future state (resp. denied).
- *Maintain (resp. avoid) goals*—concerned with system behavior related to certain required properties that should be permanently satisfied in every future state (resp. denied) unless some other property holds.
- *Optimize goals*—compare behaviors to favor those which better ensure some soft target property.

3.2.4.5 Safety and Self-* Objectives

For many NASA/ESA systems, safety is an especially important source of requirements. RE engineers can express safety requirements as a set of features and procedures that ensure predictable system performance under normal and abnormal conditions. Furthermore, ARE might rely on safety requirements to derive self-* objectives controlling the consequences of unplanned events or accidents. Safety standards might be a good source of safety requirements and consecutively on safety-related self-* objectives. Such self-* objectives may provide for fault tolerance behavior, bounding failure probability, and adhering to proven practices and standards. Therefore, in this approach fault tolerance should be expressed via self-* objectives where the latter must be explored with all the possible hazards. Explicit safety requirements provide a key way to maintain ARE knowledge of what is important for safety. In typical practice, safety-related autonomy requirements can be derived by a four-stage process:

1. *Hazard identification*—all the hazards exhibited by the system are identified. A hazard might be regarded as a condition—situation, event, etc., that may lead to an accident.
2. *Hazard analysis*—possible causes of the system's hazards are explored and recorded. Essentially, this step identifies all processes, combinations of events, and sequences that can lead from a "normal" or "safe" state to an accident. Success in this step means that we now understand how the system can get to an accident.
3. *Identifying Safety Capabilities*—a key step is to identify the capabilities the system needs to have in order to perform its goals and remain safe. It is very likely that some of the capabilities have been already identified by for the purpose of other self-* objectives.
4. *Requirements derivation*—once the set of hazards is known, and their causation is understood, engineers can derive safety requirements that either prevent the hazards occurring or mitigate the resulting accidents via self-* objectives.

For *hazard identification and analysis* we can use the Energy Trace and Barrier Analysis (ETBA) technique, a preliminary hazard analysis technique based on energy models of accidents, where accidents are viewed as the result of an undesired release of energy from a system, which may lead to harm [22]. The technique is based on the principle that if one can identify the sources of energy in a system, one can prevent an unwanted or uncontrolled release of that energy in a way that might cause harm, by using some form of barrier. Another technique for hazard identification is the Scenario Functional Failure Analysis (FFA) [28], a method for doing hazard analysis over scenarios. The FFA technique involves the analysis of different failure modes of system functions.

3.2.5 Recording Self-* Objectives

3.2.5.1 Autonomy Needs: Abstract Self-* Objectives

To record the autonomy requirements, ARE relies on both natural language and formal notation. A natural language description of a self-* objective has the following format:

- *Self-protection_1*: Autonomously detect the presence of high solar irradiation and protect (eventually turn off or shade) the electronics and instruments on board.

  - Assisting system goals:
    BepiColombo Transfer Objective
  - Actors:
    BepiColombo transfer module, the Sun, Base on Earth, BepiColombo composite module (MPO and MMO), solar irradiation, shades, power system.
  - Targets:
    electronics and instruments.

Note that this description is abstract and does not say how the self-* objective is going to be achieved. Basically, as recorded the self-* objectives define the "*autonomy needs*" of the system. How these needs are going to be met is provided by more detailed description of the self-* objectives where the latter are specified formally in more details.

3.2.5.2 Formal Notation and Natural Language, Autonomous Functions, and Requirements Chunks

ARE relies on KnowLang (Sect. 2.5.4) for the formal specification of the elicited autonomy requirements (Sect. 3.5.3). Sections 3.3, 3.4, and 3.5 provide a very detailed case study where KnowLang has been used to specify autonomy requirements for BepiColombo. The self-* objectives are specified with special *policies* associated with *goals*, *special situations*, *actions* (eventually identified as system capabilities), *metrics*, etc. Thus, the self-* objectives are represented as policies describing at an abstract level what the spacecraft will do when particular situations arise. The situations are meant to represent the conditions needed to be met in order for the system to switch to a *self-* objective* while pursuing a system goal.

Note that the policies rely on actions that are a priori-defined as functions of the spacecraft (also can be considered as system capabilities—see Sect. 3.2.4.3), e.g., *moveSpacecraftUp*, *moveSpacecraftDown*, etc. In case, such functions have not been defined yet, the needed functions should be considered as *autonomous functions* and their implementation will be justified by the ARE's selected self-* objectives. ARE does not state nor specify how the spacecraft will perform these actions. This is out of the scope of the ARE approach. Basically, any requirements engineering approach states what the software will do, not how the software will do it.

In general, a more detailed description in a natural language may precede the formal specification of the elicited autonomy requirements. Such a description might be written as a scenario describing both the conditions and sequence of actions needed to be performed in order to achieve the self-* objective in question. Note that a self-objective could be associated with multiple scenarios. The combination of a self-*

objective and a scenario ARE defines as an ARE Requirements Chunk (see Fig. 3.5). A requirements chunk can be recorded in a natural language as following:

`ARE Requirements Chunk`

- *Self-protection_1*: Autonomously detect the presence of high solar irradiation and protect (eventually turn off or shade) the electronics and instruments on board.

  - `Assisting system goals:`
    BepiColombo Transfer Objective.
  - `Actors:`
    BepiColombo transfer module, the Sun, Base on Earth, BepiColombo composite module (MPO and MMO), solar irradiation, shades, power system.
  - `Targets:`
    electronics and instruments.

- *Scenario*: If the solar radiation level is less than $90Sv$, then the MMO spacecraft shades the instruments and turns off the electronics onboard. In case the radiation level is equal to or higher than 90 Sv, MMO performs one of the following operations: (1) move the spacecraft to an upper orbit; (2) move the spacecraft to a lower orbit; and (3) the spacecraft decides what to do on its own.

3.2.5.3 Reverse Requirements Engineering for ARE

A sort of a Reverse Requirements Engineering can be used to derive scenarios from policies already specified with KnowLang. In such a case, the scenario's conditions are derived from the specification of both the *POLICY_SITUATIONS* and policy *MAPPING.CONDITIONS*, and the sequence of actions is derived from the policy actions (the *DO_ACTIONS* specification clause). For example, if we assume the following policy:

```
CONCEPT_POLICY BringMMOToOrbit {
 SPEC {
  POLICY_GOAL { MMO..MMOOrbit_Placement_Done }
  POLICY_SITUATIONS { MMO..ArrivedAtMercury }
  POLICY_RELATIONS { MMO..Policy_Situation_2}
  POLICY_ACTIONS { MMO..Action.GoToPolarOrbit }
  POLICY_MAPPINGS {
   MAPPING {
    CONDITIONS { MMO..Metric.OutsideTemperature.VALUE > 300 }
    DO_ACTIONS { MMO..Action.ShadeInstruments,
                 MMO..Action.StartCoolingSystem,
                 MMO..Action.GoToPolarOrbit }
   }
   MAPPING {
    CONDITIONS { MMO..Metric.OutsideTemperature.VALUE <= 300 }
    DO_ACTIONS { MMO..Action.GoToPolarOrbit }
   }
```

```
        }
        }
        }
```

the following scenario can be derived:
SCENARIO: *If the spacecraft has arrived at Mercury and the outside temperature is higher than 300 °C (the spacecraft is on the bright side of Mercury), then the MMO performs the following operations in a sequence: (1) shade the instruments; (2) start the cooling system; and (3) move spacecraft to a Polar Orbit. Note that the process of Reverse Requirements Engineering where ARE Requirements Chunks are derived from the specification of KnowLang policies can be automatized.*

3.2.5.4 Putting the Autonomy Requirements in the Software Requirements Specification Document

The Software Requirements Specification document is the official statement of what is required of the system developers. This document should include both *definition of user requirements* and *specification of the system requirements*. It is NOT a design document and as far as possible, it should set WHAT the system should do rather than HOW it should do it. The self-* objectives might be recorded in the form of *enriched goals models* (including both system goals and self-* objectives—see Sect. 3.5.2) and as *ARE Requirements Chunks* in a subsection (named *Self-* Objectives*) of the section devoted to the objectives of the system (see, the IEEE-Std-830/1993 standards). The assistive autonomy requirements (monitoring, adaptability, etc.) can be recorded in a distinct subsection (named *Assistive Autonomy Requirements*) of the Non-Functional Requirements section of the software requirements specification document. Similarly, the autonomous functions shall be recorded in a subsection (named Autonomous Functions) of the Functional Requirements section. In such a document, there should be cross references among these three sections. Finally, the formal model specifying all the autonomy requirements described in these three sections can be presented as an appendix named "*Autonomy Requirements Specification.*"

3.2.6 Variability Points and Degree of Goals Satisfaction in ARE

3.2.6.1 Variability Points in ARE

The introduction of "*variability points*" in the goals models is explicitly supported by the GAR model, which provides for the realization of *self-* objectives* providing both *alternative* and *supporting behavior* to the main system goals. In addition, these objectives are explicitly supported by the GAR's adaptation-assistive attributes taking shape into aspects and qualities we need to take into consideration, e.g., adaptability, dynamicity, resilience, etc. For example, the adaptability requirement (what can be adapted in the system) and the dynamicity requirement (what can be moved) along with the environmental constraints introduce *"variability points"* and assist in the realization of design drivers.

More *"variability points"* might be introduced if we build more detailed goals models where abstract goals might be decomposed into more detailed sub-goals. In this case, a main goal acts as a *"root goal"* (or parent goal), which is decomposed into sub-goals related via *AND/OR* relationships. The *AND/OR* relationships are inspired from *AND/OR* graphs in Artificial Intelligence [6, 8, 24, 30] where such are used to capture goal decomposition into more operational goals and alternative goals, respectively.

In the *AND* decomposition, all the sub-goals must be satisfied for the parent goal to be achieved whereas in the OR decomposition, if one of the alternative goals is achieved, then the parent goal is satisfied. For example, in the BepiColombo Mis-

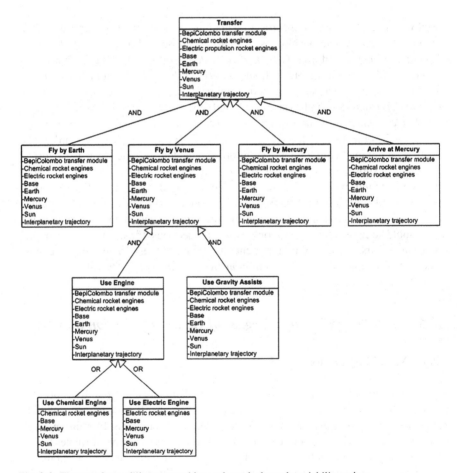

Fig. 3.4 The transfer goal decomposed into sub-goals through variability points

sion the goal Transfer might be decomposed into four sub-goals: *Fly by Earth, Fly by Venus, Fly by Mercury,* and *Arrive at Mercury* (Fig. 3.4). These four goals are sub-goals of the Transfer goal, which will be satisfied if all of its sub-goals are themselves satisfied. Further, the sub-goals are also decomposed into sub-sub-goals and so on. When the OR relationship is used we have alternatives to satisfy the parent goal.

For example, *Use Chemical Engine* and *Use Electric Engine* are sub-goals providing alternatives to the *Use Engine* goal (Fig. 3.4). This goal will be satisfied if one of the two alternative goals is satisfied. *AND* and *OR* relationships can also be used with negation.

In this approach, the inter-goal relationship is extended to support the capture of negative/positive influence between goals. A sub-goal is said to contribute partially to its parent goal. This leads to the notion of goal satisfaction where the sub-goals might contribute positively (*AND/OR*) or negatively (*NOTAND/OR*) to satisfying the parent goal. Here, goal satisfaction might be expressed in *AND/OR* graphs of goals where the relationships among goals capture positive/negative influences among goals (Fig. 3.4). Here, each goal shall be associated with scenarios (expressed as Policies and Situations in KnowLang) and the goal-scenario pairs (or requirements chunks, RCs) can be assembled together through composition, alternative and refinement relationships (Fig. 3.5). The first two lead to *AND* and *OR* structures of RCs whereas the last leads to the organization of the collection of RCs as a hierarchy of chunks of different granularity. *AND* relationships among RCs link complementary chunks in the sense that everyone requires others to define a completely functioning scenario covering a main goal. RCs linked through *OR* relationships represent alternative ways of fulfilling the same goal. RCs linked through a refinement relationship (in Fig. 3.5 denoted with the inheritance arrow) are at different levels of abstraction. Internally, the scenarios might introduce additional variability points via conditional requirements derived from the GAR's requirements such as monitoring, adaptability, dynamicity, resilience, and robustness. For example, we may introduce a monitoring-based conditional requirement in a scenario associated with the "*Use Electric Engine*" goal (Fig. 3.4) such as:

"*If the Sun can be monitored then start the electric engine.*" *Conflict relationships* are another kind of relationship among goals that can be used in ARE goals models. These relationships have been introduced [27] to capture the fact that one goal might prevent the other from being satisfied. For example, in the context of the BepiColombo Mission, a self-protection goal might have a conflict relationship with a main goal requiring high performance and heavy resource usage.

In an ARE goals model, the goals are assumed to have corresponding actions that an (external) actor or the system itself can perform to fulfill them. Currently, ARE tackles scenarios in a formal way via the specification of situations and policies with KnowLang. A RC (requirements chunk) in this formal presentation is the specification of a policy—recall that a KnowLang policy is associated with a goal. The scenario outlined by a policy is driven by the policy actions and conditions for action

execution. For example, in the following example, the specified policy outlines the
following scenario (associated with the *MMOSelf_Protection* goal):

SCENARIO: *If the solar radiation level is less than 90Sv, then the MMO spacecraft
shades the instruments and turns off the electronics onboard. In case the radiation
level is equal to or higher than 90Sv, MMO performs one of the following operations:
(1) move spacecraft to an upper orbit; (2) move spacecraft to a lower orbit; and (3)
spacecraft decides what to do on its own. In this case, the operation choice depends
on the current preference determined by the success rate. The initial preference is
set at design time to move spacecraft to an upper orbit.*

```
CONCEPT_POLICY MMOProtect_Spacecraft {
 SPEC {
  POLICY_GOAL { MMO..MMOSelf-Protection }
  POLICY_SITUATIONS { MMO..HighIrradiation }
  POLICY_RELATIONS { MMO..Policy_Situation_3 }
  POLICY_ACTIONS {
   MMO..Action.CoverInstruments, MMO..Action.TurnOffElectronics,
   MMO..Action.MoveSpacecraftUp, MMO..Action.MoveSpacecraftDown }
  POLICY_MAPPINGS {
   MAPPING {
    CONDITIONS { MMO..Metric.SolarRadiation.VALUE < 90 }
    DO_ACTIONS { MMO..Action.ShadeInstruments, MMO..Action.TurnOffElectronics } }
   MAPPING {
    CONDITIONS { MMO..Metric.SolarRadiation.VALUE >= 90 }
    DO_ACTIONS { MMO..Action.MoveSpacecraftUp }
    PROBABILITY {0.5} }
   MAPPING {
    CONDITIONS { MMO..Metric.SolarRadiation.VALUE >= 90 }
    DO_ACTIONS { MMO..Action.MoveSpacecraftDown }
    PROBABILITY {0.4} }
   MAPPING {
    CONDITIONS { MMO..Metric.SolarRadiation.VALUE >= 90 }
```

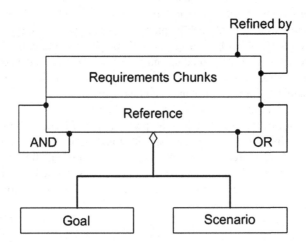

Fig. 3.5 Requirements chunks

```
      DO_ACTIONS { GENERATE_NEXT_ACTIONS(MMO..MMO_Spacecraft) }
      PROBABILITY {0.1} }
    }
  }
}
```

Note that the *operation choice* introduces another level of *variability points*, i.e., scenarios might also encompass variability points determining alternative paths within that scenario. In addition, operation preference introduces another level of variability points where common conditions might allow the execution of multiple operations rated according their success rate and initial preference.

3.2.6.2 Goals Satisfaction in ARE

The problem of evaluating alternatives with respect to degrees of goal satisfaction has been addressed by qualitative [5, 7] and quantitative reasoning techniques [19, 21]. The idea is to expose positive or negative influences of different alternatives of a goal. At the heart of conceptualizing partial goal satisfaction is identifying how to define partiality. For this, it is essential to define when a goal is achieved (satisfied completely), i.e., we cannot define partiality without knowing what complete satisfaction means. In the quantitative approach, we need a metric in terms of which (complete) satisfaction is expressed (satisfaction metric). This metric will be endowed with a partial ordering, to allow the system determine whether a goal is getting closer to completion. Such a metric can be called a progress metric of a goal, and denote it as a set A with partial order $\leq$ [18]. A goal then specifies a minimum value $a_{min} \in A$ for this metric (also called the completion value) that should be reached in order to consider the goal to have been completely satisfied. For example, the progress metric for the goal *Use Engine* (Fig. 3.4) might be defined in terms of time where complete satisfaction is achieved when the engine has been used for x hours (the time estimated to reach the point for gravity assist); or the metric may be defined as a Boolean proposition such as "*engine has been used*;" or it may be defined in terms of the number of sub-goals achieved where complete satisfaction means that at least one of the sub-goals is achieved (due to the *OR* relationships).

We may consider a wide range of *domain-independent metrics* such as: *time, utility, number of sub-goals*, etc. In addition we may define *domain-dependent metrics* such as: *number of planets to pass by in the Transfer goal, distance to Sun, distance to Mercury*, etc. Besides the metric chosen as the progress metric, the requirements engineer might have interest in additional metrics as well. For example, progress may be defined in terms of traveled distance, but elapsed time could be an additional relevant factor used to evaluate the goal satisfaction for the Transfer goal.

A fundamental reasoning concerning *partial goal satisfaction* is the so-called *progress appraisal* [14]. In this approach, the system should be able to determine in a given situation where it is in terms of goal satisfaction with respect to a progress metric. For example, if time is the progress metric, the system needs to be able to determine how long it has spent so far on pursuing a goal. In the case of time, the computation from the current state to the time spent is relatively direct. The computation may be more complex for other metrics. In the case of utility, for example, more computation might be needed to determine the current appraised value of utility in terms of other, measurable quantities, i.e., other metrics besides the progress metric. However, in all cases, the system should be able to determine, given its beliefs about current state, at least an estimation of the value of the progress metric for a goal. Note that KnowLang expresses goals with an *arrival state* and with an optional *departure state* (see the KnowLang specification model for BepiColombo in Appendix A). Moreover, KnowLang supports the specification of situations and metrics. However, the language is not currently supporting progress metrics, which drawback can be eventually overcome with the specification of multiple metrics for each member of the ordered set of a progress metric.

3.3 The Spacecraft in BepiColombo Mission

The space segment of the BepiColombo Mission consists of two orbiters: a Mercury Planetary Orbiter (MPO) and a Mercury Magnetospheric Orbiter (MMO) (Fig. 3.6). Initially, these two orbiters are packed together into a special composite module used to bring both orbiters into their proper orbits. Moreover, in order to transfer the orbiters to Mercury, the composite module is equipped with an extra electric propulsion module both forming a transfer module. The transfer module is intended to do the long cruise from Erath to Mercury by using the electric propulsion engine and the gravity assists of Moon, Venus and Mercury. Note that the environment around Mercury imposes strong requirements on the spacecraft design, particularly to the parts exposed to Sun and Mercury: solar array mechanisms, antennas, multi-layer insulation, thermal coatings and radiators.

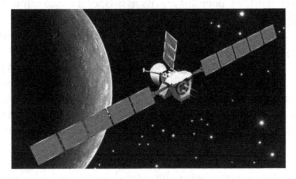

Fig. 3.6 BepiColombo arriving at Mercury, picture courtesy of ESA [10]

3.3.1 Planetary Orbiter

The Mercury Planetary Orbiter (MPO) is a three-axis-stabilised spacecraft pointing at nadir. The spacecraft shall revolve around Mercury at a relatively low altitude and will perform a series of experiments related to planet-wide remote sensing and radio science. MPO will be equipped with two rocket engines nested in two propulsion modules respectively: a *solar electric propulsion module* (SEPM) and a *chemical propulsion module* (CPM). Moreover, to perform scientific experiments, the spacecraft will carry a highly sophisticated suit of eleven instruments [4]:

- *BepiColombo Laser Altimeter* (BELA)—Characterise the topography and surface morphology of Mercury.
- *Mercury Orbiter Radio Science Experiment* (MORE)—Determine the gravity field of Mercury as well as the size and physical state of its core.
- *Italian Spring Accelerometer* (ISA)—The objectives of ISA are strongly connected with those of the MORE experiment. Together the experiments can give information on Mercury's interior structure as well as test Einstein's theory of the General Relativity.
- *Mercury Magnetometer* (MERMAG)—Detailed description of Mercury's planetary magnetic field and its source, to better understand the origin, evolution and current state of the planetary interior, as well as the interaction between Mercury's magnetosphere with the planet's itself and with the solar wind.
- *Mercury Thermal Infrared Spectrometer* (MERTIS)—Will provide detailed information about the mineralogical composition of Mercury's surface layer. Will provide global temperature maps.
- *Mercury Gamma ray and Neutron Spectrometer* (MGNS)—Determine the elemental compositions of the surface and subsurface of Mercury, and will determine the regional distribution of volatile depositions on the polar areas which are permanently shadowed from the Sun.
- *Mercury Imaging X-ray Spectrometer* (MIXS)—Use X-ray fluorescence analysis method to produce a global map of the surface atomic composition at high spatial resolution.
- *Probing of Hermean Exosphere by Ultraviolet Spectroscopy* (PHEBUS)—The spectrometer is devoted to the characterisation of Mercury's exosphere composition and dynamics. It will also search for surface ice layers in permanently shadowed regions of high-latitude craters.
- *Search for Exosphere Refilling and Emitted Neutral Abundances* (SERENA)—Study the gaseous interaction between surface, exosphere, magnetosphere and solar wind.
- *Spectrometers and Imagers for MPO BepiColombo Integrated Observatory System* (SYMBIOSYS)—Will provide global, high resolution, and IR imaging of the surface. Examine the surface geology, volcanism, global tectonics, surface age and composition, and geophysics.

- *Solar Intensity Xray Spectrometer* (SIXS)—Performs measurements of X-rays and particles of solar origin at high time resolution and a very wide field of view.

3.3.2 Mercury Magnetospheric Orbiter

The Mercury Magnetospheric Orbiter (MMO) is a spin-stabilized spacecraft in a relatively eccentric orbit carrying instruments to perform scientific experiments mostly with fields (e.g., Mercury magnetic field), waves and particles. Similar to MPO, MMO is also equipped with two propulsion modules: a *solar electric propulsion module* (SEPM) and a *chemical propulsion module* (CPM). MMO has altitude control functions, but no orbit control functions. MMO's main structure consists of: two decks (upper and lower), a central cylinder (thrust tube) and four bulkheads (Fig. 3.7) [39]. Both decks have an octagonal shape and are connected by a side panel. The side panel is divided in two parts—upper part and lower part. The upper part is covered by solar cells (54 %) and by SSM (second surface mirror) (46 %), and the lower part is entirely covered by SSM. The instruments are located on both decks. The MMO spacecraft shall carry five advanced scientific experiments, as described below [4]:

- *Instrument Science Objective Mercury Magnetometer* (MERMAG-MGF)—Provide a detailed description of Mercury's magnetosphere and of its interaction with the planetary magnetic field and the solar wind.
- *Mercury Plasma Particle Experiment* (MPPE)—Study low- and high-energetic particles in the magnetosphere.
- *Mercury Plasma Wave Instrument* (PWI)—Will make a detailed analysis of the structure and dynamics of the magnetosphere.
- *Mercury Sodium Atmospheric Spectral Imager* (MSASI)—Measure the abundance, distribution, and dynamics of sodium in Mercury's exosphere.
- *Mercury Dust Monitor* (MDM)—Study the distribution of interplanetary dust in the orbit of Mercury.

Most of the instruments are mounted on the side panel (Fig. 3.7). Inside the central cylinder are mounted batteries, a nutation damper,[1] a UHF antenna and a tank for a cold gas jet system (GN2 Tank). The side panel and the two decks form an octagonal prism divided into three parts: upper, middle and lower prism (Fig. 3.7a) [39].

---

[1] Nutation damper is a device on board a rotating spacecraft which reduces the amplitude of motions arising from perturbing torques. Despite the words used in the term, a nutation damper reduces precession as well as nutation. (ENCYCLO—Online Encyclopedia, http://www.encyclo.co.uk).

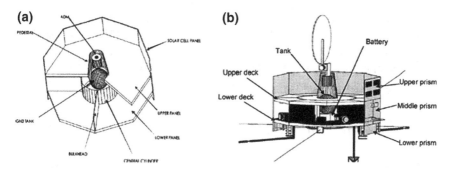

Fig. 3.7 MMO structure [39]

3.3.2.1 Communication

The UHF antenna is intended for communication with MPO. A HGA (high gain antenna) is mounted in the center of the upper deck. HGA is a helical array antenna (80 cm diameter). HGA must be pointed towards Earth with the help of a special antenna pointing mechanism (APM) comprising an antenna despun motor (ADP) and an elevation control mechanism (ECM). In addition, a medium gain antenna (MGA) (bi-reflector type antenna) is mounted on the lower deck. MGA is provided with a special extendible mechanism [39].

3.3.2.2 Thermal Control

The harsh environment near Mercury (0.31 AU from the Sun) imposes 11 solar intensities on the MMO spacecraft. Thus, a thermal control system is provided to maintain a proper temperature onboard and protect the instruments. Two design solutions have been implemented to assist the thermal control: passive thermal design technique and a combined method of passive and active techniques controlled by a thermal control system. Passive control elements: the SSMs, thermal shield, special insulation painting, insulation films and multi-layer insulation blankets (MLI). All external surfaces are electrically-conductive. The upper deck is covered by MLI and the lower deck is covered by SSMs (i.e., the thermal properties are low absorptivity and high emissivity). The lower deck works as a heat radiator. Both the batteries and the GN2 tank are covered by MLIs and are mounted inside the central cylinder which is also internally covered by a MLI. Solar cells and SSMs cover the upper prism. The middle prism is covered by SSMs outside and by MLIs inside. Both sides of the lower prism are covered by SSMs to reflect the direct solar flux. Finally, most of the internal components are black-painted for high emissivity surface. The thermal control system provides a temperature control over the batteries by relying on radiators and heaters installed on the batteries panel attached to the bottom of the central cylinder [39].

MMO is designed as a spin-stabilized spacecraft orbiting Mercury and with certain limitations on the acceptable sunlit during the Cruise Phase. MMO is activated on arrival at Mercury. While active, its thermal control system is required to maintain the onboard equipment and the spacecraft structure in proper temperature range during the entire mission phases.

3.3.3 Composite Module (MPO and MMO)

The BepiColombo Composite Module packs both MPO and MMO. The advantage is a single control mechanism while performing tasks on Mercury capture and orbiting. The composite module is MPO-CPM-SEPM and MMO-CPM-SEPM. While attached to the composite module, before Mercury arrival, both MPO and MMO are considered as dormant payload.

3.3.4 Transfer Module

The BepiColombo Transfer Module is a composition of the BepiColombo Composite Module (Sect. 3.2.3) and an additional rocket engine—a SEPM (solar electric propulsion module) [39]. The rocket engine shall assist the Transfer Module in its planetary cruise and in the Mercury orbit insertion. Actually, the electrical propulsion provided by the SEPM module is going to be combined with Venus, Mercury and even Moon gravity assists. While being a part of the Transfer Module, both MMO and MPO will stay in a dormant mode and thus there will be no active thermal control in both spacecraft. Therefore, in order to maintain the proper temperature for the instruments and internal structure, the altitude of the Transfer Module during the interplanetary cruise phase should be kept without solar input to the MMO's and MPO's upper surface, even if it is an altitude for safe hold mode [39]. Moreover, both MPO and MMO are covered with sunshield during the cruise to Mercury. Sunshield has been tested in high temperatures up to 350 °C [39].

3.3.5 Carrier Spacecraft

BepiColombo is to be launched on an Ariane 5 rocket [3, 9]. BepiColombo will weigh about 4,400 kg at launch. The spacecraft will leave the Earth with a hyperbolic excess velocity of 3.36 km/s. The Transfer Module will be connected to the upper stage of Ariane 5 launcher and after jettisoning of the launcher, it will start the cruise to Mercury.

3.4 GORE for BepiColombo

By applying GORE for ARE (Sect. 3.2.2), we build *goals models* that can help us consecutively derive and organize the *autonomy requirements* for BepiColombo. In our approach, the models provide the starting point for ARE (Autonomy Requirements Engineering) for BepiColombo by defining (1) the objectives of the mission that must be realized in (2) the system's operational environment (space, Mercury, proximity to the Sun, etc.), and by identifying the (3) problems that exist in this environment as well as (4) the immediate targets supporting the mission objectives and (5) constraints the system needs to address. Moreover, GORE helps us identify the mission actors (mission spacecraft, spacecraft components, environmental elements, base station, etc.). In this exercise, we do not categorize the objectives' actors, but for a more comprehensive requirements engineering, actors might be categorized by role or by importance (e.g., main, supporting and offstage actors). Further, the requirements goals models can be used as a *baseline for validating the system*.

3.4.1 Mission Objectives

BepiColombo's main objective is to explore Mercury and its environment. Among several investigations, BepiColombo will make a complete map of Mercury at different wavelengths. It will chart the planet's mineralogy and elemental composition, determine whether the interior of the planet is molten or not, and investigate the extent and origin of Mercury's magnetic field. In addition, the BepiColombo mission is going to addresses fundamental science and minor-body issues as described in [16].

3.4.1.1 High-Level Mission Objectives

ESA imposes to BepiColombo three high-level mission objectives:

- *Study Mercury*: Gather complimentary data about planetary formation in the hottest part of the proto-solar nebula:

  - Actors:
    MPO Spacecraft (Mercury Planetary Orbiter), MMO Spacecraft (Mercury Magnetospheric Orbiter), the Sun, Base on Earth.
  - Targets:
    Mercury

- *Study relativity*: Gather data for testing general relativity and exploring the limits of other metric theories of gravitation with unprecedented accuracy:

  - Rationale:
    The discovery of any violation of general relativity would have profound consequences to theoretical physics and cosmology.

- Actors:
  MPO Spacecraft (Mercury Planetary Orbiter), MMO Spacecraft (Mercury Magnetospheric Orbiter), the Sun, Base on Earth.

- *Possible impacts*: Observe minor bodies with semi-major axes of less than 1 AU (the so-called Atens and Inner-Earth Objects), which may possibly impact Earth:

  - Actors:
    MPO Spacecraft (Mercury Planetary Orbiter), MMO Spacecraft (Mercury Magnetospheric Orbiter), Base on Earth.
  - Targets:
    minor bodies with semi-major axes of less than 1 AU.

3.4.1.2 Middle-Level Mission Objectives

The middle-level mission objectives provide a detailed realization of the high-level mission objectives (Sect. 3.4.1.1). Thus, a high-level mission objective can be broken down into a few middle-level mission objectives, inheriting the properties of that high-level objective. The following elaborates on the middle-level objectives:

- *Unseen hemisphere*: Discover (photograph and analyze) the unseen hemisphere of Mercury:

  - Rationale:
    The Mercury's unknown hemisphere might appear to be quite different than the known one (similar to the Moon).
  - Actors:
    MPO Spacecraft, MMO Spacecraft, Mercury, Base on Earth.
  - Targets:
    Along with photographing the unseen hemisphere a supplementary target is a gigantic dome on that hemisphere (a ground-based radar observations suggest the presence of a lineament).

- *Geological evolution*: Gather data about the planet's geological evolution. Investigate inter-crater plains, scarps, faults and lineaments:

  - Rationale:
    The planet's surface has traces of various exogenic (bombardment) and endogenic processes.
  - Actors:
    MPO Spacecraft, MMO Spacecraft, Mercury, Base on Earth.
  - Targets:
    large scarps, faults and lineaments (such can be induced by phenomenons like the relaxation of the equatorial bulge, the contraction due to the cooling of the mantle, and the tidal stresses caused by the highly eccentric planet's orbit.

- *Tectonic activity*: Determine if Mercury is still tectonically active.

- Actors:
  MPO Spacecraft, MMO Spacecraft, Mercury, Base on Earth.
- Targets:
  planet's crust.

- *Chemical analysis*: Perform chemical composition analysis of the planet's surface.
  Build a mineralogical and elemental composition map of the surface.

  - Rationale:
    This will provide the means of distinguishing between various models of the
    origin and evolution of the planet.
  - Actors:
    MPO Spacecraft, MMO Spacecraft, Mercury, Base on Earth.
  - Targets:
    the ironoxide content of silicates (an indicator of the condensation temperature
    of the solar nebula during the accretion of the planet);
    the concentration ratio of key elements such as potassium, uranium, and tho-
    rium (an indicator of the temperature scale of the feeding zone where the
    body was accreted).

- *Mercury's density*: Investigate the anomaly of the high Mercury's density.

  - Rationale:
    The density of Mercury does not line up with those of the other terrestrial
    planets, including the Moon. When corrected for compression due to size, it
    is the largest of all.
  - Actors:
    MPO Spacecraft, MMO Spacecraft, Mercury, Base on Earth.
  - Targets:
    the iron concentration in the different regions on the planet's surface (sup-
    posedly, it was larger in the feeding zone where the planet accreted);
    metal oxides (supposedly, oxides were reduced to metallic form due to the
    proximity of the Sun);
    the concentration of materials with high condensation temperature (suppos-
    edly, the temperature of the young Sun was sufficient to sublimate and blow
    off silicates, thereby leaving only materials with higher condensation temper-
    atures;
    traces of gigantic impacts (supposedly, the initial composition of the planet
    has been significantly altered by gigantic impacts, which may have removed
    a substantial part of the mantle).

- *Internal structure*: Analyze the Mercury's internal structure and find out if there
  is a liquid outer core.

  - Rationale:
    The high density suggests a relatively large iron core in which 70–80 % of the
    planetary mass is concentrated, and implies a low moment of inertia factor.

- Actors:
  MPO Spacecraft, MMO Spacecraft, Mercury, Base on Earth.
- Targets:
  concentration of sulphur on the planet's surface (the presence of a small percentage of this element—1–5 %, could account for the molten shell, because this element would depress the freezing point of the core alloy);
  global shape, gravity field and rotational state (these parameters are required to estimate the radius and the mass of the core);

- *Magnetic field*: Investigate the origin of the Mercury's magnetic field.

  - Rationale:
    The existence of the Mercury's magnetic field was discovered by Mariner-10 [16]. The field is relatively weak (a few $100\,nT$ at the equator equivalent to about one hundredth of that of the Earth) and could be generated by an internal hydro-magnetic dynamo driven by a liquid shell, perhaps 500 km thick, in the outer core [16].
  - Actors:
    MPO Spacecraft, MMO Spacecraft, Mercury, Base on Earth.
  - Targets:
    magnetic field, internal dynamo (detailed mapping of the magnetic field will provide the necessary constraints on the structure and mechanism of the internal dynamo).

- *Solar wind*: Investigate the impact of the solar wind on the planetary magnetic field in the absence of any ionosphere.

  - Rationale:
    The magnetosphere of Mercury (the Hermean magnetosphere) is exposed to a solar-wind density and an interplanetary magnetic field (IMF) which are 4–9 times larger than at 1 AU.
  - Actors:
    MPO Spacecraft, MMO Spacecraft, Mercury, the Sun, Base on Earth.
  - Targets:
    solar wind, magnetosphere of Mercury, magnetospheric currents (the topology of the currents might differ significantly from that observed at the Earth, due to the absence of an ionosphere and the massive emission of photoelectrons on the dayside).
    magnetospheric sub-storms (could be triggered by the IMF reversals or internal instabilities);
    IMF reversals and IMF variations;
    possible radiation belts (could cause perturbations in planetary magnetic field);
    field-line resonances;
    reflection properties of the planetary surface (could cause field-line resonances).

- *Water ice*: Look for water ice in the permanently shadowed craters of the Polar Regions.

  - Rationale:
    Mercury is a world of extreme temperatures. The surface temperature at the sub-solar point reaches 700 K (427 °C), but it can be as low as 100 K (−173 °C) in shadowed areas.
  - Actors:
    MPO Spacecraft, MMO Spacecraft, Mercury, Base on Earth.
  - Targets:
    Mercury's Polar Regions, water ice, sulphur (a major discovery was made by radar observations in 1992 about the a possibility that water ice or sulphur may be present in permanently shadowed craters near the poles, deposited there by meteorites or diffused and trapped from the planet's crust).

- *Exosphere*: Find out the volatiles composing the exosphere of Mercury.

  - Rationale:
    Mercury has no stable atmosphere. The gaseous environment of the planet is best described as exosphere, i.e., a medium so rarefied that its neutral constituents never collide.
  - Actors:
    MPO Spacecraft, MMO Spacecraft, Mercury, Base on Earth.
  - Targets:
    the elements O, H, Ne, Na, and K (discovered in the exosphere of Mercury by Mariner-10 and by ground-based observations);
    other elements and possible ice near the poles (may be detected using UV spectroscopic observations of the limb);
    in-falling micrometeorites (solar photo and ion sputtering, and impact vaporisation may be used to study such meteorites).

- *Test relativity*: Use the proximity of the Sun to test general relativity with improved accuracy.

  - Rationale:
    A Mercury orbiter offers a unique opportunity to test general relativity and alternative theories of gravity.
  - Actors:
    MPO Spacecraft, MMO Spacecraft, the Sun, Mercury, Base on Earth.
  - Targets:
    solar occultations (solar occultations can provide for classical tests that can be repeated with improved accuracy; new experiments based upon different observable quantities can be performed due to the proximity of the Sun and the high eccentricity of Mercury's orbit);
    deflection of radio waves by the Sun, time delay of radio signals (can be used for classical test when Mercury is in its perihelion);
    perihelion of Mercury (the best time to perform relativity tests);

position tracking, gravity field of Mercury, non-gravitational accelerations due to radiation pressure (these factors influence the gravity experiments, e.g., a precision spacecraft tracking is required along with accurate measurement of non-gravitational accelerations, in particular the radiation pressure and the gravity field of Mercury).

- *Cosmic impactors*: Investigate the possible threats for the Earth coming from cosmic impactors.

  - `Rationale`:
    BepiColombo has the potential to observe cosmic impactors at distances from the Sun as small as 0.4 AU.
  - `Actors`:
    MPO Spacecraft, MMO Spacecraft, Mercury, Earth, Base on Earth.
  - `Targets`:
    small space objects between Mercury and Earth

3.4.1.3 Low-Level Mission Objectives

This level covers preliminary-stage or supporting objectives. Such objectives support the middle-level objectives. The low-level Mission Objectives are:

- *Launch*: Bring the spacecraft out of Earth's orbit.

  - `Rationale`:
    Launch opportunities of typically one-month duration for BepiColombo are dictated by positions of the Earth, Venus, and Mercury, allowing the spacecraft to follow its intricate interplanetary trajectory. The next launch opportunity to Mercury occurs in August 2015 and is consistent with the projected completion date of the spacecraft, including margins.
  - `Actors`:
    launch rocket (Ariane 5), BepiColombo spacecraft (transfer module, MPO and MMO), Earth, Venus, Mercury, Base on Earth.
  - `Targets`:
    start-journey orbit (the Earth orbit where the BepiColombo spacecraft can separate from the launch rocket and start its journey to Mercury).

- *Transfer*: Transport the BepiColombo Spacecraft to Mercury.

  - `Rationale`:
    Involves the long cruise phase including a combination of electric propulsion and gravity-assist maneuvers (once by Earth, twice by Venus, and four times by Mercury [12]). During the voyage to Mercury, the two orbiters and the carrier spacecraft, consisting of electric propulsion and traditional chemical rocket units, will form one single composite spacecraft.

– Actors:
  BepiColombo transfer module, chemical rocket engines, electric propulsion rocket engines, Earth, Venus, Mercury, the Sun, Base on Earth, BepiColombo composite module (MPO and MMO).
– Targets:
  interplanetary trajectory.

- *Orbit-placement*: Both MPO and MMO must be placed in orbit around Mercury to fulfill the mission objectives.

  – Rationale:
    When approaching Mercury in, the carrier spacecraft will be separated and the composite spacecraft will use rocket engines and a technique called weak stability boundary capture to bring it into polar orbit around the planet. When the MMO orbit is reached, the MPO will separate and lower its altitude to its own operational orbit. Observations from orbit will be taken for at least one Earth year.
  – Actors:
    BepiColombo transfer module, electric propulsion rocket engines, chemical rocket engines, Mercury, the Sun, Base on Earth, BepiColombo composite module (MPO and MMO), MPO, MMO.
  – Targets:
    MPO orbit, MMO orbit.

Figure 3.8 depicts the goals model for the BepiColombo mission. This figure puts together all the goals described in this section by relating them via particular relationships such as *inheritance* and *dependency*. Goals are depicted as boxes listing both goal actors and targets.[2] As shown, the *low-level goals* (Sect. 3.4.1.3) are preliminary goals that need to be achieved before proceeding with the *middle-level goals* (Sect. 3.4.1.2). Furthermore, the *middle-level goals* are concrete descendants of the *high-level generic goals* (Sect. 3.4.1.1).

The BepiColombo Goals Model provides the traceability mechanism for autonomy requirements. When a change in requirements is detected at runtime (e.g., a major change in the global mission goal), the goals model can be used to re-evaluate the system behavior with respect to the new requirements and to determine if system reconfiguration is needed. Moreover, the presented goals model provides a unifying intentional view of the system by relating goals assigned to actors and involving targets. Some of the actors can be eventually identified as the *autonomy components* (autonomic elements) providing a *self-adaptive behavior* when needed to keep up with the high-level system objectives.

Note that this is an initial GORE model for BepiColombo, and it does not cover the self-* objectives and other objectives stemming from the autonomy requirements. The latter shall be integrated in the model after applying the *Generic Autonomy Requirements for Space Missions* to BepiColombo (Chap. 2).

---

[2] Note that targets might be considered as a distinct class of actors.

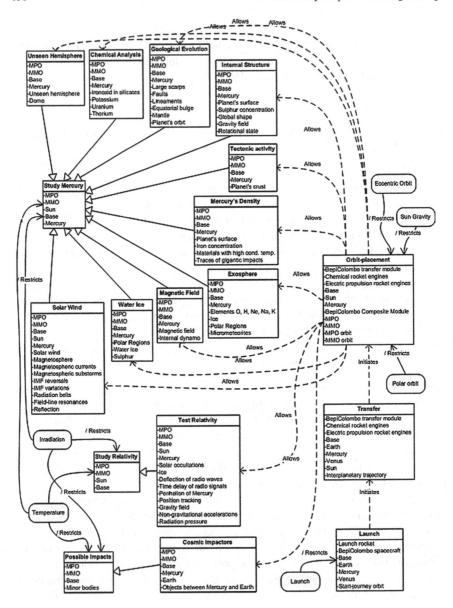

Fig. 3.8 Goals model for BepiColombo

3.4.2 Environmental Constraints for BepiColombo

The following elements express major *gravitational, thermal, radiation, orbital,* and *launch* constrains imposed by the BepiColombo's operational environment:

- *Sun gravity*: Both Orbiters must take into account the gravitational potential of the Sun.
- *Eccentric orbit*: Both Orbiters must take into account the highly-eccentric planet's orbit around the Sun.
- *Temperature*: Both Orbiters must take into account the large temperature amplitude during the complete orbiting cycle. Large heat flux increased above the dayside due to reflected sunlight and infrared emission.
- *Irradiation*: The solar irradiation[3] [18] is about 10 times larger at Mercury than at Earth.
- *Polar orbit*: The orbits need to be polar in order to ensure global coverage of the planet.
- *Launch*: Launch opportunities of typically one-month duration for BepiColombo are dictated by positions of the Earth, Venus, and Mercury, allowing the spacecraft to follow its intricate interplanetary trajectory.

More constraints can be eventually derived from both the mission and environment specifics. Next, the constraints need to be associated with the mission goals to prevent mission failures. Further, constraints shall be considered by the self-* objectives providing assistive behavior to the main mission goals. In the system goals model (Fig. 3.8), constraints are depicted as gray ellipses linked via a Restricts link to objectives.

As shown in Fig. 3.8, the Launch constraint adds on the Launch objective. The constraints Sun gravity, Eccentric orbit and Polar orbit restrict the Orbit-placement objective. Both the Temperature and Irradiation constraints restrict the three high-level mission objectives: Study Mercury, Study Relativity and Possible Impacts. Note that due to the *inheritance relationship*, these constraints are propagated to all the Middle-level Mission Objectives (Sect. 3.4.1.2).

3.5 Autonomy Requirements for BepiColombo

The BepiColombo Mission falls in the category of Interplanetary Missions and consecutively inherits the *generic autonomy requirements* (GAR) for such missions, i.e., GAR for Interplanetary Missions (Sect. 2.3.3). Considering the hierarchical structure of the mission objectives (Fig. 3.8), a good practice will be to associate the autonomy requirements with each hierarchical level of objectives. Thus, we may have autonomy requirements (including self-* objectives) associated with the Transfer Objective, the Orbit-placement Objective (Sect. 3.4.1.3), and with the Scientific Objectives, grouping all the middle-level objectives (Sect. 3.4.1.2).

---

[3] Total amount of solar radiation transmitted to the surface of the Earth's atmosphere in a given unit of time.

3.5.1 Applying GAR for Space Missions

The Generic Autonomy Requirements for Interplanetary Missions (GAR for Interplanetary Missions) were applied to BepiColombo to derive the following of autonomy requirements.

3.5.1.1 Transfer Objective Autonomy Requirements

The Interplanetary Missions involve more than one space object (planets, the Sun or satellites). Consecutively, the BepiColombo's Transfer Objective involves the planets Earth, Venus and Mercury, the Moon, and the Sun (Sect. 3.4.1.3). Hence, the transfer trajectory needs to be developed with concerns about possible perturbations caused by the gravitational influence of the Sun and the planetary bodies. By considering the Transfer Objective specifics, we derive the autonomy requirements for that objective, by applying the Generic Autonomy Requirements for Interplanetary Missions (Sect. 2.3.3):

- *self-* requirements* (autonomicity):

  - `self-trajectory`:
      autonomously acquire the most optimal trajectory to reach Mercury;
      adapt to trajectory perturbations due to gravitational influence of the Sun, the Moon, Earth, Venus and Mercury.
  - `self-protection`:
      autonomously detect the presence of high solar irradiation and:
      - protect the electronics on board and instruments;
      - change the altitude if possible by using electric propulsion and/or chemical propulsion.
      - the altitude of the Transfer Module during the interplanetary cruise should be kept without solar input to the MMO's and MPO's upper surface.
  - `self-scheduling`:
      autonomously determine when a gravity-assist maneuver is required:
      - near Earth (at transfer-starting point after launch);
      - near Venues (twice);
      - near Mercury (4 times).
  - `self-reparation`:
      autonomously restore broken communication links;
      when malfunctioning, components should be fixed autonomously where possible.

- *knowledge*:

  - mission objectives (Transfer Objective);
  - payload operational requirements;

- instruments onboard together with their characteristics (acceptable levels of radiation);
- Base on Earth;
- propulsion system (electric propulsion rockets, chemical propulsion rockets);
- communication links, data transmission format, eclipse period, altitude, communication mechanisms onboard,
- gravitational forces (Earth gravity, Moon gravity, Venus gravity, Sun gravity and Mercury gravity);

- *awareness*:

  - trajectory awareness;
  - radiation awareness;
  - instrument awareness;
  - sensitive to thermal stimuli;
  - gravitational forces awareness;
  - data-transfer awareness;
  - speed awareness;
  - communication awareness.

- *monitoring*:

  - electronic components onboard;
  - surrounding environment (e.g., radiation level, planets, the Sun and other space objects);
  - planned operations (status, progress, feasibility, etc.).

- *adaptability*:

  - adaptable mission parameters concerning the Transfer Objective (e.g., what can be adapted in pursing the Transfer Objective);
  - possibility for re-planning (adaptation) of operations;
  - adapt to loss of energy;
  - adapt to high radiation;
  - adapt to weak a satellite-ground station communication link;
  - adapt to low energy.

- *dynamicity*:

  - dynamic communication links;

- *robustness*:

  - robust to temperature changes;
  - robust to cruise trajectory perturbations;
  - robust to communication losses;

- *resilience*:

  - loss of energy is recoverable;
  - resilient to radiation.

- *mobility*:
  - information goes in and out;
  - changing trajectory.

3.5.1.2 Orbit-Placement Objective Autonomy Requirements

The Orbit-placement Objective is to place both MMO and MPO into their operational orbits around Mercury. When approaching Mercury, the BepiColombo Transfer Module will be separated by releasing the module's SEPM. Then, the BepiColombo Composite Module will use the MMO's rocket engines (mainly the CPM) (Sect. 3.3.3) and the weak stability boundary capture mechanism to move the spacecraft into polar orbit around Mercury. When the MMO orbit is reached, the MPO will separate and lower its altitude to its own operational orbit.

To derive the autonomy requirements assisting that objective, we need to identify the appropriate category of generic autonomy requirements that might be applied. Considering the Orbit-placement Objective, the BepiColombo mission falls in the category of *Interplanetary Missions using Low-thrust Trajectories* (Sect. 2.3.3.2). Such missions use spacecraft for orbit control activities in geostationary orbits, drag compensation in low orbits, planetary orbit missions and missions to comets and asteroids. These missions often have a complex mission profile utilizing ion propulsion in combination with multiple *gravity-assist manoeuvers* (similar to BepiColombo). Therefore, by considering the Orbit-placement Objective specifics, we derive the autonomy requirements for that objective, by applying GAR for Interplanetary Missions using Low-thrust Trajectories:

- *self-* requirements* (autonomicity):
  - `self-jettison`:
    the Transfer Module shall automatically release its SEPM when the right jettison attitude is reached;
    the Composite Module shall automatically release MMO when the polar orbit is reached.
  - `self-capture`:
    the Composite Module shall autonomously determine a steering law and use low thrust to achieve capture around Mercury.
  - `self-escape`:
    the Composite Module shall autonomously acquire the escape procedure and use it to leave Mercury if necessary;
  - `self-low-thrust-trajectory`:
    autonomously determine a steering law for a thrust vector and use low thrust to bring the Composite Module into polar orbit;
    autonomously determine a steering law for a thrust vector and use low thrust to bring MPO into its orbit.

– `self-protection`:

both the Composite Module and MPO shall autonomously detect the presence of high solar irradiation and:

· protect the electronics on board and instruments;

· change the altitude if possible by using electric propulsion and/or chemical propulsion.

– `self-thermal-control`:

both MMO and MPO shall maintain the onboard equipment and the spacecraft structure in proper temperature range.

– `self-scheduling`:

both the Composite Module and MPO shall autonomously determine what task to perform next in the course of pursuing the Orbit-placement Objective:

· jettison;

· start and stop engines;

· spin-up by using thrusters;

· moving by using thrusters.

- *knowledge*:

  - central force field physics;
  - steering law model for weak stability boundary capture;
  - MMO orbit;
  - MPO orbit;
  - maximum rate of change of orbital energy for MMO and MPO;
  - maximum rate of change of orbital inclination for MMO and MPO;
  - instruments onboard together with their characteristics (acceptable levels of radiation);
  - Base on Earth;
  - propulsion system (chemical propulsion rockets);
  - communication links, data transmission format, communication mechanisms onboard;
  - gravitational forces (Sun gravity and Mercury gravity);

- *awareness* (for both the Composite Module and MPO):

  - Mercury capture awareness;
  - Mercury escape awareness;
  - trajectory velocity awareness;
  - Mercury's magnetic field awareness,
  - Mercury's gravitational force awareness;
  - Sun's gravitational force awareness;
  - awareness of the spacecraft's position on the projected trajectory perturbations;
  - radiation awareness;
  - instrument awareness;
  - sensitive to thermal stimuli;
  - data-transfer awareness;
  - speed awareness;

   – communication awareness.

- *monitoring* (for both the Composite Module and MPO):

   – the environment around Mercury (e.g., radiation level, Mercury, the Sun);
   – planned operations (status, progress, feasibility, etc.).

- *adaptability* (for both the Composite Module and MPO):

   – adapt the low thrust trajectories to orbit and/or altitude perturbations.

- *dynamicity* (for both the Composite Module and MPO):

   – dynamic near-body environment;
   – dynamic trajectory following procedure (may require trajectory maneuvers);
   – dynamic communication links.

- *robustness* (for both the Composite Module and MPO):

   – robust to solar irradiation;
   – robust to temperature changes (high temperature amplitude);
   – robust to orbit-placement trajectory perturbations;
   – robust to communication losses.

- *resilience* (for both the Composite Module and MPO):

   – resilient to magnetic field changes.

- *mobility* (for both the Composite Module and MPO):

   – trajectory maneuvers for avoiding orbit and/or altitude perturbations.

3.5.1.3 Scientific Objectives Autonomy Requirements

The scientific objectives of BepiColombo address scientific tests and exploration of the Mercury's surface. As presented, the scientific objectives fall in another class of GAR (Generic Autonomy Requirements)—GAR for *Small Object "To Orbit" Missions* (Sect. 2.3.3.1). Although, Mercury is not considered as a *"small object,"* the BepiColombo's scientific objectives have characteristics similar to those of *Small Object "To Orbit" Missions*, which helped us adapt their GAR and derive the autonomy requirements for BepiColombo's Scientific Objectives. Note that the relevant environmental constraints (Sect. 3.4.2) were also used in this process.

- *self-* requirements* (autonomicity) (for both MMO and MPO):

   – `self-orbiting`:
       autonomously acquire the most optimal orbit;
       adapt to orbit perturbations due to possible large heat flux or solar irradiation;
   – `self-protection`:
       autonomously detect the presence of high solar irradiation and:
          · protect the electronics on board and instruments;

    ·   change the altitude if possible by using electric propulsion and/or chemical propulsion;

autonomously detect the presence of large heat flux and:

    ·   protect the electronics on board and instruments;

    ·   change the altitude if possible by using electric propulsion and/or chemical propulsion;

– `self-scheduling`:

autonomously determine what task to perform next in the course of pursuing the scientific objectives;

- *knowledge* (for both MMO and MPO):

  - scientific objectives (middle-level objectives—see Sect. 3.4.1.2);
  - payload operational requirements;
  - instruments onboard together with their characteristics (acceptable levels of radiation);
  - Base on Earth;
  - propulsion system (electric propulsion rockets, chemical propulsion rockets);
  - communication links, data transmission format, eclipse period, altitude, communication mechanisms onboard,
  - gravitational forces (Sun gravity and Mercury gravity);
  - physics of Mercury;
  - physics of the Sun;
  - radiation;
  - heat flux;

- *awareness* (for both MMO and MPO):

  - radiation awareness;
  - heat flux awareness;
  - Mercury's gravitational force awareness;
  - Mercury's magnetic fields awareness;
  - Sun's gravitational force awareness;
  - Mercury spin awareness;
  - Mercury speed awareness;
  - spacecraft's altitude awareness;
  - spacecraft's orbital speed awareness;
  - spacecraft's orbital period awareness;

- *monitoring* (for both MMO and MPO):

  - the environment around;
  - Mercury's surface;
  - Sun eruptions;

- *adaptability* (for both MMO and MPO):

  - adapt system operations to mission goals;

- adapt to the environment around (orbiting operations must take into consideration both orbit and altitude perturbations);

- *dynamicity* (for both MMO and MPO):

  - dynamic near-body environment;

- *robustness* (for both MMO and MPO):

  - robust to solar irradiation;
  - robust to large heat flux;

- *resilience*:

  - resilient to magnetic fields changes;

- *mobility*:

  - trajectory maneuvers for orbiting.

3.5.2 Goals Model for BepiColombo with Self-* Objectives

From the self-* requirements (autonomicity) presented in Sect. 3.5.1 we can derive self-* objectives providing mission behavior alternatives with respect to the Bepi-Colombo Mission Objectives (Fig. 3.8 and Sect. 3.4).

3.5.2.1 Self-* Objectives for BepiColmbo's Transfer Objective

The following elements describe the self-* objectives (derived from the self-* requirements presented in Sect. 3.5.1.1) assisting the BepiColombo's Transfer Objective:

- *Self-trajectory_1*: Autonomously acquire the most optimal trajectory to reach Mercury.

  - Actors:
    BepiColombo transfer module, chemical rocket engines, electric propulsion rocket engines, Earth, Venus, Mercury, the Sun, Base on Earth, BepiColombo composite module (MPO and MMO).
  - Targets:
    optimal interplanetary trajectory.

- *Self-trajectory_2*: Autonomously adapt to trajectory perturbations due to gravitational influence of the Sun, the Moon, Earth, Venus and Mercury.

  - Actors:
    BepiColombo transfer module, chemical rocket engines, electric propulsion rocket engines, Earth, Venus, Mercury, the Sun, Base on Earth, BepiColombo

composite module (MPO and MMO), trajectory perturbations, gravitational influence.

- Targets:

  interplanetary trajectory.

- *Self-protection_1*: Autonomously detect the presence of high solar irradiation and protect (eventually turn off or shade) the electronics and instruments on board.

  - Actors:

    BepiColombo transfer module, the Sun, Base on Earth, BepiColombo composite module (MPO and MMO), solar irradiation, shades, power system.

  - Targets:

    electronics and instruments.

- *Self-protection_2*: Autonomously detect the presence of high solar irradiation and get away if possible by using electric propulsion and/or chemical propulsion.

  - Actors:

    BepiColombo transfer module, chemical rocket engines, electric propulsion rocket engines, Earth, Venus, Mercury, the Sun, Base on Earth, solar irradiation.

  - Targets:

    safe position in space.

- *Self-protection_3*: Autonomously maintain a proper altitude of the Transfer Module during the interplanetary cruise, so no solar input will reach the MMO's and MPO's upper surface.

  - Actors:

    BepiColombo transfer module, chemical rocket engines, electric propulsion rocket engines, Earth, Venus, Mercury, the Sun, Base on Earth, solar input.

  - Targets:

    safe altitude.

- *Self-scheduling_1*: Autonomously determine when a gravity-assist maneuver is required near Earth.

  - Actors:

    BepiColombo transfer module, Earth, Earth gravitational influence.

  - Targets:

    gravity-assist maneuver, interplanetary trajectory.

- *Self-scheduling_2*: Autonomously determine when a gravity-assist maneuver is required near Venus.

  - Actors:

    BepiColombo transfer module, Venus, Venus gravitational influence.

  - Targets:

    gravity-assist maneuver, interplanetary trajectory.

- *Self-scheduling_3*: Autonomously determine when a gravity-assist maneuver is required near Mercury.

  – Actors:
    BepiColombo transfer module, Mercury, Mercury gravitational influence.
  – Targets:
    gravity-assist maneuver, interplanetary trajectory.

- *Self-reparation_1*: Autonomously restore broken communication links.

  – Actors:
    BepiColombo transfer module, BepiColombo composite module (MPO and MMO), communication link (state: broken).
  – Targets:
    communication link (state: operational).

- *Self-reparation_2*: Autonomously fix malfunctioning components if possible.

  – Actors:
    BepiColombo transfer module, BepiColombo composite module (MPO and MMO), component (state: malfunctioning).
  – Targets:
    component (state: operational).

Figure 3.9 depicts a partial goals model showing the relationships between the Transfer Objective and the assisting self-* objectives, providing mission behavior alternatives with respect to the Transfer Objective. As shown, most of the assisting self-* objectives inherit the Transfer Objective and consecutively, the main objective's target (the mission's interplanetary trajectory) is kept in all of those self-* objectives. The mission switches to one of the assisting objectives when alternative autonomic behavior is required (e.g., high irradiation emitted by the Sun).

3.5.2.2 Self-* Objectives for BepiColmbo's Orbit-Placement Objective

The following elements describe the *self-* objectives* (derived from the self-* requirements presented in Sect. 3.5.1.2) assisting the BepiColombo's orbit-placement objective:

- *Self-jettison_1*: Autonomously release the SEPM when the right jettison attitude is reached:

  – Actors:
    BepiColombo transfer module, SEPM, Mercury, the Sun, Base on Earth.
  – Targets:
    BepiColombo composite module.

- *Self-jettison_2*: Autonomously release MMO when the polar orbit is reached:

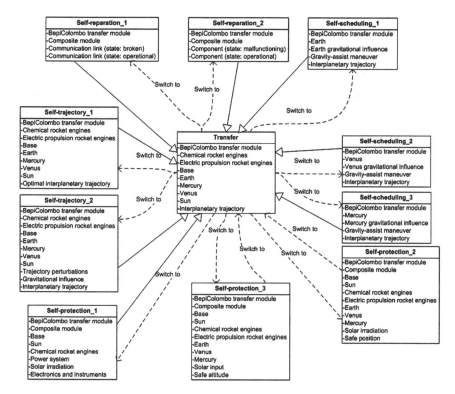

Fig. 3.9 Goals model for BepiColombo with self-* objectives assisting the transfer objective

 – Actors:
   BepiColombo composite module, MMO, Mercury, the Sun, Base on Earth.
 – Targets:
   MPO, Polar orbit.

• *Self-capture*: Autonomously determine a steering law and use low thrust to achieve capture around Mercury:

 – Actors:
   BepiColombo composite module, CPM, Mercury, the Sun, Base on Earth.
 – Targets:
   steering law, Mercury capture.

• *Self-escape*: Autonomously acquire the escape procedure and use it to leave Mercury if necessary:

 – Actors:
   BepiColombo composite module, CPM, Mercury, the Sun, Base on Earth.
 – Targets:
   escape procedure, Mercury leave.

- *Self-low-thrust-trajectory_1*: Autonomously determine a steering law for a thrust vector and use low thrust to bring the Composite Module into polar orbit (MMO's orbit):

  – Actors:
    BepiColombo composite module, CPM, Mercury, the Sun, Base on Earth.
  – Targets:
    steering law, thrust vector, MMO's orbit.

- *Self-low-thrust-trajectory_2*: Autonomously determine a steering law for a thrust vector and use low thrust to bring MPO into its orbit.

  – Actors:
    MPO, CPM, Mercury, the Sun, Base on Earth.
  – Targets:
    steering law, thrust vector, MPO's orbit.

- *Self-protection_1*: Autonomously detect the presence of high solar irradiation and protect (eventually turn off or shade) the electronics and instruments on board.

  – Actors:
    BepiColombo composite module (MMO), the Sun, Base on Earth, solar irradiation, shades, power system.
  – Targets:
    electronics and instruments.

- *Self-protection_2*: Autonomously detect the presence of high solar irradiation and get away if possible by using chemical propulsion.

  – Actors:
    BepiColombo composite module (MMO), CPM, Mercury, the Sun, Base on Earth, solar irradiation.
  – Targets:
    safe position around Mercury.

- *Self-protection_3*: Autonomously detect the presence of high solar irradiation and protect (eventually turn off or shade) the electronics and instruments on board.

  – Actors:
    MPO, the Sun, Base on Earth, solar irradiation, shades, power system.
  – Targets:
    electronics and instruments.

- *Self-protection_4*: Autonomously detect the presence of high solar irradiation and get away if possible by using chemical propulsion.

  – Actors:
    MPO, CPM, Mercury, the Sun, Base on Earth, solar irradiation.
  – Targets:
    safe position around Mercury.

- *Self-thermal-control_1*: Autonomously maintain the onboard equipment and the spacecraft structure in proper temperature range.

  – Actors:
    MMO, MMO's Thermal Control System, MMO's instruments, the Sun, Base on Earth, Mercury.
  – Targets:
    proper temperature.

- *Self-thermal-control_2*: Autonomously maintain the onboard equipment and the spacecraft structure in proper temperature range.

  – Actors:
    MPO, MPO's Thermal Control System, MPO's instruments, the Sun, Base on Earth, Mercury.
  – Targets:
    proper temperature.

- *Self-scheduling_1*: Autonomously determine what task to perform next in the course of pursuing the Orbit-placement Objective:

  – Actors:
    BepiColombo composite module, CPM, Mercury, the Sun, Base on Earth.
  – Targets:
    task jettison, start engine, stop engine, moving.

- *Self-scheduling_2*: Autonomously determine what task to perform next in the course of pursuing the Orbit-placement Objective:

  – Actors:
    MMO, CPM, Mercury, the Sun, Base on Earth.
  – Targets:
    task start engine, stop engine, spin-up, moving.

- *Self-scheduling_3*: Autonomously determine what task to perform next in the course of pursuing the Orbit-placement Objective:

  – Actors:
    MPO, CPM, Mercury, the Sun, Base on Earth.
  – Targets:
    task control engine, spin-up, moving.

Figure 3.10 depicts another partial goals model showing the relationships between the Orbit-placement Objective and the assisting self-* objectives, providing mission behavior alternatives with respect to the Orbit-placement Objective. Some of the assisting self-* objectives inherit the Orbit-placement Objective and consecutively, the main objective's target (bringing into orbit both MMO and MPO) is kept in all of those self-* objectives. The mission will switch to one of the assisting objectives when either a specific task must be performed (e.g., jettison) or alternative autonomic behavior is required (e.g., high irradiation emitted by the Sun).

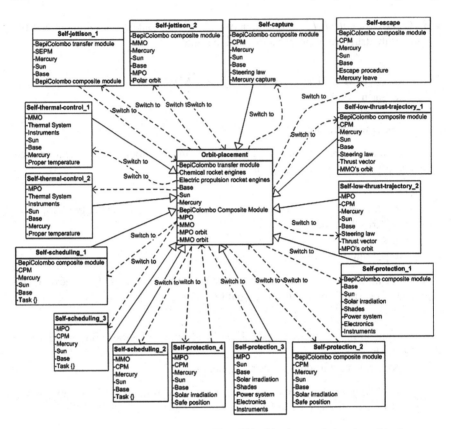

Fig. 3.10 Goals model for BepiColombo with self-* objectives assisting the orbit-placement objective

3.5.2.3 Self-* Objectives for BepiColmbo's Scientific Objectives

The following elements describe the self-* objectives (derived from the self-* requirements presented in Sect. 3.5.1.3) assisting the BepiColombo's Scientific Objectives:

- *Self-orbiting_1*: Autonomously acquire the most optimal orbit:

    – Actors:
      MMO/MPO, Mercury, the Sun, Base on Earth, SEPM, CPM.
    – Targets:
      · Optimal polar orbit.

- *Self-orbiting_2*: Autonomously adapt to orbit perturbations due to possible large heat flux:

    – Actors:

MMO/MPO, Mercury, the Sun, Base on Earth, SEPM, CPM, orbit perturbation.
- Targets:
  · Safe polar orbit.

- *Self-orbiting_3*: Autonomously adapt to orbit perturbations due to possible solar irradiation:

  - Actors:
    MMO/MPO, Mercury, the Sun, Base on Earth, SEPM, CPM, orbit perturbations, solar irradiation.
  - Targets:
    Safe polar orbit.

- *Self-protection_1*: Autonomously detect the presence of high solar irradiation and protect the electronics on board and instruments:

  - Actors:
    MMO/MPO, Mercury, the Sun, Base on Earth, shields, solar irradiation.
  - Targets:
    Electronics, instruments.

- *Self-protection_2*: Autonomously detect the presence of high solar irradiation and change the altitude if possible by using electric propulsion and/or chemical propulsion:

  - Actors:
    MMO/MPO, Mercury, the Sun, Base on Earth, SEPM, CPM, solar irradiation.
  - Targets:
    Safe polar orbit.

- *Self-protection_3*: Autonomously detect the presence of large heat flux and protect the electronics on board and instruments:

  - Actors:
    MMO/MPO, Mercury, the Sun, Base on Earth, shields, heat flux.
  - Targets:
    Electronics, instruments.

- *Self-protection_4*: Autonomously detect the presence of large heat flux and change the altitude if possible by using electric propulsion and/or chemical propulsion:

  - Actors:
    MMO/MPO, Mercury, the Sun, Base on Earth, SEPM, CPM, heat flux.
  - Targets:
    Safe polar orbit.

- *Self-scheduling*: Autonomously determine what task to perform next in the course of pursuing the scientific objectives:

  - Actors:

MMO/MPO, Mercury, the Sun, Base on Earth, instruments, objectives.
– Targets:
  Next task.

Figure 3.11 depicts another partial goals model showing the relationships between
BepiColombo's Scientific Objectives and the assisting self-* objectives, providing
mission behavior alternatives with respect to the Scientific Objectives. As shown, all
BepiColombo's Scientific Objectives are abstracted by one single *Scientific Objective*
(we may call this a Meta-level System Objective) presenting all the Middle-level
Mission Objectives (Sect. 3.4.1.2). Hence, the self-* objectives shown in Fig. 3.11
assist each one of the Scientific Objectives (the Middle-level Mission Objectives).

As shown in Fig. 3.11 and similar to the other goals models, some of the self-*
objectives require a temporal objective switching (or shifting) (see the "*Switch to*"

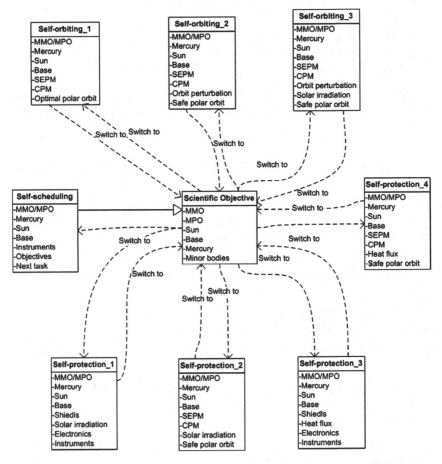

Fig. 3.11 Goals model for BepiColombo with self-* objectives assisting the scientific objectives

links) and other self-* objectives are descendant of the main mission goal (e.g., the Self-scheduling self-* objective), and inherit the main objective's target. The mission will switch to one of the assisting objectives when either a specific task must be performed (e.g., protection from solar irradiation) or alternative autonomic behavior is required.

3.5.3 Specifying the Autonomy Requirements with KnowLang

The next step after deriving the autonomy requirements per mission objectives (Sects. 3.5.1 and 3.5.2) shall be their specification, which can be considered as a form of formal specification or requirements recording. In this section, we present the KnowLang specification of the BepiColombo autonomy requirements. Note that both the specification models and accompanying rationale presented in this section are partial and intended to demonstrate how KnowLang copes with the different autonomy requirements. Moreover, a full specification model of BepiColombo is too large to be presented here and it is beyond this task's objectives. A more complete specification model (but still partial) can be found in Appendix A.

Before starting with the requirements specification, recall that specifying with KnowLang goes over a few phases (Sect. 2.5.4.1):

1. Initial knowledge requirements gathering—involves domain experts to determine the basic notions, relations and functions (operations) of the domain of interest.
2. Behavior definition—identifies situations and behavior policies as "control data" helping to identify important self-adaptive scenarios.
3. Knowledge structuring—encapsulates domain entities, situations and behavior policies into KnowLang structures like concepts, properties, functionalities, objects, relations, facts and rules.

When specifying autonomy requirements with KnowLang, another important factor to take into consideration is to know how the KnowLang framework handles these requirements at runtime. Recall that KnowLang comes with a special KnowLang Reasoner (Sect. 2.5.4.4), which operates on the specified requirements and provides the system with awareness capabilities. Moreover, the reasoner follows the architecture style of the deliberative controllers (Sect. 2.4.2.1) and provides supports both logical and statistical reasoning based on integrated Bayesian networks. Moreover, KnowLang implies layering (i.e., it might be used to handle layered controller architectures—see Sect. 2.4.2.3) for structuring functionalities and computational structures used for reasoning purposes in goal-oriented autonomy.

The KnowLang Reasoner is supplied as a component hosted by the system (e.g., BepiColombo's MMO spacecraft) and thus, it runs in the system's Operational Context as any other system's component. However, it operates in the Knowledge Representation Context (KR Context) and on the KR symbols (represented knowledge). The system talks to the reasoner via special *ASK* and *TELL* Operators allowing for knowledge queries and knowledge updates. Upon demand, the KnowLang Reasoner can also build up and return a self-adaptive behavior model—a chain of actions to be realized in the environment or in the system itself.

3.5.3.1 Knowledge

KnowLang (Sect. 2.5.4) is exclusively dedicated to knowledge specification where the latter is specified as a Knowledge Base (KB) comprising a variety of knowledge structures, e.g., *ontologies*, *facts*, *rules*, and *constraints*. Here, in order to specify the *autonomy requirements* of BepiColombo, the first step is to specify the KB representing both the external (space, Mercury, the Sun, etc.) and internal (spacecraft systems—MMO, MPO, etc.) worlds of the BepiColombo Mission. The BepiColombo KB shall contain a few ontologies structuring the knowledge domains of MMO, MPO, BepiColombo Composite Module, BepiColombo Transfer Module, and BepiColombo's operational environment (space). Note that these domains are described via domain-relevant concepts and objects (concept instances) related through relations. To handle explicit concepts like situations, goals, and policies, we grant some of the domain concepts with explicit state expressions (a state expression is a Boolean expression over ontology). Note that being part of the autonomy requirements, knowledge plays a very important role in the expression of all the autonomy requirements: *autonomicity*, *knowledge*, *awareness*, *monitoring*, *adaptability*, *dynamicity*, *robustness*, *resilience*, and *mobility* outlined by GAR (Sect. 3.2.1). To express the autonomy requirements of BepiColombo, we specified the necessary knowledge as following. Figure 3.12, depicts a graphical representation of the

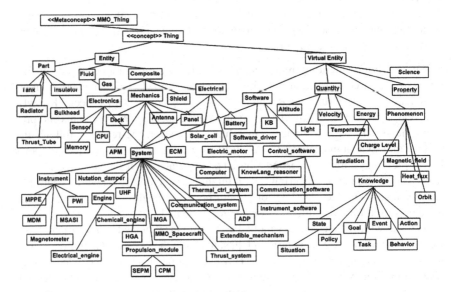

Fig. 3.12 MMO ontology: MMO thing concept tree

MMOThing concept tree relating most of the concepts within the MMO Ontology. Note that the relationships within a concept tree are "*is-a*" (inheritance), e.g., the *Part* concept is an *Entity* and the *Tank* concept is a *Part* and consecutively *Entity*, etc.

The following is a sample of the KnowLang specification representing the concepts of the MMO's propulsion modules: SEPM and CPM. As specified, the concepts in a concept tree might have properties of other concepts, functionalities (actions associated with that concept), states (Boolean expressions validating a specific state), etc. The *IMPL{}* specification directive references to the implementation of the concept in question, i.e., in the following example *SEPMSystem* is the software implementation (presuming a C++ class) of the MMO's SEPM.

```
// Propulsion modules
CONCEPT SEPM {
 CHILDREN {}
 PARENTS { MMO..System }
 STATES {
  STATE Operational {
   this.solar_cells.Functional AND this.gas_tank.Functional
   AND  this.el_engine.Operational AND this.control_soft.Functional }
  STATE Forwarding { IS_PERFORMING(this.forward) }
  STATE Reversing { IS_PERFORMING(this.forward) }
  STATE Started { LAST_PERFORMED(this, this.start) }
  STATE Stopped { LAST_PERFORMED(this, this.stop) }
  }
 PROPS {
  PROP solar_cells { TYPE {MMO..Solar_cell} CARDINALITY {200} }
  PROP gas_tank { TYPE {MMO..Tank} CARDINALITY {1} }
  PROP el_engine { TYPE {MMO..Electrical_Engine} CARDINALITY {1} }
  PROP control_soft { TYPE {MMO..Control_Software} CARDINALITY {1} }
  }
 FUNCS {
  FUNC reverse { TYPE {MMO..Action.ReverseSEPM } }
  FUNC forward { TYPE {MMO..Action.ForwardSEPM } }
  FUNC start { TYPE {MMO..Action.StartSEPM } }
  FUNC stop { TYPE {MMO..Action.StopSEPM } }
  }
 IMPL { MMO.SEPMSystem }
 }

CONCEPT CPM {
 CHILDREN {}
 PARENTS { MMO..System }
 STATES {
  STATE Operational {
   this.gas_tank.Functional AND this.chem_engine.Operational AND
   this.control_soft.Functional }
  STATE Forwarding { IS_PERFORMING(this.forward) }
  STATE Reversing { IS_PERFORMING(this.forward) }
  STATE Started { LAST_PERFORMED(this, this.stop) }
  STATE Stopped { LAST_PERFORMED(this, this.start) }
```

```
 }
 PROPS {
  PROP gas_tank { TYPE {MMO..Tank} CARDINALITY {1} }
  PROP chem_engine { TYPE {MMO..Chemical_Engine} CARDINALITY {1} }
  PROP control_soft { TYPE {MMO..Control_Software} CARDINALITY {1} }
 }
 FUNCS {
  FUNC reverse { TYPE {MMO..Action.ReverseCPM } }
  FUNC forward { TYPE {MMO..Action.ForwardCPM } }
  FUNC start { TYPE {MMO..Action.StartCPM } }
  FUNC stop { TYPE {MMO..Action.StopCPM } }
 }
 IMPL { MMO.CPMSystem }
 }
```

As mentioned, the states are specified as Boolean expressions. For example, the state *Forwarding* is true while the propulsion model is performing the reverse function. The KnowLang operator *IS_PERFORMING* evaluates actions and returns true if an action is currently performing. Similarly, the operator *LAST_PERFORMED* evaluates actions and returns true if an action is the last successfully performed action by the concept realization (a concept realization is an object instantiated from that concept, e.g., the *SEPM* object or the *CPM* object). A complex state, might be expressed as a function of other states. For example, the *Operational* state is expressed as a Boolean function of a few other states, particularly, states of the concept properties, e.g., the CPM is operational if its gas tank is functional, its chemical engine is operational, and its control software is functional:

```
 this.gas_tank.Functional AND this.chem_engine.Operational AND this.control_soft.
 Functional
```

As mentioned before, *states* are extremely important to the specification of *goals* (objectives), *situations*, and *policies*. For example, states help the KnowLang Reasoner determine at runtime whether the system is in a particular situation or a particular goal (objective) has been achieved.

The *MMO_Thing* concept tree (Fig. 3.12) is the main concept tree of the *MMOOntology* (a partial KnowLang specification of this ontology can be found in Appendix A). Note that due to space limitations, Fig. 3.12 does not show all the concept tree branches. Moreover, some of the concepts in this tree are "roots" of other trees. For example, the *Action* concept, expressing the common concept for all the actions that can be realized by MMO, is the root of the concept tree shown in Fig. 3.13. As shown, actions are grouped by subsystem (or part) they are associated with. For example, the HGA (high gain antenna) (Sect. 3.3.2.1) actions are: *PointHGA*, *SendHGA*, *ReceiveHGA*, *StopHGA*, and *StartHGA*.

The following is a partial specification of the *MMOSpacecraft* concept. Note this concept "is-a" system, i.e., it inherits the *System* concept. A system, according to the *MMOOntology* (Fig. 3.12) is a complex concept that joins the properties of four other concepts: *Electronics*, *Mechanics*, *Electrical*, and *Software*. Note that to

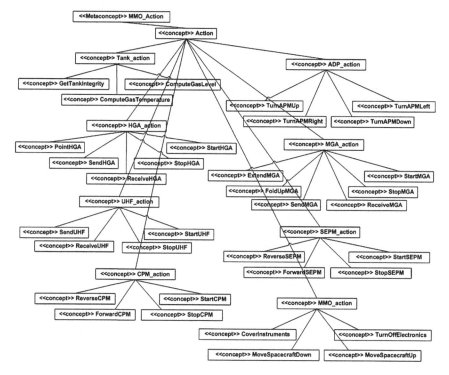

Fig. 3.13 MMO ontology: MMO action concept tree

specify MMO states, we used *metrics*. Metrics are intended to handle the *monitoring autonomy requirements* (Sect. 3.5.3.3).

```
CONCEPT MMO_Spacecraft {
 CHILDREN {}
 PARENTS { MMO..System }
 STATES {
  STATE Orbiting {}
  STATE InTransfer {}
  STATE InOrbitPlacement {}
  STATE InJettison {}
  STATE InHighIrradiation { MMO..Metric.OutsideRadiation.VALUE > 50 }
  STATE InHeatFlux { MMO..Metric.OutsideTemp.VALUE > 150 }
  STATE AtPolarOrbit { LAST_PERFORMED(this, this.moveToPolarOrbit) }
  STATE ArrivedAtMercury { MMO..Metric.MercuryAltitude.VALUE = 0.39 }
  STATE EarthCommunicationLost { MMO..Metric.EarthSignal.VALUE = 0 }
 }
 PROPS {
  PROP sepm { TYPE {MMO..SEPM} CARDINALITY {1} }
  PROP cpm { TYPE {MMO..CPM} CARDINALITY {1} }
  PROP upper_deck { TYPE {MMO..Deck} CARDINALITY {1} }
  PROP lower_deck { TYPE {MMO..Deck} CARDINALITY {1} }
  PROP thrust_tube { TYPE {MMO..Thrust_Tube} CARDINALITY {1} }
```

```
      PROP bulkhead { TYPE {MMO..Bulkhead} CARDINALITY {4} }
      PROP side_panel { TYPE {MMO..Panel} CARDINALITY {1} }
      PROP solar_cell { TYPE {MMO..Solar_cell} CARDINALITY {200} }
      PROP battery {  TYPE {MMO..Battery} CARDINALITY {1} }
      PROP nutation_damper {  TYPE {MMO..Nutation_damper} CARDINALITY {1} }
      PROP mppe_instr { TYPE {MMO..MPPE} CARDINALITY {1} }
      PROP mdm_instr { TYPE {MMO..MDM} CARDINALITY {1} }
      PROP magnetometer { TYPE {MMO..Magnetometer} CARDINALITY {1} }
      PROP msasi_instr { TYPE {MMO..MSASI} CARDINALITY {1} }
      PROP pwi_instr { TYPE {MMO..PWI} CARDINALITY {1} }
      PROP radiator { TYPE {MMO..Radiator} CARDINALITY {1} }

      PROP uhf { TYPE {MMO..UHF} CARDINALITY {1} }
      PROP mga { TYPE {MMO..MGA} CARDINALITY {1} }
      PROP hga { TYPE {MMO..HGA} CARDINALITY {1} }
      PROP control_soft { TYPE {MMO..Control_Software} CARDINALITY {1} }
      PROP communication_sys { TYPE {MMO..Communication_system} CARDINALITY {1} }
      PROP thermal_ctrl_sys { TYPE {MMO..Thermal_Ctrl_System} CARDINALITY {1} }
      }
      FUNCS {
      FUNC moveToPolarOrbit { TYPE {MMO..Action.GoToPolarOrbit} }
      FUNC waitForInstrFromEarth { TYPE {MMO..Action.WaitForInstructions} }
      }
      IMPL { MMO.MMOSystem }
      }
```

In the KnowLang specification models, the *concept instances* are considered as objects and are structured in *object trees*. The latter are a conceptualization of how objects existing in the world of interest are related to each other. The relationships in an object tree are based on the principle that objects have properties, where the value of a property is another object, which in turn also has properties. Therefore, the object trees are the realization of concepts in the ontology domain (e.g., MMO). To better understand the relationship between concepts and objects, we may think of concepts as similar to the OOP classes and objects as instances of these classes. Figure 3.14 depicts the graphical representation of the HGA object tree specified with KnowLang. Thus, as shown, in the MMO domain there is an instance of HGA called *hga_antenna_1*. The following is the specification of the *hga_antenna_1* object tree:

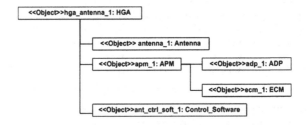

Fig. 3.14 MMO ontology: hga_antenna_1 object tree

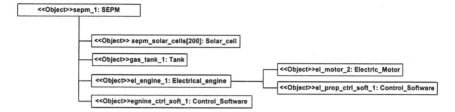

Fig. 3.15 MMO ontology: sepm_1 object tree

```
// hga_antenna_1 object tree
FINAL OBJECT antenna_1 {
 INSTANCE_OF { MMO..Antenna }
 }
FINAL OBJECT adp_1 {
 INSTANCE_OF { MMO..ADP }
 }
FINAL OBJECT ecm_1 {
 INSTANCE_OF { MMO..ECM }
 }
FINAL OBJECT apm_1 {
 INSTANCE_OF { MMO..APM }
 PROPS {
  PROP adp { MMO.OBJECT_TREES.adp_1 }
  PROP ecm { MMO.OBJECT_TREES.ecm_1 }
 }
 }
FINAL OBJECT ant_ctrl_soft_1 {
 INSTANCE_OF { MMO..Control_software }
 }
FINAL OBJECT hga_antenna_1 {
 INSTANCE_OF { MMO..HGA }
 PROPS {
  PROP hga_antenna { MMO.OBJECT_TREES.antenna_1 }
  PROP apm { MMO.OBJECT_TREES.apm_1 }
  PROP control_soft { MMO.OBJECT_TREES.ant_ctrl_soft_1 }
 }
 IMPL { MMO.HGAAntennaModule }
 }
```

Figure 3.15 depicts the object tree of the SEPM (Solar Electric Propulsion Module). The concept instance *sepm*_1 represent the MMO's SEPM. As shown, the SEPM has *solar cells* (presumably 200), a *gas tank*, an *electrical engine*, and *control software*.

3.5.3.2 Autonomicity

To specify the self-* objectives (autonomicity requirements), we use goals, policies, and situations. These are defined as explicit concepts in KnowLang and for the MMO Ontology we specified them under the concepts *Virtual_entity* → *Phenomenon* →

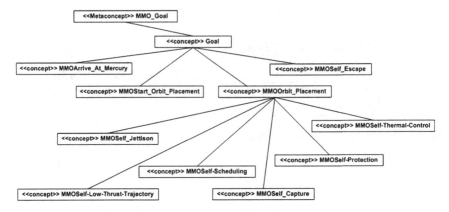

Fig. 3.16 MMO ontology: MMO_Goal concept tree

Knowledge (Fig. 3.12). Figure 3.16 depicts a concept tree with some of the goals (objectives) related to MMO. Note that most of these goals were directly interpolated from the goals models (Sects. 3.4 and 3.5.1) and more specifically, from the goals model for *self-* objectives assisting the Orbit-placement Objective* (Sect. 3.5.2.2).

KnowLang specifies goals as *functions of states* where any combination of states can be involved. A goal has an *arriving state* (Boolean function of states) and an optional *departing state* (another Boolean function of states). A goal with departing state is more restrictive, i.e., it can be achieved only if the system departs from the specific goal's departing state. The following code samples present the specification of three simple goals. Note that their arriving and departing states are single MMO states, but also can be Boolean functions involving more than one state. Recall that the states used to specify these goals are specified as part of the *MMO_Spacecraft* concept (Sect. 3.5.3.1).

```
//
//==== SC Goals ===========================================================
//

CONCEPT_GOAL MMOOrbit_Placement {
 SPEC {
  DEPART { MMO_Spacecraft.STATES.InOrbitPlacement }
  ARRIVE { MMO_Spacecraft.STATES.AtPolarOrbit }
 }
}
CONCEPT_GOAL MMOArrive_At_Mercury {
 SPEC { ARRIVE { MMO_Spacecraft.STATES.ArrivedAtMercury } }
}
CONCEPT_GOAL MMOStart_Orbit_Placement {
 SPEC {
  DEPART { MMO_Spacecraft.STATES.ArrivedAtMercury }
  ARRIVE { MMO_Spacecraft.STATES.InOrbitPlacement }
 }
}
```

The following code sample presents the specification of a goal with an arriving state expressed as a Boolean function over two *MMO_Spacecraft* states: *InHighIrradiation* and *AtPolarOrbit*.

```
//protect from solar radiation
CONCEPT_GOAL MMOSelf-Protection {
  SPEC {
    ARRIVE { NOT MMO_Spacecraft.STATES.InHighIrradiation AND MMO_Spacecraft.STATES.
    AtPolarOrbit}
  }
}
```

In order to achieve specified goals (objectives), we need to specify *policies* triggering *actions* that will change the system states, so the desired ones, required by the goals, will become effective. All the policies in KnowLang descend from the explicit *Policy* concept. Note that policies allow the specification of autonomic behavior (autonomic behavior can be associated with autonomy requirements). As a rule, we need to specify at least one policy per single goal, i.e., a policy that will provide the necessary behavior to achieve that goal. Of course, we may specify multiple policies handling same goal (objective), which is often the case with the self-* objectives and let the system decides which policy to apply taking into consideration the current situation and conditions.

The following is a formal presentation of the policy specification (Sect. 2.5.4.2). Recall that policies (Π) are specified as individual concepts providing behavior (often concurrent). A policy π has a goal (g), policy situations (Si_π), policy-situation relations (R_π), and policy conditions (N_π) mapped to policy actions (A_π) where the evaluation of N_π may eventually (with some degree of probability) imply the evaluation of actions (denoted with $N_\pi \xrightarrow{[Z]} A_\pi$, see Definition 3.2). A condition is a Boolean function over ontology (Definition 3.4), e.g., the occurrence of a certain event.

Definition 3.1 $\Pi := \{\pi_1, \pi_2, ..., \pi_n\}, n \geq 0$ (Policies)

Definition 3.2 $\pi := < g, Si_\pi, [R_\pi], N_\pi, A_\pi, map(N_\pi, A_\pi, [Z]) >$
$$A_\pi \subset A, N_\pi \xrightarrow{[Z]} A_\pi \quad (A_\pi—\text{Policy Actions})$$
$$Si_\pi \subset Si, Si_\pi := \{si_{\pi_1}, si_{\pi_2}, ..., si_{\pi_n}\}, n \geq 0$$
$$R_\pi \subset R, R_\pi := \{r_{\pi_1}, r_{\pi_2}, ..., r_{\pi_n}\}, n \geq 0$$
$$\forall r_\pi \in R_\pi \bullet (r_\pi := < si_\pi, [rn], [Z], \pi >), si_\pi \in Si_\pi$$
$$Si_\pi \xrightarrow{[R_\pi]} \pi \to N_\pi$$

Definition 3.3 $N_\pi := \{n_1, n_2, ..., n_k\}, k \geq 0$ (Conditions)

Definition 3.4 $n := be(O)$ (Condition—Boolean Expression)

Policy situations (Si_π) are situations that may trigger (or imply) a policy π, in compliance with the policy-situations relations R_π (denoted with $Si_\pi \xrightarrow{[R_\pi]} \pi$), thus implying the evaluation of the policy conditions N_π (denoted with $\pi \rightarrow N_\pi$) (Definition 3.2). Therefore, the optional policy-situation relations (R_π) justify the relationships between a policy and the associated situations (Definition 3.2). In addition, the self-adaptive behavior requires relations to be specified to connect policies with situations over an optional probability distribution (Z) where a policy might be related to multiple situations and vice versa. Probability distribution is provided to support probabilistic reasoning and to help the KnowLang Reasoner choose the most probable situation-policy "*pair*." Thus, we may specify a few relations connecting a specific situation to different policies to be undertaken when the system is in that particular situation and the probability distribution over these relations (involving the same situation) should help the KnowLang Reasoner decide which policy to choose (denoted with $Si_\pi \overset{[R_\pi]}{\rightarrow} \pi$—see Definition 3.2). Hence, the presence of probabilistic beliefs at both mappings and policy relations justifies the probability of policy execution, which may vary with time.

The following is a specification sample showing a simple policy called *Bring − MMOToOrbit*—as the name says, this policy is intended to bring MMO into polar orbit. As shown, the policy is specified to handle the goal *MMOOrbit_Placement _Done* and is triggered by the situation *ArrivedAtMercury*. Further, the policy triggers unconditionally (the *CONDITIONS{}* directive is empty) the execution of the *GoToPolarOrbit* action.

```
CONCEPT_POLICY BringMMOToOrbit {
  SPEC {
    POLICY_GOAL { MMO..MMOOrbit_Placement_Done }
    POLICY_SITUATIONS { MMO..ArrivedAtMercury }
    POLICY_RELATIONS { MMO..Policy_Situation_2 }
    POLICY_ACTIONS { MMO..Action.GoToPolarOrbit }
    POLICY_MAPPINGS {
     MAPPING {
      CONDITIONS {}
      DO_ACTIONS { MMO..Action.GoToPolarOrbit }
     }
    }
  }
}
```

As mentioned above, policies are triggered by situations. Therefore, while specifying policies handling system objectives, we need to think of important situations that may trigger those policies. A single policy requires to be associated with (related to) at least one situation, but for polices handling self-* objectives we eventually need more situations. Actually, because the *policy-situation relation* is bidirectional, it is maybe more accurate to say that a single situation may need more policies, those providing alternative behaviors.

Figure 3.17 depicts a situation concept tree. This partial tree presents some of the possible and important situations the MMO spacecraft can fall in. Recall, that

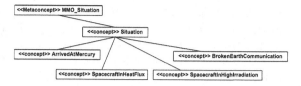

Fig. 3.17 MMO ontology: MMO situation concept tree

situations are important, because they might have impact on mission objectives. The four situations, depicted in Fig. 3.17, are specified by the following KnowLang code:

```
//
//==== SC Situations ==================================================
//
CONCEPT_SITUATION ArrivedAtMercury {
 CHILDREN {}
 PARENTS {MMO..Situation}
 SPEC {
  SITUATION_STATES { MMO_Spacecraft.STATES.ArrivedAtMercury }
  SITUATION_ACTIONS {
   MMO..Action.GoToPolarOrbit, MMO..Action.WaitForInstructions, MMO..Action.
   ScheduleNewTask
  }
 }
}
CONCEPT_SITUATION BrokenEarthCommunication {
 CHILDREN {}
 PARENTS {MMO..Situation}
 SPEC {
  SITUATION_STATES { MMO_Spacecraft.STATES.EarthCommunicationLost }
  SITUATION_ACTIONS { MMO..Action.SendPingSignalToEarth, MMO..Action.
  ScheduleNewTask }
 }
}
CONCEPT_SITUATION SpacecraftInHeatFlux {
 CHILDREN {}
 PARENTS {MMO..Situation}
 SPEC {
  SITUATION_STATES { MMO_Spacecraft.STATES.InHeatFlux }
  SITUATION_ACTIONS { MMO..Action.CoverInstruments, MMO..Action.GotoSafeAltitude }
 }
}
CONCEPT_SITUATION SpacecraftInHighIrradiation {
 CHILDREN {}
 PARENTS {MMO..Situation}
 SPEC {
  SITUATION_STATES { MMO_Spacecraft.STATES.InHighIrradiation }
  SITUATION_ACTIONS { MMO..Action.CoverInstruments, MMO..Action.GotoSafeAltitude }
 }
}
```

As shown, situations are specified with states and possible actions. To consider a situation effective (the system is currently in that situation), its associated states must be respectively effective (evaluated as true). For example, the situation *Spacecraft − InHeatFlux* is effective if the *MMOSpacecraft* state *InHeatFlux* is effective. The possible actions define what actions can be undertaken once the system falls in a particular situation. For example, the *ArrivedAtMercury* situation has three possible actions: *GoToPolarOrbit*, *WaitForInstructions*, *ScheduleNewTask*.

Recall that situations are related to policies via relations. The following code demonstrates how we related the *ArrivedAtMercury* situation to two different policies: *FollowOrbitPlacementInstrs* and *BringMMOToOrbit*. As specified, the probability distribution gives initial designer's preference about what policy should be applied if the system ends up in the *ArrivedAtMercury* situation. Note that at runtime, the KnowLang Reasoner maintains a record of all the action executions and re-computes the probability rates every time when a policy has been applied. Thus, although initially the system will apply the *FollowOrbitPlacementInstrs* policy (it has the higher probability rate of 0.9), if the policy cannot achieve the goal it is intended to handle due to action fails (e.g., the communication link with Earth is broken and instructions are not coming), then the probability distribution will be shifted in favor of the *BringMMOToOrbit* policy and the system will try to apply that policy. Note that, eventually, both policies *FollowOrbitPlacementInstrs* and *BringMMOToOrbit* share the same goal.

```
//
//==== MMO Relations ==================================================
//
RELATIONS {
 RELATION Policy_Situation_1 {
 RELATION_PAIR {MMO..ArrivedAtMercury, MMO..FollowOrbitPlacementInstrs}
 PROBABILITY {0.9}
 }

 RELATION Policy_Situation_2 {
 RELATION_PAIR {MMO..ArrivedAtMercury, MMO..BringMMOToOrbit} PROBABILITY {0.1}
 }

 RELATION Policy_Situation_3 {
 RELATION_PAIR {MMO..HighIrradiation, MMO..MMOSelf-protection}
 }

}
```

Probability distribution at the level of situation-policy relation can be omitted, presuming the relationship will not change over time (see the third relation in the code above). It is also possible to assign probability distribution within a policy where the probability values are set at the level of action execution. The following code specifies the *MMOProtect_spacecraft* policy intended to handle the *MMOSelf_Protection* objective with similar probability distribution. Probabilities are recomputed after every action execution, and thus the behavior change accordingly.

```
CONCEPT_POLICY MMOProtect_Spacecraft {
 SPEC {
  POLICY_GOAL { MMO..MMOSelf-Protection }
  POLICY_SITUATIONS { MMO..HighIrradiation }
  POLICY_RELATIONS { MMO..Policy_Situation_3 }
  POLICY_ACTIONS {
   MMO..Action.CoverInstruments, MMO..Action.TurnOffElectronics,
   MMO..Action.MoveSpacecraftUp, MMO..Action.MoveSpacecraftDown }
  POLICY_MAPPINGS {
   MAPPING {
    CONDITIONS { MMO..Metric.SolarRadiation.VALUE < 90 }
    DO_ACTIONS { MMO..Action.ShadeInstruments, MMO..Action.TurnOffElectronics }
   }
   MAPPING {
    CONDITIONS { MMO..Metric.SolarRadiation.VALUE >= 90 }
    DO_ACTIONS { MMO..Action.MoveSpacecraftUp }
    PROBABILITY {0.5}
   }
   MAPPING {
    CONDITIONS { MMO..Metric.SolarRadiation.VALUE >= 90 }
    DO_ACTIONS { MMO..Action.MoveSpacecraftDown }
    PROBABILITY {0.4}
   }
   MAPPING {
    CONDITIONS { MMO..Metric.SolarRadiation.VALUE >= 90 }
    DO_ACTIONS { GENERATE_NEXT_ACTIONS(MMO..MMO_Spacecraft) }
    PROBABILITY {0.1}
   }
  }
 }
}
```

To increase the goal-oriented autonomicity, in this policy's specification, we use the special KnowLang operator *GENERATE_NEXT_ACTIONS*, which will automatically generate the most appropriate actions to be undertaken by the MMO spacecraft. The action generation is based on the computations performed by a special reward function implemented by the KnowLang Reasoner. The KnowLang Reward Function (KLRF) observes the outcome of the actions to compute the possible successor states of every possible action execution and grants the actions with special reward number considering the current system state (or states, if the current state is a composite state) and goals. KLRF is based on past experience and uses Discrete Time Markov Chains [13] for probability assessment after action executions (Sect. 2.5.4.3).

Note that when generating actions, the *GENERATE_NEXT_ACTIONS* operator follows a sequential decision-making algorithm where actions are selected to maximize the total reward. This means that the immediate reward of the execution of the first action, of the generated list of actions, might not be the highest one, but the overall reward of executing all the generated actions will be the highest possible one. Moreover, note that, the generated actions are selected from the predefined set of actions (e.g., the possible MMO actions—see Fig. 3.13). The principle of the decision-making algorithm used to select actions is as follows:

1. The average cumulative reward of the reinforcement learning system is calculated.
2. For each policy-action mapping, the KnowLang Reasoner learns the value function, which is relative to the sum of average reward.
3. According to the value function and *Bellman Optimality Principle*,[4] is generated the optimal sequence of actions.

3.5.3.3 Monitoring

The *monitoring autonomy requirement* is handled via the explicit *Metric* concept. In general, a self-adaptive system has sensors that connect it to the world and eventually help it listen to its internal components. These sensors generate *raw data* that represents the physical characteristics of the world. In our approach, we assume that MMO's sensors are controlled by software drivers (e.g., implemented in C++) where appropriate methods are used to control a sensor and read data from it. By specifying a *Metric* concept we introduce a class of sensors to the KB and by specifying objects, instances of that class, we represent the real sensor. KnowLang allows the specification of four different types of metrics:

- *RESOURCE*—measures resources like capacity;
- *QUALITY*—measures qualities like performance, response time, etc.;
- *ENVIRONMENT*—measures environment qualities and resources;
- *ENSEMBLE*—measures complex qualities and resources where the metric might be a function of multiple metrics both of *RESOURCE* and *QUALITY* type.

The following is a specification of metrics mainly used to assist the specification of states and policy conditions:

```
//Metrics
CONCEPT_METRIC OutsideRadiation {
 SPEC {
  METRIC_TYPE { ENVIRONMENT }
  METRIC_SOURCE { RadiationMeasure.OutsideRadiation }
  DATA { DATA_TYPE { MMO..Sievert } VALUE { 1 } }
 }
}
CONCEPT_METRIC OutsideTemp {
 SPEC {
  METRIC_TYPE { ENVIRONMENT }
  METRIC_SOURCE { TempMeasure.OutsideTemp }
  DATA { DATA_TYPE { MMO..Celsius } VALUE { 1 } }
```

---

[4] The Bellman optimality principle: If a given state-action sequence is optimal, and we were to remove the first state and action, the remaining sequence is also optimal (with the second state of the original sequence now acting as initial state).

```
    }
    }
CONCEPT_METRIC MercuryAltitude {
  SPEC {
    METRIC_TYPE { ENVIRONMENT }
    METRIC_SOURCE { AltitudeMeasure.Mercury }
    DATA { DATA_TYPE { MMO..AU } VALUE { 1 } }
  }
}
CONCEPT_METRIC EarthSignal {
  SPEC {
    METRIC_TYPE { QUALITY }
    METRIC_SOURCE { EarthCommLink.SignalStrength }
    DATA { VALUE { 1 } }
  }
}
CONCEPT_METRIC SolarRadiation {
  SPEC {
    METRIC_TYPE { ENVIRONMENT }
    METRIC_SOURCE { IrradiationMeasure.GetLevel }
    DATA { DATA_TYPE { MMO..Lumen } VALUE { 1 } }
  }
}
```

3.5.3.4 Awareness

The *awareness autonomy requirements* are handled by the KnowLang Reasoner (Sect. 2.5.2). However, still we need to specify concepts and objects that will support the reasoner in its awareness capabilities. For example, we need to specify *metrics* that support both *self-* and *environment monitoring* (Sect. 3.5.3.3). Next, by specifying states where metrics are used, we introduce *awareness capabilities* for *self-awareness* and *context-awareness*. Finally, with the specification of situations (Sect. 3.5.3.2) we introduce the basis for *situational awareness*.

Other classes of awareness could draw attention to specific states and situations, such as operational conditions and performance (*operational awareness*), control processes (*control awareness*), interaction processes (*interaction awareness*), and navigation processes (*navigation awareness*).

3.5.3.5 Resilience, Robustness, Mobility, Dynamicity, and Adaptability

Resilience, robustness, mobility, dynamicity, and adaptability *autonomy requirements* might be handled by specifying special *soft goals*. For example, the requirement "*robustness: robust to communication losses*" and "*resilience: resilient to solar radiation*." These requirements can be specified as soft goals leading the system towards "*reducing and copying with communication losses*" and "*preventing the MMO from taking self-protective actions if the radiation is relatively low*." Note that specifying soft goals is not an easy task. The problem is that there is no clear-cut satisfaction condition for a soft goal. Soft goals are related to the notion of satisfaction. Unlike regular goals, soft goals can seldom be accomplished or satisfied. For soft goals, eventually, we need to find solutions that are "*good enough*" where soft goals are satisfied to a sufficient degree. Thus, when specifying robustness and resilience autonomy requirements we need to set the desired degree of satisfaction, e.g., by using probabilities and/or policy conditions (see the specification of the *MMOProtect_Spacecraft* policy in Sect. 3.5.3.2).

Mobility, dynamicity, and adaptability might also be specified as soft goals, but with relatively high degree of satisfaction. These three types of autonomy requirements represent important quality requirements that the system in question need to meet to provide conditions making autonomicity possible. Thus, their *degree of satisfaction* should be relatively high. Eventually, adaptability requirements might be defined as *hard goals* because they determine what parts of the system in question can be adapted (not how).

3.6 Summary

This chapter has outlined our ARE (Autonomy Requirements Engineering) approach along with a proof-of-concept case study. This case study targets ARE for ESA's BepiColombo Mission where we have applied the proposed ARE model to a real ESA mission. Moreover, we have demonstrated how ARE can be used to both elicit and express autonomy requirements for space missions. In our approach, ARE relies on Goal-Oriented Requirements Engineering (GORE) to elicit and define the system goals, and uses the Generic Autonomy Requirements (GAR) model, put in the context of space missions, to derive and define *assistive* and eventually *alternative goals* (or objectives). The system may pursue these "*self-* objectives*" in the presence of factors threatening the achievement of the initial system goals. Once identified, the autonomy requirements including the self-* objectives have been further specified with KnowLang. The specification of the BepiColombo's autonomy requirements along with accompanying rationale have also been presented in this chapter.

References

1. Amoroso, E.: Fundamentals of Computer Security. Prentice-Hall, Upper Saddle River (1994)
2. Anton, A., Potts, C.: The use of goals to surface requirements for evolving systems. In: Proceedings of the 20th International Conference on Software Engineering (ICSE-98), Kyoto. IEEE Computer Society (1998)
3. Arianespace: Arianespace to launch BepiColombo spacecraft on first European mission to Mercury. arianespace.com (2011). http://www.arianespace.com/news-press-release/2011/9-15-2011-BepiColombo.asp

4. Benkhoff, J.: BepiColombo: overview and latest updates. European Planetary Science Congress, EPSC Abstracts 7 (2012)
5. Boehm, H., Rodgers, B., Deutsch, T.M.: Applying WinWin to quality requirements: a case study. In: Proceedings of the 23rd International Conference on Software Engineering, pp. 555–564 (2001)
6. Bubenko, J., Rolland, C., Loucopoulos, P., de Antonellis, V.: Facilitating "fuzzy to formal" requirements modeling. In: Proceedings of the IEEE 1st Conference on Requirements Engineering (ICRE94), pp. 154–158. IEEE (1994)
7. Chung, L., Nixon, B., Yu, E., Mylopoulos, J. (eds.): Non-Functional Requirements in Software Engineering. Kluwer Academic, Boston (2000)
8. Dardenne, A., van Lamsweerde, A., Fickas, S.: Goal-directed requirements acquisition. Sci. Comput. Prog. Elsevier **20**, 3–50 (1993)
9. ESA: BepiCcolombo Mercury explorer to be launched on Ariane. esa.int. http://www.esa.int/Our_Activities/Space_Science/BepiColombo_Mercury_explorer_to_be_launched_on_Ariane
10. ESA: BepiColombo Mercury mission to be launched in 2015. sci.esa.int (2012). http://sci.esa.int/science-e/www/object/index.cfm?fobjectid=50105
11. ESA: BepiColombo overview. esa.int (2012). http://www.esa.int/Our_Activities/Space_Science/BepiColombo_overview2
12. ESA: BepiColombo—the interdisciplinary cornerstone mission to the planet Mercury—an overview of the system and technology study. ESA, BR-165 (2000)
13. Ewens, W.J., Grant, G.R.: Statistical Methods in Bioinformatics, 2nd edn, Chap. Stochastic processes (i): poison processes and Markov Chains. Springer, New York (2005)
14. Feather, M.S., Cornford, S.L., Dunphy, J., Hicks, K.: A quantitative risk model for early life-cycle decision making. In: Proceedings of the Conference on Integrated Design and Process Technology, Pasadena, California, USA (2002)
15. Fortescue, P., Swinerd, G., Stark, J. (eds.): Spacecraft Systems Engineering. Wiley, Chichester (2011)
16. Grard, R., Novara, M., Scoon, G.: BepiColombo—a multidisciplinary mission to a hot planet. ESA Bull. **103**, 11–19 (2000)
17. Haumer, P., Pohl, K., Weidenhaupt, K.: Requirements elicitation and validation with real world scenes. In: IEEE Transactions on Software Engineering, Special Issue on Scenario Management, pp. 1036–1054 (1998)
18. Jessa, T.: Solar irradiation. Universe Today, universetoday.com (2011). http://www.universetoday.com/85045/solar-irradiation/
19. Kazman, R., Barbacci, M., Klein, M., Carriere, S.J.: Experience with performing architecture tradeoff analysis. In: Proceedings of ICSE99, Los Angeles, CA, USA, pp. 54–63 (1999)
20. Kirwan, B., Ainsworth, L.K.: A Guide to Task Analysis. CRC Press, Boca Raton (1992)
21. Lamsweerde, A., van Letier, E.: Handling obstacles in goal-oriented requirements engineering. In: IEEE Transactions on Software Engineering, Special Issue on Exception Handling (2000)
22. Leveson, N.G.: Safeware: System Safety and Computers. ACM Press, New York (1995)
23. Montagnon, E.: International collaboration on BepiColombo. Ask Magazine, NASA (46) (2012). http://www.nasa.gov/offices/oce/appel/ask/issues/46/46s_international_collaboration.html
24. Mylopoulos, J., Chung, K.L., Yu, E.: From object-oriented to goal-oriented requirements analysis. Comm. ACM **42**(1), 31–37 (1999)
25. Nixon, B.A.: Dealing with performance requirements during the development of information systems. In: Proceedings of the 1st International IEEE Symposium on Requirements Engineering (RE93), pp. 42–49. IEEE (1993)
26. Novara, M.: The BepiColombo ESA cornerstone mission to Mercury. Acta Astronaut. **51**(1–9), 387–395 (2002)
27. Nuseibeh, B., Kramer, J., Finkelstein, A.: A framework for expressing the relationships between multiple views in requirements specification. IEEE Trans. Softw. Eng. **20**, 760–773 (1994)

28. Pumfrey, D.J.: The principled design of computer system safety analyses. Ph.D. thesis, University of York (1999)
29. Robinson, W.N.: Integrating multiple specifications using domain goals. In: Proceedings of the 5th International Workshop on Software Specification and Design (IWSSD-5), pp. 219–225. IEEE (1989)
30. Rolland, C., Souveyet, C., Achour, C.B.: Guiding goal-modeling using scenarios. In: IEEE Transactions on Software Engineering, Special Issue on Scenario Management, pp. 1055–1071 (1998)
31. Ross, D., Schoman, K.: Structured analysis for requirements definition. IEEE Trans. Softw. Eng. **3**(1), 6–15 (1977)
32. The EIT Consortium: The SOHO extreme ultraviolet imaging telescope, NASA Goddard Space Flight Center, Solar Physics Branch/Code 682 Greenbelt. umbra.nascom.nasa.gov. http://umbra.nascom.nasa.gov/eit/
33. van Lamsweerde, A., Darimont, R., Letier, E.: Managing conflicts in goal-driven requirements engineering. In: IEEE Transactions on Software Engineering, Special Issue on Inconsistency Management in Software Development (1998)
34. van Lamsweerde, A., Darimont, R., Massonet, P.: Goal-directed elaboration of requirements for a meeting scheduler: problems and lessons learnt. In: Proceedings of the 2nd International IEEE Symposium on Requirements Engineering, pp. 194–203. IEEE Computer Society (1995)
35. van Lamsweerde, A.: Requirements engineering in the Year 00: a research perspective. In: Proceedings of the 22nd IEEE International Conference on Software Engineering (ICSE-2000), pp. 5–19. ACM (2000)
36. Vassev, E., Hinchey, M.: Knowledge representation for cognitive robotic systems. In: Proceedings of the 15th IEEE International Symposium on Object/Component/Service-Oriented Real-Time Distributed Computing Workshops (ISCORCW 2012), pp. 156–163. IEEE Computer Society (2012)
37. Vassev, E., Hinchey, M.: ASSL: a software engineering approach to autonomic computing. IEEE Comput. **42**(6), 106–109 (2009)
38. Wertz, J., Larson, W. (eds.): Space Mission Analysis and Design. Microcosm Press, Hawthorne (1999)
39. Yamakawa, H., et al.: Current status of the BepiColombo/MMO spacecraft design. Adv. Space Res. **33**(12), 2133–2141 (2004)

Chapter 4
Verification and Validation of Autonomy Requirements

Abstract Verification of autonomy requirements needs to show a proof of compliance with the requirements the system can meet, i.e., each self-* objective is proven through performance of a test, analysis, inspection, or demonstration. Validation of autonomy requirements needs to demonstrate that the system pursuing a space mission accomplishes the intended self-* objectives in the intended environment (e.g., outer space or Mercury's orbit) and under specific constraints, i.e., the system's behavior meets the expectations defined by the autonomy requirements. However, due to their large state space, non-determinism, and the changing nature, traditional verification and validation of unmanned space systems is not adequate. This chapter reasons on the subject and presents a possible approach to verification and validation of autonomy requirements. The approach called AdaptiV uses the combination of stabilization science, HPC simulations, compositional verification, and traditional verification techniques where a self-adaptive system is linearized into stable and unstable (or adaptive) components verified separately first and then as a whole using compositional verification techniques.

4.1 Introduction

As discussed in Chap. 1, both *verification* and *validation* are similar in nature, but follow fundamentally different objectives. Verification of *autonomy requirements* needs to show a proof of compliance with the requirements the system can meet, i.e., each *self-* objective* is proven through performance of a test, analysis, inspection, or demonstration. Validation of autonomy requirements needs to demonstrate that the system pursuing a space mission accomplishes the intended self-* objectives in the intended environment (e.g., outer space or Mercury's orbit) and under specific constraints, i.e., the system's behavior meets the expectations defined by the autonomy requirements as shown through performance of a test, analysis, inspection, or demonstration. Note that *verification* relates back to the specified autonomy requirements and can be performed either on the requirements specification models or on the system's implementation. It is important to mention that ARE specification models establish an *autonomy behavior baseline*. This baseline acts as a global *autonomy*

© Springer International Publishing Switzerland 2014

E. Vassev and M. Hinchey, *Autonomy Requirements Engineering for Space Missions*,
NASA Monographs in Systems and Software Engineering,
DOI 10.1007/978-3-319-09816-6_4

verification/validation directive, which might be modified at a later time. Without this baseline and appropriate configuration controls, the verification and validation of autonomy requirements will not be possible.

In this chapter, we reason on the subject and present a possible approach to verification and validation of autonomy requirements.

4.2 Background

Usually, verification is done using scenario-based testing. In such testing, the software component to be verified is embedded into a test bed that connects to the inputs and outputs of that component, and drives it through a suite of test runs. Each test run is an alternate sequence of provided inputs and expected outputs, corresponding to one scenario of execution of the tested component. An error is signaled when the received output does not meet the expected one.

Even for simple systems, the design and maintenance of test suites is a difficult and expensive process. It requires a good understanding of the system to be tested, to ensure that a maximum number of different situations are covered using a minimum number of test cases. Running the tests is also a time-consuming task, because the whole model (or implementation) has to be executed and everything must be re-initialized before each test run. In the development of complex systems, it is quite common that testing the software actually takes more resources than developing it.

Complete testing of autonomous and self-adaptive systems will be nearly (if not completely) impossible since the situations triggering the self-* objectives can be difficult or impossible to forecast and because there are may be limited to no opportunities to effectively monitor and adjust such systems during operation (especially for deep space missions). Therefore, system and software verification will be critical to these systems' correct operation after deployment [5]. The problem is that verification of these systems using traditional verification techniques is not adequate. Due to the nature of these systems' need to adjust/adapt their behavior on the fly, the state space of the systems can be astronomical.

A practical example demonstrating the inefficiency of the traditional testing when applied to autonomous systems is the so-called Remote Agent Experiment (RAX), which indeed provided a striking example [8]. After a year of extensive testing, Remote Agent was put in control of NASA's Deep Space One mission on May 17, 1999. A few hours later, RAX had to be stopped after a deadlock had been detected. After analysis, it turns out that the deadlock was caused by a highly unlikely race condition between two concurrent threads inside Remote Agent's executive. The scheduling conditions that caused the problem to manifest never happened during testing but indeed showed up in flight. RAX was re-activated 2 days later and successfully completed all its objectives. Note that redundancy, which is the usual solution to increase reliability, is not appropriate for software. As opposed to hardware components, which fail statistically because of wear or external damage, programs fail almost exclusively due to latent design errors. Failure of an active system is thus

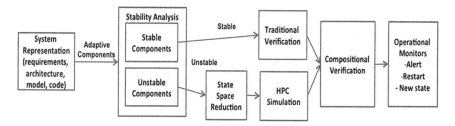

Fig. 4.1 Process for verification of adaptive systems [10]

highly correlated with failure of a duplicate back-up system (unless the systems use different software designs, as in the Shuttle's on-board computers).

Aggressive state space reduction is required for modern automated verification techniques to work. Unfortunately, this leads to the need to reduce the granularity of the system models (e.g., ARE models), which results in low-precision models that no longer adequately represent the original system. To address these and other verification issues for autonomous and self-adaptive systems, a special *Adaptive Verification* (AdpatiV) platform needs to be developed [10]. AdaptiV should provide a tool chain and methodology (Fig. 4.1) for verifying autonomous and self-adaptive systems that alleviates the above challenges. AdaptiV consists of the following parts:

(1) *a stability analysis capability* that identifies instabilities given a system model and partitions the system model into stable and unstable component models;
(2) *a state-space reduction capability* that prunes the state space of an unstable component model without loss of critical fidelity;
(3) *high performance computing (HPC) simulations* to explore component behavior over a wide range of an unstable component's reduced state space and produce a statistical verification for the component;
(4) *a compositional verification capability* that aggregates individual component verifications; and
(5) *operational monitors* to detect and take action to correct undesired unstable behavior of the system during operation.

4.3 AdaptiV

Systems like BepiColombo have massive state spaces. This is particularly true for the autonomous components (or modules) pursuing autonomy objectives. In such modules, often subsystems run concurrently, interact with each other and the environment, and react in response to changes in the environment. The huge state spaces are the result of the combinatorial explosion caused by non-deterministic interaction (interleaving) of component operations and the environment. Typical modern automated verification/validation techniques, such as *automated theorem proving* and *model checking*, do not scale to support such large state spaces. For these techniques to be effective, the state space of the targeted systems must be substantially reduced. State space reduction is achieved by aggregating state transitions into an *abstract* (coarser-grained) *finite state model* of the system. The technique effectively reduces the total number of states to be considered, but also reduces the fidelity of the system model. The key is that the abstract model must remain precise enough to adequately represent the original system in dimensions of interest. Thus, a tradeoff exists between the size and precision of the models. Today, only very abstract, low fidelity models can be automatically verified. What's needed for autonomous systems are techniques to support automated verification of a much larger state space.

Stabilization science has been used to verify the stability of a trained neural network, which is one form of an self-adaptive system [9, 11–14]. AdaptiV is building on this body of work to verify a broader range of autonomous and self-adaptive systems. It is using stability analysis to identify the unstable parts of an adaptive system. These parts will be further analyzed using HPC simulation over a large number of runs to compute a confidence level in their ability to converge around a stable operating point or region. While adaptive systems may be inherently unstable because of operational needs—e.g., the need to adapt in real time—this is not necessarily a reason for failing verification. An unstable system may still converge, even though complete verification may not be possible.

The above results will then be combined to yield a probabilistic measure of confidence in component behavior and provide state space convergence parameters that identify potential symptoms of unstable behavior. Where comprehensive verification is not possible, operational monitors can be deployed with the adaptive system. Monitors will be able to be automatically generated and deployed to detect non-convergence symptoms during operation and guide the adaptation towards stable behavior.

4.3.1 Model Checking

A promising, and lately popular, technique for software verification is model checking [1]. This approach advocates formal verification tools whereby software programs are automatically checked for specific design flaws by considering *correctness properties* expressed in a *temporal logic* (TL). A temporal logic augments propositional logic with modal and fix-point operators. In general, model checking provides an automated method for verifying finite state systems by relying on efficient graph-search algorithms. The latter help to determine whether or not system behavior described with temporal correctness properties holds for the system's state graph.

A general model-checking problem is: given a software system A and its formal specification a, determine in the system's state graph g whether or not the behavior of A, expressed with the correctness properties p, meets the specification a. Formally, this can be presented as a triple $(a; p; g)$. Note that g is the state graph constructed from the formal specification in a *labeled transition system* (LTS) [1] format. Formally, an

LTS can be presented as a Kripke Structure [1], which is a tuple $(S; S_0; Act; R; AP; L)$ where:

- S is the set of all possible system states;
- $S_0 \subseteq S$ is a set of initial states;
- Act is the set of actions;
- $R \subseteq S \times Act \times S$ are the possible state transitions;
- AP is a set of special atomic propositions;
- $L : S \rightarrow 2^{AP}$ is a labeling function relating a set $L(s) \in 2^{AP}$ of atomic propositions to any state s, i.e., a set of atomic propositions true in that state.

Note that in order to make an LTS appropriate for model checking, each state s must be associated with a set of atomic propositions AP true in that state. Therefore, if we turn a software system into a state machine, we can use temporal logics to express temporal correctness properties of the program. The most common such property is the *global invariant*, i.e., a property that holds in all reachable states of a state machine, or equivalently, always holds during the execution of a program.

The biggest issue model checking is facing today is the so-called *state explosion problem* [1]. In general, the size of a state graph is at least exponential in the number of tiers running as concurrent processes, because the state space of the entire system is built as the Cartesian product of the local state of the concurrent processes. To overcome this problem, modern model checking tools strive to reduce the state space of the targeted software systems.

Note that a straightforward model of a contemporary concurrent software system has a large and complicated state space and reduction is an important technique for reducing the size of that state space by aggregating state transitions into coarser-grained state transitions. State-space reduction is achieved by constructing an abstract (coarser-grained) finite state model of the system, which eventually is still powerful enough to verify properties of interest. The technique effectively reduces the total amount of states to be considered but is likely to reduce the granularity of the system to a point where it no longer adequately represents that system. The problem is that although the abstract model is relatively small it should also be precise to adequately represent the original system. The latter requirement tends to make the abstract models large, because the size of a transition system is exponential in the number of variables, concurrent components and communication channels. However, large models make automated verification extremely inefficient, thus introducing trade-offs between the size and precision of the models which considerably reduces their effectiveness.

Model checking is the most prominent automatic verification mechanism today. However it requires finite state models in order to perform automatic verification of all the possible execution paths of a system. However, adaptive systems (or individual adaptive components) are *intrinsically non-deterministic*, which means that they may have a huge state space. As a result, abstract models needed by model checking are difficult to set up and to use. Hence, validation by using model checking is possible neither for the whole system nor for the individual adaptive components. In such a

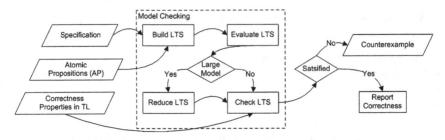

Fig. 4.2 The model-checking approach

case, to perform limited model checking on some of the components, we need to determine the non-adaptive and adaptive (unstable) parts of an adaptive system.

Figure 4.2 depicts a generic view of the model-checking verification method. Note that in the case that a correctness property is not satisfied, the method returns a *counterexample* [1]. The latter is an execution path of the LTS for which the desired correctness property is not true. If model checking has been performed on the entire LTS, then the property does not hold for the original system specification. Otherwise, in the case that a reduced LTS has been used (state-explosion techniques have been applied), the information provided by the counterexample is then used to refine the reduced model. Numerous formal tools allowing verification by model-checking have been developed, such as Spin, Emc, Tav, Mec, XTL, etc. Despite best efforts and the fact that model checking has proved to be a revolutionary advance in addressing the correctness of critical systems, software assurance for large and highly-complex software is still a tedious task. The reason is that high complexity is a source of software failures, and standard model checking approaches do not scale to handle large systems very well due to the state-explosion problem.

Model checking is the most prominent automatic verification mechanism today. However it requires finite state models in order to perform automatic verification of all the possible execution paths of a system. However, the adaptive systems (or individual adaptive components) are *intrinsically non-deterministic*, which means that they may have a huge state space. As a result, abstract models needed by model checking are difficult to set up and to use. Hence, validation by using model checking is possible neither for the whole system nor for the individual adaptive components. In such a case, to perform limited model checking on some of the components, we need to determine the non-adaptive and adaptive (unstable) parts of an adaptive system.

4.3.2 Stabilization Science

Stabilization science [3] provides a common approach to studying system stability, where a system is linearized around its operating point to determine a small-signal linearized model of that operating point. The stability of the system is then determined using linear system stability analysis methods such as: *Routh-Hurwitz, Root Locus, Bode Plot,* and *Nyquist Criterion.* AdaptiV will use stabilization science on a model of an self-adaptive system to partition it into a collection of *stable (deterministic)* and *unstable (non-deterministic)* components (usually such components follow self-* objectives), apply traditional techniques to verify the stable components, apply high performance computing simulation to explore the state space of unstable components, compute a verification confidence for each component, and use compositional verification techniques to produce an overall verification and verification confidence for the whole system.

Identifying the *unstable parts* of an adaptive system is a key to our verification approach. The unstable parts introduce *uncertainty* in system behavior where, in contrast, a stable system transits from one safe state to another *safe state.* ARE may help us deduct the unstable parts by analyzing the actors participating in the self-* objectives (Sect. 3.5.2).

Currently, there is no efficient way to determine the overall stability of a complex concurrent system, such as spacecraft. Due to the state-space explosion problem, a system-level stability check may suggest divergent behavior since over an infinite state space there may be an infinite sequence of successively weaker assertions, none of which is stable. To address this problem, we are using *stabilization science* to model an adaptive system and analyze it to identify and partition the model into a collection of *stable and unstable components.* We are using the results of the stability analysis to create *small-signal linearized models* for all the system components. We anticipate that the linearized models of system components will yield a relatively small state space, enabling their effective analysis. Automatic stability analysis of the components might be best performed via time domain simulation using small-signal models. It should be noted that the lack of unstable components does not automatically guarantee system stability and compositional verification will need to be performed to ensure the desired system behavior.

The main challenge in building *linearized models of concurrent systems,* such as spacecraft, is dealing with *interference,* i.e., the possibility that concurrent processes may concurrently make changes to shared resources, e.g., memory. A possible solution to the problem is defining a *synchronization scheme* to avoid interference. Most of such schemes rely on some form of access denial, such as locks. Though locks make it easy to reason about correctness, they may also cause loss of efficiency as processes wait to acquire access to needed resources. Therefore, a *locking scheme* may become increasingly fine-grained, attempting to deny access to the smallest possible size of resource, to minimize waiting and maximize concurrency. A linearized model must implicitly or explicitly take the actions of other processes into account. Broadly speaking, a linearized model of an operating point should encode the environment and the concurrent processes into the proof: all pre- and post-conditions must be shown to be unaffected (or stable) under the actions of the environment or the other concurrent processes. Once non-interference has been established, the proof can be carried forward exactly as for a *sequential program.* Note that automatically ensuring such non-interference can be problematic in many cases.

Partitioning the system into components, verifying each component, then using compositional techniques to provide an overall verification for the system is not new. What is unique is the *application of stabilization science to partition the system into stable and unstable components*. Stable components represent *deterministic* or *non-adaptive behavior*, and can be verified using traditional techniques. Unstable components-those providing *non-deterministic* or *adaptive behavior* (ARE actors participating in the *self-* objectives*)—require state space exploration beyond that which can be achieved using traditional techniques.

4.3.3 State Space Reduction

Stable components identified during the stability analysis represent deterministic or non-adaptive behavior. These components will be verified using traditional techniques. Unstable components may require state space exploration beyond that which can be achieved using traditional techniques. For these components, we are:

(1) Pruning the state space by identifying isomorphic elements in the state space.
(2) Examine patterns in the state space (using clustering, categorization, or other pattern identification approaches) to further reduce the state space.

As needed, we will examine other ways to reduce the state space in ways that provide sufficient confidence that model behavior appropriately represents actual system behavior.

4.3.4 High Performance Computing

Stability analysis methods perform exhaustive exploration of all possible behaviors. Partitioning the system into stable and unstable components will reduce the size of the state space requiring exploration and will help to speed up the exploration of the remaining state space. In spite of this, we anticipate that it will still be impossible to explore the entire state space of a large adaptive system with limited memory resources and limited time. To reduce memory, we will take a lightweight snapshot of an unstable component's state—consisting of a state's signature (a hash compaction of an actual state) and the trace (the sequence of return values from its path decision function). To restore the component's state, AdaptiV will replay the sequence of choices from the initial state. However, reconstructing states is a slow and CPU-intensive process, especially when traces are deeper.

To reduce runtime, we will use HPC to determine if and how the unstable components found during stability analysis will converge during adaptation. Parallelizing simulations will allow multiple state-space explorations to occur simultaneously. We plan to investigate the use of HPC to achieve exhaustive exploration on the unstable components. All *HPC nodes'* (or processing elements) will reconstruct and clone the states from their traces concurrently and explore them on different nodes. Checkpoints of actual component states on one node can be efficiently distributed to other nodes, through live operating system processes that use thin virtualization techniques. In addition, such techniques facilitate the use of distributed hash tables, treating the lightweight snapshot of the states as network objects to achieve fair load balancing and reduce the network communication for status exchange between the divided components.

As we indicated previously, even with the help of HPC, we do not anticipate that any computational model will ever be fully verified, given limited memory and time resources. To overcome this limitation, AdaptiV will provide a percentage of confidence level or confidence measure. The basic confidence measure will be calculated by following equation:

$$Cm = x * (2 * 0.5^y)$$

where Cm is the *confidence level measure*, x is the *total number of inputs*, and y is *number of optimal samples*. How to optimize the sample results to maximize coverage of the state space is an open research question that will be explored on this project. How to integrate the confidence measures of the unstable components for generating the whole complex system's confidence measure needs further stochastic research. Even so, AdaptiV can increase the statistical confidence level beyond that of traditional model checking tools.

4.3.5 Compositional Verification

Adaptation significantly complicates system design because adaptation of one component may affect the quality of its provided services, which may in turn cause adaptations in other components. The mutual interaction among system components affects overall system behavior. Hence, it is not sufficient to verify each component separately to ensure system correctness. What's needed is an ability to check the adaptation process as a whole. This is a complex and error-prone task. In our approach, we will apply *compositional verification* [2, 4] techniques to produce an overall system-wide verification. We will consider combinations that characterize important invariants, classified into: mission goal invariants, behavior invariants, interaction invariants and resource invariants. Here, behavior invariants are over-approximations of components' reachability of safe states, and interaction invariants are global constraints on the states of components involved in interactions. Selecting the most appropriate set of invariants and determining heuristics for computing invariants (e.g., interaction invariants) are major difficulties in designing a compositional verification technique for adaptive systems. We explore this selection process as part of the ongoing research.

A set of possible abstraction rules for generating the compositional model is provided in [6, 7]. These seven conflict-preserving abstraction rules will be analyzed for applicability to compositional verification for adaptive systems. Let α and ω be propositions as follows: α specifies a set of states from which terminal states are required to be reachable, and ω represents a set of terminal states. Initial abstraction rules to investigate involve [7]:

- Observation equivalence
- Removal of α-markings
- Removal of ω-markings
- Removal of non-coreachable states
- Determination of non-α states
- Removal of τ-transitions leading to non-α states
- Removal of τ-transitions originating from non-α states

While compositional verification alone cannot guarantee complete correctness of an adaptive system, it can prove such things as deadlock-freedom and overall mission-goal reachability.

4.3.6 Operational Monitors

Because an adaptive system cannot be completely verified, even with the above proposed approach, operational monitors should be deployed with the end system that monitor the adaptations. These monitors would be based on the results of the stability analysis and the HPC simulations. They would monitor either all or only those adaptive components that had trouble converging during the simulations. The monitors can provide alerts that the system is not converging during an adaptation within a given time, restart components of the system that are not converging, or force the system into a known state if any adaptations do not converge within a specified amount of time. Alerts could be adjusted by ground control based on the severity, known issues, etc. Software patches could be made during a mission based on convergence issues (which could be different from those found during simulations), reduce the amount of adaptation, or even increase the amount of adaptation if it is going well.

Instead of one large monitor, we anticipate that it will be more advantageous from a system efficiency standpoint to deploy multiple monitors with the end system-one or more for each adaptive component. To reduce overhead processing, the monitors would only have to operate when an adaptive component is executing; otherwise, they could remain dormant.

The monitors would be configured with information from the HPC simulations regarding convergence times for an adaptive component during adaptation. These times would provide bounds for how long an adaptive component may take to converge. When the convergence is outside these bounds, appropriate action, as noted above, could be taken. In addition, end states (variable values, etc.) that indicate that adaptation has completed would also be used by the monitors. When these end states are reached the monitor would know that the adaptation has converged successfully and that the monitor can do any necessary reporting and go back to sleep.

4.3.7 System Inputs

The inputs to the AdaptiV will consist of a model of the adaptive system. The model would be derived from either the system requirements or the system design. In the beginning we anticipate that this conversion will be a manual one, but there are tools that could be used as a starting point that could automatically produce the needed model. This could range from modified UML tools or other systems specification and verification tools. The type and structure of the model used for the stability analysis will depend on the type of stability analysis used (this is an area of research for the project). The parts of the adaptive system that are determined to be stable could be verified using the same techniques as the non-adaptive components of the system, which are more traditional techniques. We are currently concentrating on the unstable parts of the system so the verification of the components that are deemed stable are outside our current research thrust.

4.4 Summary

Due to their large state space, non-determinism, and their changing nature, traditional verification of autonomous and self-adaptive systems is not adequate. The combination of stabilization science, HPC simulations, compositional verification and traditional verification techniques, plus operational monitors, provides a complete approach to verification and deployment of adaptive systems that has not been used before. This chapter discussed the details of such a verification approach called AdaptiV. The stabilization science would check for unstable adaptive components of an *autonomous and self-adaptive system*. The stable components would be verified using traditional verification techniques. The unstable components would have their state space reduced and then simulated using high performance computing to determine whether they converge. Components that do not converge in a given time period would need to be redesigned. Unstable components that do converge would be deemed verified and then would be verified with the stable components using compositional verification techniques. Operational monitors would also be deployed with the system to monitor adaptations to make sure they converge. If they do not converge in a predetermined amount of time the monitors would stop the adaptation and put the system back into a known state. Note that under *"convergence"* we assume following an alternative path of execution provided by the *self-* objectives* determined with our ARE approach.

References

1. Baier, C., Katoen, J.P.: Principles of Model Checking. MIT Press, Cambridge (2008)
2. de Roever, W.P., de Boer, F., Hanneman, U., Hooman, J., Lakhnech, Y., Poel, M., Zwiers, J.: Concurrency Verification: Introduction to Compositional and Non-compositional Methods. Cambridge University Press, Cambridge (2001)
3. Emadi, A., Ehsani, M.: Aircraft power systems: technology, state of the art, and future trends. Aerosp. Electron. Syst. Mag. **15**(1), 28–32 (2000)
4. Francis, R.: An implementation of a compositional approach for verifying generalized nonblocking. The University of Waikato, Department of Computer Science, Hamilton, NZ, Technical report (2011)
5. Hinchey, M., Rash, J., Truszkowski, W., Rouff, C., Sterritt, R.: You can't get there from here! Problems and potential solutions in developing new classes of complex computer systems. In: Conquering Complexity. Springer, Heidelberg (2012)
6. Leduc, R., Malik, R.: A compositional approach for verifying generalized nonblocking. In: Proceedings of 7th International Conference on Control and Automation (ICCA '09), Christchurch, NZ, pp. 448–453 (2009)
7. Leduc, R., Malik, R.: Seven abstraction rules preserving generalized nonblocking. The University of Waikato, Department of Computer Science, Hamilton, NZ, Technical report (2009)
8. Nayak, P.P. et al.: Validating the DS1 remote agent experiment. In: Proceedings of the 5th International Symposium on Artificial Intelligence, Robotics and Automation in Space (iSAIRAS-99). ESTEC, Noordwijk (1999)
9. Phattanasri, P., Loparo, K., Soares, F. (eds.): Verification and Validation of Complex Adaptive Systems. EECS Department, Case Western Reserve University, Contek Research, Inc. (2005)
10. Pullum, L., Cui, X., Vassev, E., Hinchey, M., Rouff, C., Buskens, R.: Verification of adaptive systems. In: Proceedings of (Infotech@Aerospace) Conference 2012, Garden Grove, California, USA, pp. 2012–2478. AIAA, Reston (2012)
11. Pullum, L., Darrah, M., Taylor, B.: Independent verification and validation of neural networks—developing practitioner assistance. Software Tech News (2004)
12. Pullum, L., Taylor, B., Darrah, M.: Guidance for the Verification and Validation of Neural Networks. Wiley-IEEE Computer Society Press, chichester (2007)
13. Taylor, B. (ed.): Methods and Procedures for the Verification and Validation of Neural Networks. Springer, Heidelberg (2005)
14. Yerramalla, S., Fuller, E., Mladenovski, M., Cukic, B.: Lyapunov analysis of neural network stability in an adaptive flight control system. Self Stab. Syst. 77–91 (2003)

Chapter 5
Summary and Future Work

From the NASA roadmaps and Space Technology Grand Challenges, it is clear that the use of autonomous and self-adaptive systems will be important for future space systems and missions as well as other life critical systems. Contemporary software-intensive systems, such as modern spacecraft and unmanned exploration platforms (e.g., ExoMars) generally exhibit a number of autonomic features resulting in complex behavior and complex interactions with the operational environment, often leading to a need of self-adaptation. To properly develop such systems, it is very important to handle the autonomy requirements properly. However, the integration and promotion of autonomy in unmanned space missions is an extremely challenging task. Among the many challenges the engineers must overcome are those related to the elicitation and expression of autonomy requirements.

This book has presented a new approach to Autonomy Requirements Engineering (ARE). The approach has been presented in a step-wise manner.

As a necessary background, the book has presented first the state-of-the-art of software engineering for aerospace. Aerospace systems need to meet a variety of standards and also have high safety requirements, and therefore, the development of aerospace systems emphasizes verification, validation, certification, and testing. The book discussed the complexity of software development along with the software engineering process currently employed by leading aerospace organizations such as NASA, ESA, Boeing and Lockheed Martin. Their software development projects apply a spiral-based methodology where the emphasis is on verification. Methods, techniques, and architecture approaches for aerospace are also discussed. The same methodology is used for the development of autonomous aerospace systems (such as UAV and robotic space-exploration systems). Such systems incorporate features like integrated health management, self-monitoring and on-board decision making. However, the lack of proper, yet dedicated software engineering for autonomous aerospace systems is the reason for many inherent problems related to requirements, modeling and implementation. Requirements engineering for autonomous systems appears to be a wide open research area with only a limited number of approaches yet considered.

© Springer International Publishing Switzerland 2014
E. Vassev and M. Hinchey, *Autonomy Requirements Engineering for Space Missions*,
NASA Monographs in Systems and Software Engineering,
DOI 10.1007/978-3-319-09816-6_5

Further, the book has discussed the notion of autonomy in the context of ESA Missions, and outlined aspects of requirements engineering along with specification models and formal methods for aerospace. The discussion has gone in depth about special generic autonomy requirements for space missions along with controller architectures for robotic systems controlling such missions. A discussion about formal methods and approaches that cope with both generic autonomy requirements and controller architectures has been presented. Formal methods, like ASSL and KnowLang, have been analysed as methods that can lay the foundations of the new ARE approach dedicated to autonomic features of space missions.

Next, the book has drawn upon the discussion and results presented in the first two chapters to define and outline an Autonomy Requirements Engineering (ARE) method. ARE targets the integration and promotion of autonomy in unmanned space missions by providing a mechanism and methodology for elicitation and expression of autonomy requirements. ARE relies on goal-oriented requirements engineering to elicit and define the system goals, and uses the generic autonomy requirements model to derive and define assistive and eventually alternative objectives. The system may pursue these "self-* objectives" in the presence of factors threatening the achievement of the initial system goals. Once identified, the autonomy requirements are specified with the KnowLang language. A proof-of-concept case study demonstrating the ARE's ability to handle autonomy requirements has been presented and discussed in detail. The presented case study is a requirements engineering case study on the discovery and expression of autonomy requirements for ESA's BepiColombo Mission.

Finally, the book has discussed the verification and validation of autonomy requirements. Due to their large state space, non-determinism, and the changing nature, traditional verification and validation of unmanned space systems is not adequate. The book has reasoned on the problem and presented a new approach to verification and validation of autonomy requirements. The approach called AdaptiV uses the combination of stabilization science, HPC simulations, compositional verification, and traditional verification techniques where a self-adaptive system is linearized into stable and unstable (or adaptive) components verified separately first and then as a whole using compositional verification techniques.

Future work is mainly concerned with development of tools for our ARE model and AdaptiV approach. An efficient ARE Tool Suite incorporating the AdaptiV validation approach is the next logical step needed to complete the ARE Framework. Moreover, an efficient ARE Framework will adopt KnowLang as a formal notation and provide tools for specification and validation of autonomy requirements. The validation tools will adopt our AdaptiV approach. Runtime knowledge representation and reasoning shall be provided along with monitoring mechanisms to support the autonomy behavior of a system at runtime. We need to build an ARE Test Bed tool that will integrate the KnowLang Reasoner and will allow for validation of self-* objectives based on simulation and testing. This will help engineers validate self-* objectives by evaluating the system's ability to perceive the internal and external environment and react to changes. Therefore, with the ARE Test Bed tool, we shall be able to evaluate capabilities that might manifest system awareness about situations and conditions. Ideally, both the autonomy requirements model specified in the form of knowledge representation and the reasoner, can be further implemented in autonomous spacecraft as an engine responsible for the adaptive behavior. Eventually, a code generator will be able to generate stubs supporting the operations of the KnowLang Reasoner. These stubs can be further used as a basis for the real implementation of the mechanism controlling the autonomic behavior of the system.

In addition, an intelligent GAR (Generic Autonomy Requirements) framework will be integrated in the ARE framework to provide special GAR patterns assisting engineers in the development of autonomous systems. The integration of GORE (Goal-Oriented Requirements Engineering) in the ARE framework will go with tools for handling the SMA (Space Mission Analysis) activities along with capturing autonomy requirements stemming from SMA and self-* objectives derived from both constraints and safety requirements. Moreover, we need to develop ARE tools for handling variability points in the autonomy requirements along with qualitative and quantitative reasoning techniques for evaluating alternative scenarios introduced by variability points with respect to degrees of goal satisfaction.

All of this will make ARE not simply a framework for capturing autonomy requirements but a tool where a smooth transition from requirements to design to implementation of the autonomy features will be ensured.

Appendix A
Requirements for Cognitive Capabilities of UAS

Awareness Cognitive Capability

Functions

1. Identify threat level to platform.
2. Generate operational capabilities of platform such as endurance, load, etc.
3. Generate Information Exchange Requirements (IERs) for current ROEs (Rules of Engagement).
4. Monitor status of command chain and current authorized entities above and below this one.
5. Configuration control of information from external sources and data generated on the platform.
6. Generation of anticipated air or surface scenes using updated pre-mission data.
7. Generate actual scene in format for comparison with anticipated scene.
8. Detect differences between actual and anticipated scene.
9. Derive parameters and confidence levels for differences.

Inputs

1. Current ROE status.
2. Pre-mission data and updates in flight.
3. Current situation from sensors.
4. Network status.
5. Recognized air picture.
6. Recognized ground picture.
7. Current platform flight path and intent.
8. Current vehicle status.

Outputs to Understanding cognitive capability

1. Threat level to platform.
2. Location of friendly forces.
3. Location of hostile forces.
4. Location and flight paths of other platforms in area.
5. ROE status as IERs.

© Springer International Publishing Switzerland 2014

E. Vassev and M. Hinchey, *Autonomy Requirements Engineering for Space Missions*,
NASA Monographs in Systems and Software Engineering,
DOI 10.1007/978-3-319-09816-6

6. Differences between anticipated and actual scene.
7. Quantified parameters for differences between anticipated and actual scenes.
8. Current weapon status.

Understanding Cognitive Capability

Functions

1. Classification of scene differences into object types.
2. Identification of prohibited target areas.
3. Geolocate potential targets and probability of correct classification.
4. Geolocate non-targets.
5. Compare quantified scene-difference parameters and potential targets with ROE IERs.
6. Identify missing information, if any, between scene and ROE IERs.
7. Propose sources of missing information between scene and ROE IERs.
8. Contingency planning for changes to platform status or loss of command link.

Inputs

1. These will be the outputs from the Awareness capability.
2. Data from on-board data bases; e.g., on-board weapon range and blast damage area.
3. Network status.

Outputs to Deliberation Capability

1. Threat level.
2. Objects of military significance with:

   • Probability of correct classification;
   • Military significance;
   • Missing information to give higher probability of correct classification;
   • Proximity to friendly forces;
   • Prohibited target areas.

3. Civilian objects giving restrictions on attack plans.
4. Location of friendly forces.
5. Command chain status.

Deliberation Cognitive Capability

Functions

1. Generate self-preservation commands if threat level is high.
2. Predict effect of use of on-board weapons and capabilities.

3. Decide if ROE IERs are met and generate options available to platform.
4. Identify options that can be chosen autonomously.
5. Quantified method of ranking available options.
6. Decide if one or more options meet mission aims.
7. Decide on potential sources of missing ROE IERs, including tasking another asset.
8. Test that current command chain has given AUAS the authority to act.
9. Identify if decision must be referred to another authorized entity.
10. Generate list of reasons why a command decision cannot be made in AUAS.

Inputs

1. These will be the outputs from the Awareness capability.
2. Data from on-board data bases e.g. on-board weapon range and blast damage area.

Outputs

1. Commands to effectors if allowed.
2. Information for transfer of decision to other authorized entity.

Appendix B
ASSL Specification of Voyager Image-Processing Behavior

© Springer International Publishing Switzerland 2014   193
E. Vassev and M. Hinchey, *Autonomy Requirements Engineering for Space Missions*,
NASA Monographs in Systems and Software Engineering,
DOI 10.1007/978-3-319-09816-6

```
//============================== autonomic system VOYAGER MISSION ========================
//============================== IMAGE-PROCESSING self-management policy ==================
//
// This is the full specification of the Voyager2 mission.
// All the four antennas are operational.
//
// Note:
// - the voyager's cameras are set to apply three filters blue, red, and green;
// - the wide-angle camera takes pictures 100 x 50 pixels;
// - the narrow-angle camera takes pictures 50 x 50 pixels.
// - to trigger the self-management mechanism we specified a PERIOD ( 60 sec )
//   activation in the Voyager's timeToTakePicture event.
//
//================================================================================
AS VOYAGER_MISSION {

  TYPES { Pixel }
  VARS { integer numPixelsPerImage    } // determines the image size in pixels

  ASSELF_MANAGEMENT {
    OTHER_POLICIES {
      POLICY IMAGE_PROCESSING {
        FLUENT inProcessingImage_AntAustralia {
          INITIATED_BY { EVENTS.imageAntAustraliaReceived } TERMINATED_BY { EVENTS.imageAntAustraliaProcessed }
        }
        FLUENT inProcessingImage_AntJapan {
          INITIATED_BY { EVENTS.imageAntJapanReceived } TERMINATED_BY { EVENTS.imageAntJapanProcessed }
        }
        FLUENT inProcessingImage_AntCalifornia {
          INITIATED_BY { EVENTS.imageAntCaliforniaReceived } TERMINATED_BY { EVENTS.imageAntCaliforniaProcessed }
        }
        FLUENT inProcessingImage_AntSpain {
          INITIATED_BY { EVENTS.imageAntSpainReceived } TERMINATED_BY { EVENTS.imageAntSpainProcessed }
        }
        MAPPING {
          CONDITIONS { inProcessingImage_AntAustralia}
```

```
      DO_ACTIONS  { ACTIONS.processImage("Antenna_Australia") }
    }
    MAPPING {
      CONDITIONS  { inProcessingImage_AntJapan }
      DO_ACTIONS  { ACTIONS.processImage("Antenna_Japan") }
    }
    MAPPING {
      CONDITIONS  { inProcessingImage_AntCalifornia }
      DO_ACTIONS  { ACTIONS.processImage("Antenna_California") }
    }
    MAPPING {
      CONDITIONS  { inProcessingImage_AntSpain}
      DO_ACTIONS  { ACTIONS.processImage("Antenna_Spain") }
    }
  }
} // ASELF_MANAGEMENT

ASARCHITECTURE {
AELIST {AES.Voyager, AES.Antenna_Australia, AES.Antenna_Japan, AES.Antenna_California, AES.Antenna_Spain}
DIRECT_DEPENDENCIES {
DEPENDENCY AES.Antenna_Australia ( AES.Voyager )
DEPENDENCY AES.Antenna_Japan ( AES.Voyager )
DEPENDENCY AES.Antenna_California ( AES.Voyager )
DEPENDENCY AES.Antenna_Spain ( AES.Voyager )
}
GROUPS {
GROUP VoyagerGroup {
MEMBERS {AES.Voyager, AES.Antenna_Australia, AES.Antenna_Japan, AES.Antenna_California, AES.Antenna_Spain}
}
} // ASARCHITECTURE

ACTIONS {
ACTION IMPL processImage { // process an image sent by a specific antenna
PARAMETERS ( string antennaName )
```

```
GUARDS { ASSELF_MANAGEMENT.OTHER_POLICIES.IMAGE_PROCESSING.inProcessingImage_AntAustralia OR
         ASSELF_MANAGEMENT.OTHER_POLICIES.IMAGE_PROCESSING.inProcessingImage_AntJapan OR
         ASSELF_MANAGEMENT.OTHER_POLICIES.IMAGE_PROCESSING.inProcessingImage_AntCalifornia OR
         ASSELF_MANAGEMENT.OTHER_POLICIES.IMAGE_PROCESSING.inProcessingImage_AntSpain }

TRIGGERS {
    IF antennaName = "Antenna_Australia" THEN EVENTS.imageAntAustraliaProcessed      END
    ELSE
    IF antennaName = "Antenna_Japan" THEN EVENTS.imageAntJapanProcessed END
        ELSE
    IF antennaName = "Antenna_California" THEN EVENTS.imageAntCaliforniaProcessed END
        ELSE IF antennaName = "Antenna_Spain" THEN EVENTS.imageAntSpainProcessed END END
    END
    END
}
} // ACTIONS

EVENTS { // these events are used in the fluents specification
EVENT imageAntAustraliaReceived { ACTIVATION { RECEIVED { ASIP.MESSAGES.msgImageAntAustralia } } }
EVENT imageAntJapanReceived { ACTIVATION { RECEIVED { ASIP MESSAGES.msgImageAntJapan } } }
EVENT imageAntCaliforniaReceived { ACTIVATION { RECEIVED { ASIP.MESSAGES.msgImageAntCalifornia } } }
EVENT imageAntSpainReceived { ACTIVATION { RECEIVED { ASIP.MESSAGES.msgImageAntSpain } } }

EVENT imageAntAustraliaProcessed { }
EVENT imageAntJapanProcessed { }
EVENT imageAntCaliforniaProcessed { }
EVENT imageAntSpainProcessed { }
} // EVENTS

} // AS VOYAGER_MISSION

//================== AS interaction protocol ===========
ASIP {
MESSAGES {
    MESSAGE msgImageAntAustralia { SENDER (AES.Antenna_Australia) RECEIVER (ANY) PRIORITY (1) MSG_TYPE (BIN) }
    MESSAGE msgImageAntJapan { SENDER (AES.Antenna_Japan) RECEIVER (ANY) PRIORITY (1) MSG_TYPE (BIN) }
```

```
MESSAGE msgImageAntCalifornia { SENDER {AES.Antenna_California} RECEIVER {ANY} PRIORITY {1} MSG_TYPE {BIN} }
MESSAGE msgImageAntSpain { SENDER {AES.Antenna_Spain} RECEIVER {ANY} PRIORITY {1} MSG_TYPE {BIN} }
} // MESSAGES

CHANNELS {
CHANNEL IMG_Link {
ACCEPTS { ASIP.MESSAGES.msgImageAntAustralia, ASIP.MESSAGES.msgImageAntJapan,
          ASIP.MESSAGES.msgImageAntCalifornia, ASIP.MESSAGES.msgImageAntSpain }
ACCESS { SEQUENTIAL }
DIRECTION { INOUT } }
} // CHANNELS

FUNCTIONS {
FUNCTION sendImageMsg {
PARAMETERS { string antennaName }
DOES {
  IF antennaName = "Antenna_Australia" THEN ASIP.MESSAGES.msgImageAntAustralia >> ASIP.CHANNELS.IMG_Link END
  ELSE
  IF antennaName = "Antenna_Japan" THEN ASIP.MESSAGES.msgImageAntJapan >> ASIP.CHANNELS.IMG_Link END
  ELSE
  IF antennaName = "Antenna_California" THEN ASIP.MESSAGES.msgImageAntCalifornia >> ASIP.CHANNELS.IMG_Link END
  ELSE
  IF antennaName = "Antenna_Spain" THEN ASIP.MESSAGES.msgImageAntSpain >> ASIP.CHANNELS.IMG_Link END
  END
  END
  END
}
}

FUNCTION receiveImageMsg {
PARAMETERS { string antennaName }
DOES {
  IF antennaName = "Antenna_Australia" THEN ASIP.MESSAGES.msgImageAntAustralia << ASIP.CHANNELS.IMG_Link END
  ELSE
  IF antennaName = "Antenna_Japan" THEN ASIP.MESSAGES.msgImageAntJapan << ASIP.CHANNELS.IMG_Link END
  ELSE
  IF antennaName = "Antenna_California" THEN ASIP.MESSAGES.msgImageAntCalifornia << ASIP.CHANNELS.IMG_Link END
```

```
      ELSE
        IF antennaName = "Antenna_Spain" THEN ASIP.MESSAGES.msgImageAntSpain << ASIP.CHANNELS.IMG_Link END
      END
    END
  END
  }
  } // FUNCTIONS
}

//==================== autonomic elements ========================
AES {

//==================== AE Voyager ========================
AE Voyager {

  VARS { boolean isWideAngleImage } //determines the type of picture (wide-angle or narrow-angle)

  AESELF_MANAGEMENT {
    OTHER_POLICIES {
      POLICY IMAGE_PROCESSING {
        FLUENT inTakingPicture {
          INITIATED_BY { EVENTS.timeToTakePicture }
          TERMINATED_BY { EVENTS.pictureTaken }
        }
        FLUENT inProcessingPicturePixels {
          INITIATED_BY { EVENTS.pictureTaken }
          TERMINATED_BY { EVENTS.pictureProcessed }
        }
        MAPPING {
          CONDITIONS { inTakingPicture }
          DO_ACTIONS { ACTIONS.takePicture }
        }
        MAPPING {
          CONDITIONS { inProcessingPicturePixels }
          DO_ACTIONS { ACTIONS.processPicture }
```

```
        }
      }
    }
  } // AESELF_MANAGEMENT

  //====== AEs that can use the messages and channels specified by this AE ======
  FRIENDS {
    AELIST { AES.Antenna_Australia, AES.Antenna_Japan, AES.Antenna_California, AES.Antenna_Spain }
  }

  //==================== AE interaction protocol ====================
  AEIP {
    MESSAGES {
      MESSAGE msgImagePixel {
        SENDER { AES.Voyager }
        RECEIVER { AES.Antenna_Australia, AES.Antenna_Japan, AES.Antenna_California, AES.Antenna_Spain }
        MSG_TYPE { BIN }
      }

      // session messages to be received by Antenna_Australia
      MESSAGE msgBlueSessionBeginAus {
        SENDER { AES.Voyager }
        RECEIVER { AES.Antenna_Australia }
        MSG_TYPE { NEGOTIATION }
        BODY { BEGIN }
      }

      MESSAGE msgBlueSessionEndAus {
        SENDER { AES.Voyager }
        RECEIVER { AES.Antenna_Australia }
        MSG_TYPE { NEGOTIATION }
        BODY { END }
      }

      MESSAGE msgRedSessionBeginAus {
        SENDER { AES.Voyager }
        RECEIVER { AES.Antenna_Australia }
        MSG_TYPE { NEGOTIATION }
```

```
      BODY { BEGIN }
}

MESSAGE msgRedSessionEndAus {
   SENDER { AES.Voyager }
   RECEIVER { AES.Antenna_Australia }
   MSG_TYPE { NEGOTIATION }
   BODY { END }
}

MESSAGE msgGreenSessionBeginAus {
   SENDER { AES.Voyager }
   RECEIVER { AES.Antenna_Australia }
   MSG_TYPE { NEGOTIATION }
   BODY { BEGIN }
}

MESSAGE msgGreenSessionEndAus {
   SENDER { AES.Voyager }
   RECEIVER { AES.Antenna_Australia }
   MSG_TYPE { NEGOTIATION }
   BODY { END }
}

// session messages to be received by Antenna_Japan
MESSAGE msgBlueSessionBeginJpn {
   SENDER { AES.Voyager }
   RECEIVER { AES.Antenna_Japan }
   MSG_TYPE { NEGOTIATION }
   BODY { BEGIN }
}

MESSAGE msgBlueSessionEndJpn {
   SENDER { AES.Voyager }
   RECEIVER { AES.Antenna_Japan }
   MSG_TYPE { NEGOTIATION }
   BODY { END }
}

MESSAGE msgRedSessionBeginJpn {
   SENDER { AES.Voyager }
```

```
    RECEIVER { AES.Antenna_Japan }
    MSG_TYPE { NEGOTIATION }
    BODY { BEGIN }
}

MESSAGE msgRedSessionEndJpn {
    SENDER { AES.Voyager }
    RECEIVER { AES.Antenna_Japan }
    MSG_TYPE { NEGOTIATION }
    BODY { END }
}

MESSAGE msgGreenSessionBeginJpn {
    SENDER { AES.Voyager }
    RECEIVER { AES.Antenna_Japan }
    MSG_TYPE { NEGOTIATION }
    BODY { BEGIN }
}

MESSAGE msgGreenSessionEndJpn {
    SENDER { AES.Voyager }
    RECEIVER { AES.Antenna_Japan }
    MSG_TYPE { NEGOTIATION }
    BODY { END }
}

// session messages to be received by Antenna_California
MESSAGE msgBlueSessionBeginCfn {
    SENDER { AES.Voyager }
    RECEIVER { AES.Antenna_California }
    MSG_TYPE { NEGOTIATION }
    BODY { BEGIN }
}

MESSAGE msgBlueSessionEndCfn {
    SENDER { AES.Voyager }
    RECEIVER { AES.Antenna_California }
    MSG_TYPE { NEGOTIATION }
    BODY { END }
}
```

```
MESSAGE msgRedSessionBeginCfn {
  SENDER { AES.Voyager }
  RECEIVER { AES.Antenna_California }
  MSG_TYPE { NEGOTIATION }
  BODY { BEGIN }
}

MESSAGE msgRedSessionEndCfn {
  SENDER { AES.Voyager }
  RECEIVER { AES.Antenna_California }
  MSG_TYPE { NEGOTIATION }
  BODY { END }
}

MESSAGE msgGreenSessionBeginCfn {
  SENDER { AES.Voyager }
  RECEIVER { AES.Antenna_California }
  MSG_TYPE { NEGOTIATION }
  BODY { BEGIN }
}

MESSAGE msgGreenSessionEndCfn {
  SENDER { AES.Voyager }
  RECEIVER { AES.Antenna_California }
  MSG_TYPE { NEGOTIATION }
  BODY { END }
}

// session messages to be received by Antenna_Spain
MESSAGE msgBlueSessionBeginSpn {
  SENDER { AES.Voyager }
  RECEIVER { AES.Antenna_Spain }
  MSG_TYPE { NEGOTIATION }
  BODY { BEGIN }
}

MESSAGE msgBlueSessionEndSpn {
  SENDER { AES.Voyager }
  RECEIVER { AES.Antenna_Spain }
  MSG_TYPE { NEGOTIATION }
```

```
    BODY { END }
  }

  MESSAGE msgRedSessionBeginSpn {
    SENDER { AES.Voyager }
    RECEIVER { AES.Antenna_Spain }
    MSG_TYPE { NEGOTIATION }
    BODY { BEGIN }
  }

  MESSAGE msgRedSessionEndSpn {
    SENDER { AES.Voyager }
    RECEIVER { AES.Antenna_Spain }
    MSG_TYPE { NEGOTIATION }
    BODY { END }
  }

  MESSAGE msgGreenSessionBeginSpn {
    SENDER { AES.Voyager }
    RECEIVER { AES.Antenna_Spain }
    MSG_TYPE { NEGOTIATION }
    BODY { BEGIN }
  }

  MESSAGE msgGreenSessionEndSpn {
    SENDER { AES.Voyager }
    RECEIVER { AES.Antenna_Spain }
    MSG_TYPE { NEGOTIATION }
    BODY { END }
  }
} // MESSAGES

CHANNELS {
  CHANNEL VOYAGER_Link {
    ACCEPTS { AEIP.MESSAGES.msgImagePixel,
              AEIP.MESSAGES.msgBlueSessionBeginAus, AEIP.MESSAGES.msgBlueSessionEndAus,
              AEIP.MESSAGES.msgRedSessionBeginAus, AEIP.MESSAGES.msgRedSessionEndAus,
              AEIP.MESSAGES.msgGreenSessionBeginAus, AEIP.MESSAGES.msgGreenSessionEndAus,
              AEIP.MESSAGES.msgBlueSessionBeginJpn, AEIP.MESSAGES.msgBlueSessionEndJpn,
```

```
      AEIP.MESSAGES.msgRedSessionBeginJpn, AEIP.MESSAGES.msgRedSessionEndJpn,
      AEIP.MESSAGES.msgGreenSessionBeginJpn, AEIP.MESSAGES.msgGreenSessionEndJpn,

      AEIP.MESSAGES.msgBlueSessionBeginCfn, AEIP.MESSAGES.msgBlueSessionEndCfn,
      AEIP.MESSAGES.msgRedSessionBeginCfn, AEIP.MESSAGES.msgRedSessionEndCfn,
      AEIP.MESSAGES.msgGreenSessionBeginCfn, AEIP.MESSAGES.msgGreenSessionEndCfn,

      AEIP.MESSAGES.msgBlueSessionBeginSpn, AEIP.MESSAGES.msgBlueSessionEndSpn,
      AEIP.MESSAGES.msgRedSessionBeginSpn, AEIP.MESSAGES.msgRedSessionEndSpn,
      AEIP.MESSAGES.msgGreenSessionBeginSpn, AEIP.MESSAGES.msgGreenSessionEndSpn
   }
   ACCESS { DIRECT }
   DIRECTION { INOUT }
 }
}

FUNCTIONS {
  FUNCTION sendImagePixelMsg {
    DOES { AEIP.MESSAGES.msgImagePixel >> AEIP.CHANNELS.VOYAGER_Link }
  }
  FUNCTION sendBeginSessionMsgs {
    PARAMETERS { string filterName }
    DOES {
      IF filterName = "blue" THEN
        AEIP.MESSAGES.msgBlueSessionBeginAus >> AEIP.CHANNELS.VOYAGER_Link;
        AEIP.MESSAGES.msgBlueSessionBeginJpn >> AEIP.CHANNELS.VOYAGER_Link;
        AEIP.MESSAGES.msgBlueSessionBeginCfn >> AEIP.CHANNELS.VOYAGER_Link;
        AEIP.MESSAGES.msgBlueSessionBeginSpn >> AEIP.CHANNELS.VOYAGER_Link
      END
      ELSE
      IF filterName = "red" THEN
        AEIP.MESSAGES.msgRedSessionBeginAus >> AEIP.CHANNELS.VOYAGER_Link;
        AEIP.MESSAGES.msgRedSessionBeginJpn >> AEIP.CHANNELS.VOYAGER_Link;
        AEIP.MESSAGES.msgRedSessionBeginCfn >> AEIP.CHANNELS.VOYAGER_Link;
        AEIP.MESSAGES.msgRedSessionBeginSpn >> AEIP.CHANNELS.VOYAGER_Link
      END
```

```
    ELSE
      IF filterName = "green" THEN
        AEIP.MESSAGES.msgGreenSessionBeginAus >> AEIP.CHANNELS.VOYAGER_Link;
        AEIP.MESSAGES.msgGreenSessionBeginJpn >> AEIP.CHANNELS.VOYAGER_Link;
        AEIP.MESSAGES.msgGreenSessionBeginCfn >> AEIP.CHANNELS.VOYAGER_Link;
        AEIP.MESSAGES.msgGreenSessionBeginSpn >> AEIP.CHANNELS.VOYAGER_Link
      END
    END
  END
}

FUNCTION sendEndSessionMsgs {
  PARAMETERS { string filterName }
  DOES {
    IF filterName = "blue" THEN
      AEIP.MESSAGES.msgBlueSessionEndAus >> AEIP.CHANNELS.VOYAGER_Link;
      AEIP.MESSAGES.msgBlueSessionEndJpn >> AEIP.CHANNELS.VOYAGER_Link;
      AEIP.MESSAGES.msgBlueSessionEndCfn >> AEIP.CHANNELS.VOYAGER_Link;
      AEIP.MESSAGES.msgBlueSessionEndSpn >> AEIP.CHANNELS.VOYAGER_Link
    END
    ELSE
      IF filterName = "red" THEN
        AEIP.MESSAGES.msgRedSessionEndAus >> AEIP.CHANNELS.VOYAGER_Link;
        AEIP.MESSAGES.msgRedSessionEndJpn >> AEIP.CHANNELS.VOYAGER_Link;
        AEIP.MESSAGES.msgRedSessionEndCfn >> AEIP.CHANNELS.VOYAGER_Link;
        AEIP.MESSAGES.msgRedSessionEndSpn >> AEIP.CHANNELS.VOYAGER_Link
      END
      ELSE
        IF filterName = "green" THEN
          AEIP.MESSAGES.msgGreenSessionEndAus >> AEIP.CHANNELS.VOYAGER_Link;
          AEIP.MESSAGES.msgGreenSessionEndJpn >> AEIP.CHANNELS.VOYAGER_Link;
          AEIP.MESSAGES.msgGreenSessionEndCfn >> AEIP.CHANNELS.VOYAGER_Link;
          AEIP.MESSAGES.msgGreenSessionEndSpn >> AEIP.CHANNELS.VOYAGER_Link
        END
      END
    END
```

```
     }
   }
} // FUNCTIONS

MANAGED_ELEMENTS {
  MANAGED_ELEMENT wideAngleCamera {
    INTERFACE_FUNCTION takePicture { }
    INTERFACE_FUNCTION applyFilterBlue { }
    INTERFACE_FUNCTION applyFilterRed { }
    INTERFACE_FUNCTION applyFilterGreen { }
    INTERFACE_FUNCTION getPixel { }
    INTERFACE_FUNCTION countInterestingObjects { RETURNS { integer } }
  }

  MANAGED_ELEMENT narrowAngleCamera {
    INTERFACE_FUNCTION takePicture { }
    INTERFACE_FUNCTION applyFilterBlue { }
    INTERFACE_FUNCTION applyFilterRed { }
    INTERFACE_FUNCTION applyFilterGreen { }
    INTERFACE_FUNCTION getPixel { }
  }
} // AEIP

ACTIONS {
  ACTION takePicture { // take a picture of an interesting spot/object
    GUARDS { AESELF_MANAGEMENT.OTHER_POLICIES.IMAGE_PROCESSING.inTakingPicture }
    DOES {
      IF AES.Voyager.isWideAngleImage THEN
        call AEIP.MANAGED_ELEMENTS.wideAngleCamera.takePicture;
        AES.Voyager.isWideAngleImage = false;
        AS.numPixelsPerImage = 100*50  // an image has 100 x 50 pixels
      END
      ELSE
        call AEIP.MANAGED_ELEMENTS.narrowAngleCamera.takePicture;
        AES.Voyager.isWideAngleImage = true;
        AS.numPixelsPerImage = 50*50  // an image has 50 x 50 pixels
```

```
END
}
TRIGGERS { EVENTS.pictureTaken }
}

ACTION processFilteredPicture {
PARAMETERS { string filterName }
VARS { integer numPixels }
DOES {
IF AES.Voyager.isWideAngleImage THEN
  IF filterName = "blue" THEN
    call AEIP.MANAGED_ELEMENTS.wideAngleCamera.applyFilterBlue
  END;
  IF filterName = "red" THEN
    call AEIP.MANAGED_ELEMENTS.wideAngleCamera.applyFilterRed
  END;
  IF filterName = "green" THEN
    call AEIP.MANAGED_ELEMENTS.wideAngleCamera.applyFilterGreen
  END
ELSE
  IF filterName = "blue" THEN
    call AEIP.MANAGED_ELEMENTS.narrowAngleCamera.applyFilterBlue
  END;
  IF filterName = "red" THEN
    call AEIP.MANAGED_ELEMENTS.narrowAngleCamera.applyFilterRed
  END;
  IF filterName = "green" THEN
    call AEIP.MANAGED_ELEMENTS.narrowAngleCamera.applyFilterGreen
  END
END;

call AEIP.FUNCTIONS.sendBeginSessionMsgs (filterName);

numPixels = 0;
DO {
```

```
//call ACTIONS.prepareImagePixelMsg;
call AEIP.MANAGED_ELEMENTS.narrowAngleCamera.getPixel;
call AEIP.FUNCTIONS.sendImagePixelMsg;
numPixels = numPixels + 1
} WHILE numPixels < AS.numPixelsPerImage;

call AEIP.FUNCTIONS.sendEndSessionMsgs (filterName)
}
}

ACTION processPicture { // process all picture pixels - apply filters and send pixels to Earth
GUARDS { AESELF_MANAGEMENT.OTHER_POLICIES.IMAGE_PROCESSING.inProcessingPicturePixels }
DOES {
    call ACTIONS.processFilteredPicture("blue");
    call ACTIONS.processFilteredPicture("red");
    call ACTIONS.processFilteredPicture("green")
}
TRIGGERS { EVENTS.pictureProcessed }
}
} // ACTIONS

EVENTS {
EVENT timeToTakePicture {
    ACTIVATION { CHANGED { METRICS.interestingObjects} OR PERIOD { 60 SEC } }
}
EVENT pictureTaken { }
EVENT pictureProcessed { }
} // EVENTS

METRICS {
METRIC interestingObjects { // increments when a new interesting spot or object has been found
METRIC_TYPE { RESOURCE }
METRIC_SOURCE { AEIP.MANAGED_ELEMENTS.wideAngleCamera.countInterestingObjects }
DESCRIPTION {"counts the interesting spots and objects to be taken pictures of"}
VALUE { 0 }
THRESHOLD_CLASS { integer [0"] }
```

```
}
}
} // AE Voyager

//================== AE Antenna_Australia ==================
AE Antenna_Australia {

  AESELF_MANAGEMENT {
  OTHER_POLICIES {
  POLICY IMAGE_PROCESSING {
    FLUENT inStartingBlueImageSession {
      INITIATED_BY { EVENTS.blueImageSessionIsAboutToStart }
      TERMINATED_BY { EVENTS.imageSessionStartedBlue }
    }

    FLUENT inStartingRedImageSession {
      INITIATED_BY { EVENTS.redImageSessionIsAboutToStart }
      TERMINATED_BY { EVENTS.imageSessionStartedRed }
    }

    FLUENT inStartingGreenImageSession {
      INITIATED_BY { EVENTS.greenImageSessionIsAboutToStart }
      TERMINATED_BY { EVENTS.imageSessionStartedGreen }
    }

    FLUENT inCollectingImagePixelsBlue {
      INITIATED_BY { EVENTS.imageSessionStartedBlue }
      TERMINATED_BY { EVENTS.imageSessionEndedBlue }
    }

    FLUENT inCollectingImagePixelsRed {
      INITIATED_BY { EVENTS.imageSessionStartedRed }
      TERMINATED_BY { EVENTS.imageSessionEndedRed }
    }

    FLUENT inCollectingImagePixelsGreen {
      INITIATED_BY { EVENTS.imageSessionStartedGreen }
      TERMINATED_BY { EVENTS.imageSessionEndedGreen }
    }

    FLUENT inSendingImage {
```

```
INITIATED_BY { EVENTS.imageSessionEndedGreen }
TERMINATED_BY { EVENTS.imageAntAustraliaSent }

}
MAPPING {
   CONDITIONS { inStartingBlueImageSession }
   DO_ACTIONS { ACTIONS.startImageCollectSession ("blue") }
}
MAPPING {
   CONDITIONS { inStartingRedImageSession }
   DO_ACTIONS { ACTIONS.startImageCollectSession ("red") }
}
MAPPING {
   CONDITIONS { inStartingGreenImageSession }
   DO_ACTIONS { ACTIONS.startImageCollectSession ("green") }
}
MAPPING {
   CONDITIONS { inCollectingImagePixelsBlue }
   DO_ACTIONS { ACTIONS.collectImagePixels ("blue") }
}
MAPPING {
   CONDITIONS { inCollectingImagePixelsRed }
   DO_ACTIONS { ACTIONS.collectImagePixels ("red") }
}
MAPPING {
   CONDITIONS { inCollectingImagePixelsGreen }
   DO_ACTIONS { ACTIONS.collectImagePixels ("green") }
}
MAPPING {
   CONDITIONS { inSendingImage }
   DO_ACTIONS { ACTIONS.sendImage }
}

} // AESELF_MANAGEMENT

//====== AEIP for this AE ======
```

```
AEIP {
  FUNCTIONS {
    FUNCTION receiveImagePixelMsg {
      DOES { AES.Voyager.AEIP.MESSAGES.msgImagePixel << AES.Voyager.AEIP.CHANNELS.VOYAGER_Link }
    }
    FUNCTION receiveSessionBeginMsg {
      PARAMETERS { string filterName }
      DOES {
        IF filterName = "blue" THEN
          AES.Voyager.AEIP.MESSAGES.msgBlueSessionBeginAus << AES.Voyager.AEIP.CHANNELS.VOYAGER_Link
        END
        ELSE
          IF filterName = "red" THEN
            AES.Voyager.AEIP.MESSAGES.msgRedSessionBeginAus << AES.Voyager.AEIP.CHANNELS.VOYAGER_Link
          END
          ELSE
            IF filterName = "green" THEN
              AES.Voyager.AEIP.MESSAGES.msgGreenSessionBeginAus << AES.Voyager.AEIP.CHANNELS.VOYAGER_Link
            END
          END
        END
    }
    FUNCTION receiveSessionEndMsg {
      PARAMETERS {  string filterName }
      DOES {
        IF filterName = "blue" THEN
          AES.Voyager.AEIP.MESSAGES.msgBlueSessionEndAus << AES.Voyager.AEIP.CHANNELS.VOYAGER_Link
        END
        ELSE
          IF filterName = "red" THEN
            AES.Voyager.AEIP.MESSAGES.msgRedSessionEndAus << AES.Voyager.AEIP.CHANNELS.VOYAGER_Link
          END
          ELSE
            IF filterName = "green" THEN
              AES.Voyager.AEIP.MESSAGES.msgGreenSessionEndAus << AES.Voyager.AEIP.CHANNELS.VOYAGER_Link
```

```
          END
        END
      END
    }
  }
}

MANAGED_ELEMENTS { }
}

ACTIONS {
ACTION startImageCollectSession {
  PARAMETERS { string filterName }
  GUARDS { AESELF_MANAGEMENT.OTHER_POLICIES.IMAGE_PROCESSING.inStartingBlueImageSession OR
           AESELF_MANAGEMENT.OTHER_POLICIES.IMAGE_PROCESSING.inStartingRedImageSession OR
           AESELF_MANAGEMENT.OTHER_POLICIES.IMAGE_PROCESSING.inStartingGreenImageSession }
  DOES {
    CALL AEIP.FUNCTIONS.receiveSessionBeginMsg (filterName)
  }
}

ACTION collectImagePixels {
  PARAMETERS { string filterName }
  GUARDS { AESELF_MANAGEMENT.OTHER_POLICIES.IMAGE_PROCESSING.inCollectingImagePixelsBlue OR
           AESELF_MANAGEMENT.OTHER_POLICIES.IMAGE_PROCESSING.inCollectingImagePixelsRed OR
           AESELF_MANAGEMENT.OTHER_POLICIES.IMAGE_PROCESSING.inCollectingImagePixelsGreen }
  VARS { integer numPixels }
  DOES {
    numPixels = 0;
    DO {
      CALL AEIP.FUNCTIONS.receiveImagePixelMsg;
      numPixels = numPixels + 1
    } WHILE numPixels < AS.numPixelsPerImage ;

    CALL AEIP.FUNCTIONS.receiveSessionEndMsg (filterName)
  }
}
```

```
ACTION IMPL prepareImage { }
ACTION sendImage {
  GUARDS { AESELF_MANAGEMENT.OTHER_POLICIES.IMAGE_PROCESSING.inSendingImage }
  DOES {
    CALL IMPL ACTIONS.prepareImage;
    CALL ASIP.FUNCTIONS.sendImageMsg("Antenna_Australia");
    CALL ASIP.FUNCTIONS.receiveImageMsg("Antenna_Australia")
  }
}
} // ACTIONS

EVENTS {
  EVENT blueImageSessionIsAboutToStart { ACTIVATION { SENT { AES.Voyager.AEIP.MESSAGES.msgBlueSessionBeginAus } } }
  EVENT redImageSessionIsAboutToStart { ACTIVATION { SENT { AES.Voyager.AEIP.MESSAGES.msgRedSessionBeginAus } } }
  EVENT greenImageSessionIsAboutToStart { ACTIVATION { SENT { AES.Voyager.AEIP.MESSAGES.msgGreenSessionBeginAus } } }
  EVENT imageSessionStartedBlue { ACTIVATION { RECEIVED { AES.Voyager.AEIP.MESSAGES.msgBlueSessionBeginAus } } }
  EVENT imageSessionEndedBlue { ACTIVATION { RECEIVED { AES.Voyager.AEIP.MESSAGES.msgBlueSessionEndAus } } }
  EVENT imageSessionStartedRed { ACTIVATION { RECEIVED { AES.Voyager.AEIP.MESSAGES.msgRedSessionBeginAus } } }
  EVENT imageSessionEndedRed { ACTIVATION { RECEIVED { AES.Voyager.AEIP.MESSAGES.msgRedSessionEndAus } } }
  EVENT imageSessionStartedGreen { ACTIVATION { RECEIVED { AES.Voyager.AEIP.MESSAGES.msgGreenSessionBeginAus } } }
  EVENT imageSessionEndedGreen { ACTIVATION { RECEIVED { AES.Voyager.AEIP.MESSAGES.msgGreenSessionEndAus } } }
  EVENT imageAntAustraliaSent { ACTIVATION { SENT { ASIP.MESSAGES.msgImageAntAustralia } } }
} // EVENTS

}

//======================== AE Antenna_Japan ========================
AE Antenna_Japan {

  AESELF_MANAGEMENT {
    OTHER_POLICIES {
      POLICY IMAGE_PROCESSING {
        FLUENT inStartingBlueImageSession {
          INITIATED_BY { EVENTS.blueImageSessionIsAboutToStart }
          TERMINATED_BY { EVENTS.imageSessionStartedBlue }
        }
```

```
FLUENT inStartingRedImageSession {
    INITIATED_BY { EVENTS.redImageSessionIsAboutToStart }
    TERMINATED_BY { EVENTS.imageSessionStartedRed }
}
FLUENT inStartingGreenImageSession {
    INITIATED_BY { EVENTS.greenImageSessionisAboutToStart }
    TERMINATED_BY { EVENTS.imageSessionStartedGreen }
}
FLUENT inCollectingImagePixelsBlue {
    INITIATED_BY { EVENTS.imageSessionStartedBlue }
    TERMINATED_BY { EVENTS.imageSessionEndedBlue }
}
FLUENT inCollectingImagePixelsRed {
    INITIATED_BY { EVENTS.imageSessionStartedRed }
    TERMINATED_BY { EVENTS.imageSessionEndedRed }
}
FLUENT inCollectingImagePixelsGreen {
    INITIATED_BY { EVENTS.imageSessionStartedGreen }
    TERMINATED_BY { EVENTS.imageSessionEndedGreen }
}
FLUENT inSendingImage {
    INITIATED_BY { EVENTS.imageSessionEndedGreen }
    TERMINATED_BY { EVENTS.imageAntJapanSent }
}
MAPPING {
    CONDITIONS { inStartingBlueImageSession }
    DO_ACTIONS { ACTIONS.startImageCollectSession ("blue") }
}
MAPPING {
    CONDITIONS { inStartingRedImageSession }
    DO_ACTIONS { ACTIONS.startImageCollectSession ("red") }
}
MAPPING {
    CONDITIONS { inStartingGreenImageSession }
    DO_ACTIONS { ACTIONS.startImageCollectSession ("green") }
}
```

```
MAPPING {
    CONDITIONS { inCollectingImagePixelsBlue }
    DO_ACTIONS { ACTIONS.collectImagePixels ("blue") }
}

MAPPING {
    CONDITIONS { inCollectingImagePixelsRed }
    DO_ACTIONS { ACTIONS.collectImagePixels ("red") }
}

MAPPING {
    CONDITIONS { inCollectingImagePixelsGreen }
    DO_ACTIONS { ACTIONS.collectImagePixels ("green") }
}

MAPPING {
    CONDITIONS { inSendingImage }
    DO_ACTIONS { ACTIONS.sendImage }
}
}
} // AESELF_MANAGEMENT

//======= AEIP for this AE ======
AEIP {
    FUNCTIONS {
        FUNCTION receiveImagePixelMsg {
            DOES { AES.Voyager.AEIP.MESSAGES.msgImagePixel << AES.Voyager.AEIP.CHANNELS.VOYAGER_Link }
        }
        FUNCTION receiveSessionBeginMsg {
            PARAMETERS { string filterName }
            DOES {
                IF filterName = "blue" THEN
                    AES.Voyager.AEIP.MESSAGES.msgBlueSessionBeginJpn << AES.Voyager.AEIP.CHANNELS.VOYAGER_Link
                END
                ELSE
                    IF filterName = "red" THEN
                        AES.Voyager.AEIP.MESSAGES.msgRedSessionBeginJpn << AES.Voyager.AEIP.CHANNELS.VOYAGER_Link
                    END
```

```
          ELSE
            IF filterName = "green" THEN
              AES.Voyager.AEIP.MESSAGES.msgGreenSessionBeginJpn << AES.Voyager.AEIP.CHANNELS.VOYAGER_Link
            END
          END
        END
      }

      FUNCTION receiveSessionEndMsg {
        PARAMETERS { string filterName }
        DOES {
          IF filterName = "blue" THEN
            AES.Voyager.AEIP.MESSAGES.msgBlueSessionEndJpn << AES.Voyager.AEIP.CHANNELS.VOYAGER_Link
          END
          ELSE
            IF filterName = "red" THEN
              AES.Voyager.AEIP.MESSAGES.msgRedSessionEndJpn << AES.Voyager.AEIP.CHANNELS.VOYAGER_Link
            END
            ELSE
              IF filterName = "green" THEN
                AES.Voyager.AEIP.MESSAGES.msgGreenSessionEndJpn << AES.Voyager.AEIP.CHANNELS.VOYAGER_Link
              END
            END
          END
        }
      }

      MANAGED_ELEMENTS { }
    }

    ACTIONS {
      ACTION startImageCollectSession {
        PARAMETERS { string filterName }
        GUARDS { AESELF_MANAGEMENT.OTHER_POLICIES.IMAGE_PROCESSING.inStartingBlueImageSession OR
                 AESELF_MANAGEMENT.OTHER_POLICIES.IMAGE_PROCESSING.inStartingRedImageSession OR
                 AESELF_MANAGEMENT.OTHER_POLICIES.IMAGE_PROCESSING.inStartingGreenImageSession }
```

```
    DOES {
        CALL AEIP.FUNCTIONS.receiveSessionBeginMsg (filterName)
    }

    ACTION collectImagePixels {
        PARAMETERS { string filterName }
        GUARDS { AESELF_MANAGEMENT.OTHER_POLICIES.IMAGE_PROCESSING.inCollectingImagePixelsBlue OR
                 AESELF_MANAGEMENT.OTHER_POLICIES.IMAGE_PROCESSING.inCollectingImagePixelsRed OR
                 AESELF_MANAGEMENT.OTHER_POLICIES.IMAGE_PROCESSING.inCollectingImagePixelsGreen }
        VARS { integer numPixels }
        DOES {
            numPixels = 0;
            DO {
                CALL AEIP.FUNCTIONS.receiveImagePixelMsg;
                numPixels = numPixels + 1
            } WHILE numPixels < AS.numPixelsPerImage ;

            CALL AEIP.FUNCTIONS.receiveSessionEndMsg (filterName)
        }
    }

    ACTION IMPL prepareImage { }
    ACTION sendImage {
        GUARDS { AESELF_MANAGEMENT.OTHER_POLICIES.IMAGE_PROCESSING.inSendingImage }
        DOES {
            CALL IMPL ACTIONS.prepareImage;
            CALL ASIP.FUNCTIONS.sendImageMsg("Antenna_Japan");
            CALL ASIP.FUNCTIONS.receiveImageMsg("Antenna_Japan")
        }
    }
} // ACTIONS

EVENTS {
    EVENT blueImageSessionIsAboutToStart { ACTIVATION { SENT { AES.Voyager.AEIP.MESSAGES.msgBlueSessionBeginJpn } } }
    EVENT redImageSessionIsAboutToStart { ACTIVATION { SENT { AES.Voyager.AEIP.MESSAGES.msgRedSessionBeginJpn } } }
    EVENT greenImageSessionIsAboutToStart { ACTIVATION { SENT { AES.Voyager.AEIP.MESSAGES.msgGreenSessionBeginJpn } } }
    EVENT imageSessionStartedBlue { ACTIVATION { RECEIVED { AES.Voyager.AEIP.MESSAGES.msgBlueSessionBeginJpn } } }
```

```
     EVENT imageSessionEndedBlue { ACTIVATION { RECEIVED { AES.Voyager.AEIP.MESSAGES.msgBlueSessionEndJpn } } }
     EVENT imageSessionStartedRed { ACTIVATION { RECEIVED { AES.Voyager.AEIP.MESSAGES.msgRedSessionBeginJpn } } }
     EVENT imageSessionEndedRed { ACTIVATION { RECEIVED { AES.Voyager.AEIP.MESSAGES.msgRedSessionEndJpn } } }
     EVENT imageSessionStartedGreen { ACTIVATION { RECEIVED { AES.Voyager.AEIP.MESSAGES.msgGreenSessionBeginJpn } } }
     EVENT imageSessionEndedGreen { ACTIVATION { RECEIVED { AES.Voyager.AEIP.MESSAGES.msgGreenSessionEndJpn } } }
     EVENT imageAntJapanSent { ACTIVATION { SENT { ASIP.MESSAGES.msgImageAntJapan } } }
  } // EVENTS
}

//================ AE Antenna_California ========================
AE Antenna_California {

  AESELF_MANAGEMENT {
    OTHER_POLICIES {
      POLICY IMAGE_PROCESSING {
        FLUENT inStartingBlueImageSession {
          INITIATED_BY { EVENTS.blueImageSessionIsAboutToStart }
          TERMINATED_BY { EVENTS.imageSessionStartedBlue }
        }
        FLUENT inStartingRedImageSession {
          INITIATED_BY { EVENTS.redImageSessionIsAboutToStart }
          TERMINATED_BY { EVENTS.imageSessionStartedRed }
        }
        FLUENT inStartingGreenImageSession {
          INITIATED_BY { EVENTS.greenImageSessionIsAboutToStart }
          TERMINATED_BY { EVENTS.imageSessionStartedGreen }
        }
        FLUENT inCollectingImagePixelsBlue {
          INITIATED_BY { EVENTS.imageSessionStartedBlue }
          TERMINATED_BY { EVENTS.imageSessionEndedBlue }
        }
        FLUENT inCollectingImagePixelsRed {
          INITIATED_BY { EVENTS.imageSessionStartedRed }
          TERMINATED_BY { EVENTS.imageSessionEndedRed }
        }
        FLUENT inCollectingImagePixelsGreen {
```

```
INITIATED_BY { EVENTS.imageSessionStartedGreen }
TERMINATED_BY { EVENTS.imageSessionEndedGreen }

FLUENT inSendingImage {
INITIATED_BY { EVENTS.imageSessionEndedGreen }
TERMINATED_BY { EVENTS.imageAntCaliforniaSent }
}

MAPPING {
CONDITIONS { inStartingBlueImageSession }
DO_ACTIONS { ACTIONS.startImageCollectSession ("blue") }
}

MAPPING {
CONDITIONS { inStartingRedImageSession }
DO_ACTIONS { ACTIONS.startImageCollectSession ("red") }
}

MAPPING {
CONDITIONS { inStartingGreenImageSession }
DO_ACTIONS { ACTIONS.startImageCollectSession ("green") }
}

MAPPING {
CONDITIONS { inCollectingImagePixelsBlue }
DO_ACTIONS { ACTIONS.collectImagePixels ("blue") }
}

MAPPING {
CONDITIONS { inCollectingImagePixelsRed }
DO_ACTIONS { ACTIONS.collectImagePixels ("red") }
}

MAPPING {
CONDITIONS { inCollectingImagePixelsGreen }
DO_ACTIONS { ACTIONS.collectImagePixels ("green") }
}

MAPPING {
CONDITIONS { inSendingImage }
DO_ACTIONS { ACTIONS.sendImage }
}
}
```

```
} // AESELF_MANAGEMENT

//====== AEIP for this AE ======
AEIP {
  FUNCTIONS {
    FUNCTION receiveImagePixelMsg {
      DOES { AES.Voyager.AEIP.MESSAGES.msgImagePixel << AES.Voyager.AEIP.CHANNELS.VOYAGER_Link  }
    }
    FUNCTION receiveSessionBeginMsg {
      PARAMETERS { string filterName }
      DOES {
        IF filterName = "blue" THEN
          AES.Voyager.AEIP.MESSAGES.msgBlueSessionBeginCfn << AES.Voyager.AEIP.CHANNELS.VOYAGER_Link
        END
        ELSE
        IF filterName = "red" THEN
          AES.Voyager.AEIP.MESSAGES.msgRedSessionBeginCfn << AES.Voyager.AEIP.CHANNELS.VOYAGER_Link
        END
        ELSE
        IF filterName = "green" THEN
          AES.Voyager.AEIP.MESSAGES.msgGreenSessionBeginCfn << AES.Voyager.AEIP.CHANNELS.VOYAGER_Link
        END
        END
        END
    }
    FUNCTION receiveSessionEndMsg {
      PARAMETERS { string filterName }
      DOES {
        IF filterName = "blue" THEN
          AES.Voyager.AEIP.MESSAGES.msgBlueSessionEndCfn << AES.Voyager.AEIP.CHANNELS.VOYAGER_Link
        END
        ELSE
        IF filterName = "red" THEN
          AES.Voyager.AEIP.MESSAGES.msgRedSessionEndCfn << AES.Voyager.AEIP.CHANNELS.VOYAGER_Link
```

```
      END
      ELSE
        IF filterName = "green" THEN
          AES.Voyager.AEIP.MESSAGES.msgGreenSessionEndCfn << AES.Voyager.AEIP.CHANNELS.VOYAGER_Link
        END
      END
    END
  }
}

MANAGED_ELEMENTS { }
}

ACTIONS {
  ACTION startImageCollectSession {
    PARAMETERS { string filterName }
    GUARDS { AESELF_MANAGEMENT.OTHER_POLICIES.IMAGE_PROCESSING.inStartingBlueImageSession OR
             AESELF_MANAGEMENT.OTHER_POLICIES.IMAGE_PROCESSING.inStartingRedImageSession OR
             AESELF_MANAGEMENT.OTHER_POLICIES.IMAGE_PROCESSING.inStartingGreenImageSession }
    DOES {
      CALL AEIP.FUNCTIONS.receiveSessionBeginMsg (filterName)
    }
  }

  ACTION collectImagePixels {
    PARAMETERS {   string filterName }
    GUARDS { AESELF_MANAGEMENT.OTHER_POLICIES.IMAGE_PROCESSING.inCollectingImagePixelsBlue OR
             AESELF_MANAGEMENT.OTHER_POLICIES.IMAGE_PROCESSING.inCollectingImagePixelsRed OR
             AESELF_MANAGEMENT.OTHER_POLICIES.IMAGE_PROCESSING.inCollectingImagePixelsGreen }
    VARS { integer numPixels }
    DOES {
      numPixels = 0;
      DO {
        CALL AEIP.FUNCTIONS.receiveImagePixelMsg;
        numPixels = numPixels + 1
      } WHILE numPixels < AS.numPixelsPerImage;
```

```
      CALL AEIP.FUNCTIONS.receiveSessionEndMsg (filterName)
    }

    ACTION IMPL prepareImage { }
    ACTION sendImage {
      GUARDS { AESELF_MANAGEMENT.OTHER_POLICIES.IMAGE_PROCESSING.inSendingImage }
      DOES {
        CALL IMPL ACTIONS.prepareImage;
        CALL ASIP.FUNCTIONS.sendImageMsg("Antenna_California");
        CALL ASIP.FUNCTIONS.receiveImageMsg("Antenna_California")
      }
    }
  } // ACTIONS

  EVENTS {
    EVENT blueImageSessionIsAboutToStart { ACTIVATION { SENT { AES.Voyager.AEIP.MESSAGES.msgBlueSessionBeginCfn } } }
    EVENT redImageSessionIsAboutToStart { ACTIVATION { SENT { AES.Voyager.AEIP.MESSAGES.msgRedSessionBeginCfn } } }
    EVENT greenImageSessionIsAboutToStart { ACTIVATION { SENT { AES.Voyager.AEIP.MESSAGES.msgGreenSessionBeginCfn } } }
    EVENT imageSessionStartedBlue { ACTIVATION { RECEIVED { AES.Voyager.AEIP.MESSAGES.msgBlueSessionBeginCfn } } }
    EVENT imageSessionEndedBlue { ACTIVATION { RECEIVED { AES.Voyager.AEIP.MESSAGES.msgBlueSessionEndCfn } } }
    EVENT imageSessionStartedRed { ACTIVATION { RECEIVED { AES.Voyager.AEIP.MESSAGES.msgRedSessionBeginCfn } } }
    EVENT imageSessionEndedRed { ACTIVATION { RECEIVED { AES.Voyager.AEIP.MESSAGES.msgRedSessionEndCfn } } }
    EVENT imageSessionStartedGreen { ACTIVATION { RECEIVED { AES.Voyager.AEIP.MESSAGES.msgGreenSessionBeginCfn } } }
    EVENT imageSessionEndedGreen { ACTIVATION { RECEIVED { AES.Voyager.AEIP.MESSAGES.msgGreenSessionEndCfn } } }
    EVENT imageAntCaliforniaSent { ACTIVATION { SENT { ASIP.MESSAGES.msgImageAntCalifornia } } }
  } // EVENTS
}

//================== AE Antenna_Spain ====================
AE Antenna_Spain {

  AESELF_MANAGEMENT {
    OTHER_POLICIES {
      POLICY IMAGE_PROCESSING {
        FLUENT inStartingBlueImageSession {
          INITIATED_BY { EVENTS.blueImageSessionIsAboutToStart }
```

```
    TERMINATED_BY { EVENTS.imageSessionStartedBlue }
}
FLUENT inStartingRedImageSession {
    INITIATED_BY { EVENTS.redImageSessionIsAboutToStart }
    TERMINATED_BY { EVENTS.imageSessionStartedRed }
}
FLUENT inStartingGreenImageSession {
    INITIATED_BY { EVENTS.greenImageSessionIsAboutToStart }
    TERMINATED_BY { EVENTS.imageSessionStartedGreen }
}
FLUENT inCollectingImagePixelsBlue {
    INITIATED_BY { EVENTS.imageSessionStartedBlue }
    TERMINATED_BY { EVENTS.imageSessionEndedBlue }
}
FLUENT inCollectingImagePixelsRed {
    INITIATED_BY { EVENTS.imageSessionStartedRed }
    TERMINATED_BY { EVENTS.imageSessionEndedRed }
}
FLUENT inCollectingImagePixelsGreen {
    INITIATED_BY { EVENTS.imageSessionStartedGreen }
    TERMINATED_BY { EVENTS.imageSessionEndedGreen }
}
FLUENT inSendingImage {
    INITIATED_BY { EVENTS.imageSessionEndedGreen }
    TERMINATED_BY { EVENTS.imageAntSpainSent }
}
MAPPING {
    CONDITIONS { inStartingBlueImageSession }
    DO_ACTIONS { ACTIONS.startImageCollectSession ("blue") }
}
MAPPING {
    CONDITIONS { inStartingRedImageSession }
    DO_ACTIONS { ACTIONS.startImageCollectSession ("red") }
}
MAPPING {
    CONDITIONS { inStartingGreenImageSession }
```

```
    DO_ACTIONS { ACTIONS.startImageCollectSession ("green") }
  }
  MAPPING {
    CONDITIONS { inCollectingImagePixelsBlue }
    DO_ACTIONS { ACTIONS.collectImagePixels ("blue") }
  }
  MAPPING {
    CONDITIONS { inCollectingImagePixelsRed }
    DO_ACTIONS { ACTIONS.collectImagePixels ("red") }
  }
  MAPPING {
    CONDITIONS { inCollectingImagePixelsGreen }
    DO_ACTIONS { ACTIONS.collectImagePixels ("green") }
  }
  MAPPING {
    CONDITIONS { inSendingImage }
    DO_ACTIONS { ACTIONS.sendImage }
  }
}
} // AESELF_MANAGEMENT

//===== AEIP for this AE ======
AEIP {
  FUNCTIONS {
    FUNCTION receiveImagePixelMsg {
      DOES { AES.Voyager.AEIP.MESSAGES.msgImagePixel << AES.Voyager.AEIP.CHANNELS.VOYAGER_Link }
    }
    FUNCTION receiveSessionBeginMsg {
      PARAMETERS { string filterName }
      DOES {
        IF filterName = "blue" THEN
          AES.Voyager.AEIP.MESSAGES.msgBlueSessionBeginSpn << AES.Voyager.AEIP.CHANNELS.VOYAGER_Link
        END
        ELSE
          IF filterName = "red" THEN
```

```
        AES.Voyager.AEIP.MESSAGES.msgRedSessionBeginSpn << AES.Voyager.AEIP.CHANNELS.VOYAGER_Link
      END
      ELSE
        IF filterName = "green" THEN
          AES.Voyager.AEIP.MESSAGES.msgGreenSessionBeginSpn << AES.Voyager.AEIP.CHANNELS.VOYAGER_Link
        END
      END
    END
  }

  FUNCTION receiveSessionEndMsg {
    PARAMETERS { string filterName }
    DOES {
      IF filterName = "blue" THEN
        AES.Voyager.AEIP.MESSAGES.msgBlueSessionEndSpn << AES.Voyager.AEIP.CHANNELS.VOYAGER_Link
      END
      ELSE
        IF filterName = "red" THEN
          AES.Voyager.AEIP.MESSAGES.msgRedSessionEndSpn << AES.Voyager.AEIP.CHANNELS.VOYAGER_Link
        END
        ELSE
          IF filterName = "green" THEN
            AES.Voyager.AEIP.MESSAGES.msgGreenSessionEndSpn << AES.Voyager.AEIP.CHANNELS.VOYAGER_Link
          END
        END
      END
    }
  }

  MANAGED_ELEMENTS { }
} // AEIP

ACTIONS {
  ACTION startImageCollectSession {
    PARAMETERS { string filterName }
    GUARDS { AESELF_MANAGEMENT.OTHER_POLICIES.IMAGE_PROCESSING.inStartingBlueImageSession OR
```

```
          AESELF_MANAGEMENT.OTHER_POLICIES.IMAGE_PROCESSING.inStartingRedImageSession OR
          AESELF_MANAGEMENT.OTHER_POLICIES.IMAGE_PROCESSING.inStartingGreenImageSession }
    DOES {
        CALL AEIP.FUNCTIONS.receiveSessionBeginMsg (filterName)
    }
}

ACTION collectImagePixels {
    PARAMETERS { string filterName }
    GUARDS { AESELF_MANAGEMENT.OTHER_POLICIES.IMAGE_PROCESSING.inCollectingImagePixelsBlue OR
             AESELF_MANAGEMENT.OTHER_POLICIES.IMAGE_PROCESSING.inCollectingImagePixelsRed OR
             AESELF_MANAGEMENT.OTHER_POLICIES.IMAGE_PROCESSING.inCollectingImagePixelsGreen }
    VARS { integer numPixels }
    DOES {
        numPixels = 0;
        DO {
            CALL AEIP.FUNCTIONS.receiveImagePixelMsg;
            numPixels = numPixels + 1
        } WHILE numPixels < AS.numPixelsPerImage ;
    }
}

CALL AEIP.FUNCTIONS.receiveSessionEndMsg (filterName)
}

ACTION IMPL prepareImage { }
ACTION sendImage {
    GUARDS { AESELF_MANAGEMENT.OTHER_POLICIES.IMAGE_PROCESSING.inSendingImage }
    DOES {
        CALL IMPL ACTIONS.prepareImage;
        CALL ASIP.FUNCTIONS.sendImageMsg("Antenna_Spain");
        CALL ASIP.FUNCTIONS.receiveImageMsg("Antenna_Spain")
    }
}
} // ACTIONS

EVENTS {
    EVENT blueImageSessionIsAboutToStart { ACTIVATION { SENT { AES.Voyager.AEIP.MESSAGES.msgBlueSessionBeginSpn } } }
    EVENT redImageSessionIsAboutToStart { ACTIVATION { SENT { AES.Voyager.AEIP.MESSAGES.msgRedSessionBeginSpn } } }
```

```
EVENT greenImageSessionIsAboutToStart { ACTIVATION { SENT { AES.Voyager.AEIP.MESSAGES.msgGreenSessionBeginSpn } } }
EVENT imageSessionStartedBlue { ACTIVATION { RECEIVED { AES.Voyager.AEIP.MESSAGES.msgBlueSessionBeginSpn } } }
EVENT imageSessionEndedBlue { ACTIVATION { RECEIVED { AES.Voyager.AEIP.MESSAGES.msgBlueSessionEndSpn } } }
EVENT imageSessionStartedRed { ACTIVATION { RECEIVED { AES.Voyager.AEIP.MESSAGES.msgRedSessionBeginSpn } } }
EVENT imageSessionEndedRed { ACTIVATION { RECEIVED { AES.Voyager.AEIP.MESSAGES.msgRedSessionEndSpn } } }
EVENT imageSessionStartedGreen { ACTIVATION { RECEIVED { AES.Voyager.AEIP.MESSAGES.msgGreenSessionBeginSpn } } }
EVENT imageSessionEndedGreen { ACTIVATION { RECEIVED { AES.Voyager.AEIP.MESSAGES.msgGreenSessionEndSpn } } }
EVENT imageAntSpainSent { ACTIVATION { SENT {    ASIP.MESSAGES.msgImageAntSpain } } }
} // EVENTS

} // AES
```

Appendix C
BepiColombo Autonomy Requirements Specification with KnowLang

© Springer International Publishing Switzerland 2014

E. Vassev and M. Hinchey, *Autonomy Requirements Engineering for Space Missions*,
NASA Monographs in Systems and Software Engineering,
DOI 10.1007/978-3-319-09816-6

```
// KnowLang Speccification
// MMO
//===================================================================
CORPUS BepiColombo {

ONTOLOGY MMO { //MMO's ontology

METACONCEPTS {
   METACONCEPT MMO_Thing {
      CONCEPT_NAME { MMO.CONCEPT_TREES.Thing }
      INTERPRETATION { }
   }
}

//concept trees
CONCEPT_TREES {
   CONCEPT Thing {
      META { MMO.MMO_Thing }
      PARENTS {}
      CHILDREN {Entity, Virtual_Entity}
      PROPS {
         PROP Physical {
            TYPE ( BOOLEAN }
      }
   }

//Entity concept tree
CONCEPT Entity {
   PARENTS {MMO.Thing}
   CHILDREN {MMO..Part, MMO..Fluid, MMO..Composite}
   PROPS {
      PROP Physical {
         TYPE ( True }
   }
}
```

```
//Part
CONCEPT Part {
    PARENTS {MMO..Entity}
    CHILDREN {MMO..Tank, MMO..Radiator, MMO..Thrust_Tube, MMO..Insulator, MMO..Bulkhead}
    PROPS {
        PROP Part_Shape { MMO..Shape }
    }
    FUNCS {
        FUNC Get_Integrity { }
    }
    STATES {
        STATE Functional { this.FUNCS.Get_Integrity = 100% }
    }
}

CONCEPT Tank {
    PARENTS {MMO..Part}
    CHILDREN {}
    PROPS {
        PROP Part_Shape { MMO..Shape }
        PROP Cont_gas { MMO..Gas }
    }
    FUNCS {
        FUNC Get_Integrity { TYPE { MMO..ACTION.GetTankIntegrity } }
        FUNC Get_GasLevel { TYPE { MMO..ACTION.ComputeGasLevel } }
        FUNC Get_GasTemperature { TYPE { MMO..ACTION.ComputeGasTemperature } }
    }
    STATES {
        STATE HasGas{ this.FUNCS.Get_GasLevel > 1% }
    }
}

CONCEPT Fluid {
    PARENTS {MMO..Entity}
    CHILDREN { MMO..Gas }
    PROPS {}
}

CONCEPT Gas {
```

```
PARENTS {MMO..Fluid}
CHILDREN {}
PROPS {}
}

CONCEPT Composite {
PARENTS {MMO..Entity}
CHILDREN {MMO..Electronics, MMO..Mechanics, MMO..Shield, MMO..Electrical}
PROPS {}
}

CONCEPT Electronics {
PARENTS {MMO..Composite}
CHILDREN {MMO..CPU, MMO..Sensor, MMO..Memory, MMO..System}
STATES {STATE operational {} STATE on {} STATE off {}}
}

CONCEPT Mechanics {
PARENTS {MMO..Composite}
CHILDREN {MMO..Deck, MMO..APM, MMO..Antenna, MMO..ECM, MMO..System}
STATES {STATE operational {}}
}

CONCEPT Electrical {
PARENTS {MMO..Composite}
CHILDREN {MMO..System, MMO..Solar_Cell, MMO..Battery}
STATES {STATE operational {} STATE on {} STATE off {}}
}

CONCEPT System {
PARENTS {MMO..Electronics, MMO..Mechanics, MMO..Electrical, MMO..Software}
CHILDREN {
MMO..Instrument, MMO..Nutation_Damper, MMO..Engine, MMO..HGA, MMO..MGA,
MMO..UHF, MMO..Extendible_Mechanism, MMO..Computer, MMO..Propulsion_module,
MMO..Communication_System, MMO..Thermal_Ctrl_System
}
STATES {STATE operational {} STATE on {} STATE off {} STATE active() STATE idle()}
}

// antenna related concepts
CONCEPT ADP {
```

```
    PARENTS {MMO..Electrical}
    CHILDREN {}
    STATES { STATE operational {} }
}
CONCEPT ECM {
    PARENTS {MMO..Mechanics}
    CHILDREN {}
    STATES { STATE operational {} }
}
CONCEPT APM {
    PARENTS {MMO..Mechanics}
    CHILDREN {}
    STATES {
        STATE operational { this.ecm.operational AND this.adp.operational }
    }
    PROPS {
        PROP ecm { TYPE {MMO..ECM} CARDINALITY {1} }
        PROP adp { TYPE {MMO..ADP} CARDINALITY {1} }
    }
    FUNCS {
        FUNC turnUp { TYPE {MMO..Action.TurnAPMUp} }
        FUNC turnDown { TYPE {MMO..Action.TurnAPMDown} }
        FUNC turnLeft { TYPE {MMO..Action.TurnAPMLeft} }
        FUNC turnRight { TYPE {MMO..Action.TurnAPMRight} }
    }
    IMPL { MMO.APMMechanism }
}
//antennas
CONCEPT HGA {
    CHILDREN {}
    PARENTS { MMO..System }
    STATES {
        STATE operational {
            this.hga_antenna.operational AND this.apm.operational
            AND this.control_soft.functional
```

```
        }
        STATE pointed {}
        STATE receiving {}
        STATE sending {}
        STATE off {} }
        STATE on {}
    }
    PROPS {
        PROP hga_antenna { TYPE {MMO..Antenna} CARDINALITY {1} }
        PROP apm { TYPE {MMO..APM} CARDINALITY {1} }
        PROP control_soft { TYPE {MMO..Control_Software} CARDINALITY {1} }
    }
    FUNCS {
        FUNC point { TYPE {MMO..Action.PointHGA } }
        FUNC send { TYPE {MMO..Action.SendHGA } }
        FUNC receive { TYPE {MMO..Action.ReceiveHGA } }
        FUNC start { TYPE {MMO..Action.StartHGA } }
        FUNC stop { TYPE {MMO..Action.StopHGA } }
    }
    IMPL { MMO.HGASystem }
}
CONCEPT MGA {
    CHILDREN {}
    PARENTS { MMO..System }
    STATES {
        STATE operational {
            this.mga_antenna.operational AND this.ext_mechanism.operational
            AND this.control_soft.functional
        }
        STATE extended {}
        STATE receiving {}
        STATE sending {}
        STATE off {}
        STATE on {}
    }
    PROPS {
```

```
    PROP mga_antenna { TYPE {MMO..Antenna} CARDINALITY {1} }
    PROP ext_mechanism { TYPE {MMO..Extendible_mechanism} CARDINALITY {1} }
    PROP control_soft { TYPE {MMO..Control_Software} CARDINALITY {1} }
    }
    FUNCS {
        FUNC extend { TYPE {MMO..Action.ExtendMGA } }
        FUNC fold_up { TYPE {MMO..Action.FoldUpMGA } }
        FUNC send { TYPE {MMO..Action.SendMGA } }
        FUNC receive { TYPE {MMO..Action.ReceiveMGA } }
        FUNC start { TYPE {MMO..Action.StartMGA } }
        FUNC stop { TYPE {MMO..Action.StopMGA } }
    }
    IMPL { MMO.MGASystem }

CONCEPT UHF {
    CHILDREN {}
    PARENTS { MMO..System }
    STATES {
        STATE operational {
            this.uhf_antenna.operational AND this.control_soft.functional

        STATE receiving {}
        STATE sending {}
        STATE off {}
        STATE on {}
    }
    PROPS {
        PROP uhf_antenna { TYPE {MMO..Antenna} CARDINALITY {1} }
        PROP control_soft { TYPE {MMO..Control_Software} CARDINALITY {1} }
    }
    FUNCS {
        FUNC send { TYPE {MMO..Action.SendUHF } }
        FUNC receive { TYPE {MMO..Action.ReceiveUHF } }
        FUNC start { TYPE {MMO..Action.StartUHF } }
        FUNC stop { TYPE {MMO..Action.StopUHF } }
    }
```

```
IMPL { MMO.UHFSystem }
}

// propulsion modules
CONCEPT SEPM {
  CHILDREN {}
  PARENTS { MMO..System }
  STATES {
    STATE Operational {
      this.solar_cells.Functional AND this.gas_tank.Functional AND
      this.el_engine.Operational AND this.control_soft.Functional }
    STATE Forwarding { IS_PERFORMING(this.forward) }
    STATE Reversing { IS_PERFORMING(this.forward) }
    STATE Started { LAST_PERFORMED(this, this.start) }
    STATE Stopped { LAST_PERFORMED(this, this.stop) }
  }
  PROPS {
    PROP solar_cells { TYPE {MMO..Solar_cell} CARDINALITY {200} }
    PROP gas_tank { TYPE {MMO..Tank} CARDINALITY {1} }
    PROP el_engine { TYPE {MMO..Electrical_Engine} CARDINALITY {1} }
    PROP control_soft { TYPE {MMO..Control_Software} CARDINALITY {1} }
  }
  FUNCS {
    FUNC reverse { TYPE {MMO..Action.ReverseSEPM } }
    FUNC forward { TYPE {MMO..Action.ForwardSEPM } }
    FUNC start { TYPE {MMO..Action.StartSEPM } }
    FUNC stop { TYPE {MMO..Action.StopSEPM } }
  }
  IMPL { MMO.SEPMSystem }
}

CONCEPT CPM {
  CHILDREN {}
  PARENTS { MMO..System }
  STATES {
    STATE Operational {
```

```
        this.gas_tank.Functional AND this.chem_engine.Operational
        AND this.control_soft.Functional }
    STATE Forwarding ( IS_PERFORMING(this.forward) )
    STATE Reversing ( IS_PERFORMING(this.forward) )
    STATE Started { LAST_PERFORMED(this, this.stop) )
    STATE Stopped ( LAST_PERFORMED(this, this.start) )
    }
    PROPS {
    PROP gas_tank { TYPE {MMO..Tank} CARDINALITY {1} }
    PROP chem_engine { TYPE {MMO..Chemical_Engine} CARDINALITY {1} }
    PROP control_soft { TYPE {MMO..Control_Software} CARDINALITY {1} }
    }
    FUNCS {
    FUNC reverse { TYPE {MMO..Action.ReverseCPM } }
    FUNC forward { TYPE {MMO..Action.ForwardCPM } }
    FUNC start { TYPE {MMO..Action.StartCPM } }
    FUNC stop { TYPE {MMO..Action.StopCPM } }
    }
    IMPL { MMO.CPMSystem }
}

// MMO
CONCEPT MMO_Spacecraft {
    CHILDREN {}
    PARENTS { MMO..System }
    STATES {
    STATE Orbiting {}
    STATE InTransfer {}
    STATE InOrbitPlacement {}
    STATE InJettison {}
    STATE InHighIrradiation { MMO..Metric.OutsideRadiation.VALUE > 50 }
    STATE InHeatFlux { MMO..Metric.OutsideTemp.VALUE > 150 }
    STATE AtPolarOrbit { LAST_PERFORMED(this, this.moveToPolarOrbit) }
    STATE ArrivedAtMercury { MMO..Metric.MercuryAltitude.VALUE = 0.39 }
    STATE EarthCommunicationLost { MMO..Metric.EarthSignal.VALUE = 0 }
    }
```

```
PROPS (
    PROP sepm ( TYPE {MMO..SEPM} CARDINALITY {1} )
    PROP cpm ( TYPE {MMO..CPM} CARDINALITY {1} )

    PROP upper_deck ( TYPE {MMO..Deck} CARDINALITY {1} )
    PROP lower_deck ( TYPE {MMO..Deck} CARDINALITY {1} )
    PROP thrust_tube ( TYPE {MMO..Thrust_Tube} CARDINALITY {1} )
    PROP bulkhead ( TYPE {MMO..Bulkhead} CARDINALITY {4} )
    PROP side_panel ( TYPE {MMO..Panel} CARDINALITY {1} )
    PROP solar_cell ( TYPE {MMO..Solar_cell} CARDINALITY {200} )
    PROP battery ( TYPE {MMO..Battery} CARDINALITY {1} )
    PROP nutation_damper ( TYPE {MMO..Nutation_damper} CARDINALITY {1} )

    PROP mppe_instr ( TYPE {MMO..MPPE} CARDINALITY {1} )
    PROP mdm_instr ( TYPE {MMO..MDM} CARDINALITY {1} )
    PROP magnetometer ( TYPE {MMO..Magnetometer} CARDINALITY {1} )
    PROP msasi_instr ( TYPE {MMO..MSASI} CARDINALITY {1} )
    PROP pwi_instr ( TYPE {MMO..PWI} CARDINALITY {1} )

    PROP radiator ( TYPE {MMO..Radiator} CARDINALITY {1} )

    PROP uhf ( TYPE {MMO..UHF} CARDINALITY {1} )
    PROP mga ( TYPE {MMO..MGA} CARDINALITY {1} )
    PROP hga ( TYPE {MMO..HGA} CARDINALITY {1} )

    PROP control_soft ( TYPE {MMO..Control_Software} CARDINALITY {1} )
    PROP communication_sys ( TYPE {MMO..Communication_system} CARDINALITY {1} )
    PROP thermal_ctrl_sys ( TYPE {MMO..Thermal_Ctrl_System} CARDINALITY {1} )
)

FUNCS (
    FUNC moveToPolarOrbit ( TYPE {MMO..Action.GoToPolarOrbit} )
    FUNC waitForInstrFromEarth ( TYPE {MMO..Action.WaitForInstructions} )

IMPL ( MMO.MMOSystem )
}
```

```
//metrics
CONCEPT_METRIC OutsideRadiation {
    SPEC {
        METRIC_TYPE { ENVIRONMENT }
        METRIC_SOURCE { RadiationMeasure.OutsideRadiation }
        DATA { DATA_TYPE { MMO..Sievert } VALUE { 1 } }
    }
}
CONCEPT_METRIC OutsideTemp {
    SPEC {
        METRIC_TYPE { ENVIRONMENT }
        METRIC_SOURCE { TempMeasure.OutsideTemp }
        DATA { DATA_TYPE { MMO..Celsius } VALUE { 1 } }
    }
}
CONCEPT_METRIC MercuryAltitude {
    SPEC {
        METRIC_TYPE { ENVIRONMENT }
        METRIC_SOURCE { AltitudeMeasure.Mercury }
        DATA { DATA_TYPE { MMO..AU } VALUE { 1 } }
    }
}
CONCEPT_METRIC EarthSignal {
    SPEC {
        METRIC_TYPE { QUALITY }
        METRIC_SOURCE { EarthCommLink.SignalStrength }
        DATA { VALUE { 1 } }
    }
}
CONCEPT_METRIC OutsideRadiation {
    SPEC {
        METRIC_TYPE { ENVIRONMENT }
        METRIC_SOURCE { IrradiationMeasure.GetLevel }
        DATA { DATA_TYPE { MMO..Sievert } VALUE { 1 } }
    }
}
```

```
// goals
CONCEPT_GOAL MMOOrbit_Placement {
    SPEC {
        DEPART { MMO_Spacecraft.STATES.InOrbitPlacement }
        ARRIVE { MMO_Spacecraft.STATES.AtPolarOrbit }
    }
}

CONCEPT_GOAL MMOArrive_At_Mercury {
    SPEC { ARRIVE { MMO_Spacecraft.STATES.ArrivedAtMercury } }
}

CONCEPT_GOAL MMOStart_Orbit_Placement {
    SPEC {
        DEPART { MMO_Spacecraft.STATES.ArrivedAtMercury }
        ARRIVE { MMO_Spacecraft.STATES.InOrbitPlacement }
    }
}

//protect from solar radiation
CONCEPT_GOAL MMOSelf_Protection {
    SPEC {
        ARRIVE { NOT MMO_Spacecraft.STATES.InHighIrradiation
            AND MMO_Spacecraft.STATES.AtPolarOrbit }
    }
}

//
//=== MMO Situations ===================================================
//
CONCEPT_SITUATION ArrivedAtMercury {
    CHILDREN {}
    PARENTS {MMO..Situation}
    SPEC {
        SITUATION_STATES { MMO_Spacecraft.STATES.ArrivedAtMercury }
        SITUATION_ACTIONS {
            MMO..Action.GoToPolarOrbit, MMO..Action.WaitForInstructions,
            MMO..Action.ScheduleNewTask
```

```
	}
}

CONCEPT_SITUATION BrokenEarthCommunication {
	CHILDREN {}
	PARENTS {MMO..Situation}
	SPEC {
		SITUATION_STATES { MMO_Spacecraft.STATES.EarthCommunicationLost }
		SITUATION_ACTIONS { MMO..Action.SendPingSignalToEarth, MMO..Action.ScheduleNewTask }
	}
}

CONCEPT_SITUATION SpacecraftInHeatFlux {
	CHILDREN {}
	PARENTS {MMO..Situation}
	SPEC {
		SITUATION_STATES { MMO_Spacecraft.STATES.InHeatFlux }
		SITUATION_ACTIONS { MMO..Action.CoverInstruments, MMO..Action.GotoSafeAltitude }
	}
}

CONCEPT_SITUATION SpacecraftInHighIrradiation {
	CHILDREN {}
	PARENTS {MMO..Situation}
	SPEC {
		SITUATION_STATES { MMO_Spacecraft.STATES.InHighIrradiation }
		SITUATION_ACTIONS {
			MMO..Action.CoverInstruments, MMO..Action.TurnOffElectronics,
			MMO..Action.MoveSpacecraftUp, MMO..Action.MoveSpacecraftDown
		}
	}
}

//
//=== SC Policies ===========================================================
//

CONCEPT_POLICY BringMMOToOrbit {
	SPEC {
		POLICY_GOAL { MMO..MMOOrbit_Placement_Done }
```

```
        POLICY_SITUATIONS { MMO..ArrivedAtMercury }
        POLICY_RELATIONS { MMO..Policy_Situation_2 }
        POLICY_ACTIONS { MMO..Action.GoToPolarOrbit }
        POLICY_MAPPINGS (
            MAPPING (
                CONDITIONS { }
                DO_ACTIONS { MMO..Action.GoToPolarOrbit }
            }
        }
    }

CONCEPT_POLICY MMOProtect_spacecraft (
    SPEC (
        POLICY_GOAL { MMO..MMOSelf-Protection }
        POLICY_SITUATIONS { MMO..HighIrradiation }
        POLICY_RELATIONS { MMO..Policy_Situation_3 }
        POLICY_ACTIONS {
            MMO..Action.CoverInstruments, MMO..Action.TurnOffElectronics,
            MMO..Action.MoveSpacecraftUp, MMO..Action.MoveSpacecraftDown }
        POLICY_MAPPINGS (
            MAPPING (
                CONDITIONS { MMO..Metric.SolarRadiation.VALUE < 90 }
                DO_ACTIONS { MMO..Action.ShadeInstruments,
                    MMO..Action.TurnOffElectronics }
            }

            MAPPING (
                CONDITIONS { MMO..Metric.SolarRadiation.VALUE >= 90 }
                DO_ACTIONS { MMO..Action.MoveSpacecraftUp }
                PROBABILITY {0.5}
            }

            MAPPING (
                CONDITIONS { MMO..Metric.SolarRadiation.VALUE >= 90 }
                DO_ACTIONS { MMO..Action.MoveSpacecraftDown }
                PROBABILITY {0.4}
            }
```

```
MAPPING {
    CONDITIONS { MMO..Metric.SolarRadiation.VALUE >= 90 }
    DO_ACTIONS { GENERATE_NEXT_ACTIONS(MMO..MMO_Spacecraft) }
    PROBABILITY {0.1}
    }
    }
    }
} // concept trees

//
//=== MMO Relations ==================================================================================
//
RELATIONS {
    RELATION Policy_Situation_1 {
        RELATION_PAIR (MMO..ArrivedAtMercury, MMO..FollowOrbitPlacementInstrs) PROBABILITY {0.9}
    }

    RELATION Policy_Situation_2 {
        RELATION_PAIR (MMO..ArrivedAtMercury, MMO..BringMMOToOrbit) PROBABILITY {0.1}
    }

    RELATION Policy_Situation_3 {
        RELATION_PAIR (MMO..HighIrradiation, MMO..MMOSelf-protection)
    }

    RELATION Instance_Of {
        RELATION_PAIR (object.mmo_1, MMO..MMO_Spacecraft)
    }
}

//
//=== MMO Object Trees ==============================================================================
//
OBJECT_TREES {
    // hga_antenna_1 object tree
```

```
FINAL OBJECT antenna_1 {
    INSTANCE_OF { MMO..Antenna }
}

FINAL OBJECT adp_1 {
    INSTANCE_OF { MMO..ADP }
}

FINAL OBJECT ecm_1 {
    INSTANCE_OF { MMO..ECM }
}

FINAL OBJECT apm_1 {
    INSTANCE_OF { MMO..APM }
    PROPS {
        PROP adp { MMO.OBJECT_TREES.adp_1 }
        PROP ecm { MMO.OBJECT_TREES.ecm_1 }
    }
}

FINAL OBJECT ant_ctrl_soft_1 {
    INSTANCE_OF { MMO..Control_software }
}

FINAL OBJECT hga_antenna_1 {
    INSTANCE_OF { MMO..HGA }
    PROPS {
        PROP hga_antenna { MMO.OBJECT_TREES.antenna_1 }
        PROP apm { MMO.OBJECT_TREES.apm_1 }
        PROP control_soft { MMO.OBJECT_TREES.ant_ctrl_soft_1 }
    }
    IMPL { MMO.HGAAntennaModule }
}

// mga_antenna_1 object tree
FINAL OBJECT antenna_2 {
    INSTANCE_OF { MMO..Antenna }
}

FINAL OBJECT arm_1 {
    INSTANCE_OF { MMO..Mechanism }
}
```

```
FINAL OBJECT el_motor_1 {
    INSTANCE_OF { MMO..Electric_motor }
}

FINAL OBJECT ant_ctrl_soft_3 {
    INSTANCE_OF { MMO..Control_software }
}

FINAL OBJECT ext_mechanism_1 {
    INSTANCE_OF { MMO..Extendible_Mechanism }
    PROPS {
        PROP arm { MMO.OBJECT_TREES.arm_1 }
        PROP el_motor { MMO.OBJECT_TREES.el_motor_1 }
        PROP control_soft { MMO.OBJECT_TREES.ant_ctrl_soft_3 }
    }
    IMPL { MMO.MGAExtMechanism }
}

FINAL OBJECT ant_ctrl_soft_2 {
    INSTANCE_OF { MMO..Control_software }
}

FINAL OBJECT mga_antenna_1 {
    INSTANCE_OF { MMO..MGA }
    PROPS {
        PROP mga_antenna { MMO.OBJECT_TREES.antenna_2 }
        PROP ext_mechanism { MMO.OBJECT_TREES.ext_mechanism_1 }
        PROP control_soft { MMO.OBJECT_TREES.ant_ctrl_soft_2 }
    }
    IMPL { MMO.MGAAntennaModule }
}

// sepm_1 object tree
FINAL OBJECT_ARRAY sepm_sollar_cells [200] {
    INSTANCE_OF { MMO..Sollar_cell }
}

FINAL OBJECT gas_tank_1 {
    INSTANCE_OF { MMO..Tank }
}

FINAL OBJECT el_motor_2 {
```

```
        INSTANCE_OF { MMO..Electric_motor }
    }
    FINAL OBJECT el_prop_ctrl_soft_1 {
        INSTANCE_OF { MMO..Control_software }
    }
    FINAL OBJECT el_engine_1 {
        INSTANCE_OF { MMO..Electrical_engine }
        PROPS {
            PROP el_motor { MMO.OBJECT_TREES.el_motor_2 }
            PROP control_soft { MMO.OBJECT_TREES.el_prop_ctrl_soft_1 }
        }
        IMPL { MMO.SEPMElEngine }
    }
    FINAL OBJECT sepm_1 {
        INSTANCE_OF { MMO..SEPM }
        PROPS {
            PROP sollar_cells { MMO.OBJECT_TREES.sepm_sollar_cells }
            PROP gas_tank { MMO.OBJECT_TREES.gas_tank_1 }
            PROP el_engine { MMO.OBJECT_TREES.el_engine_1 }
            PROP control_soft { MMO.OBJECT_TREES.engine_ctrl_soft_1 }
        }
        IMPL { MMO.SEPMModule }
    }
} // end of MMO Object Trees
} //end of MMO Ontology } //end of BepiColombo Corpus
```

Index

A

Adaptability, 54, 109, 114, 121, 123, 141, 144, 169
Aeromaneuvering missions, 69
Aerospace, 1, 2, 16, 33, 47, 50
Aerospace development process, 5
Aerospace Industry, 1, 2, 16, 26, 33, 40
Aerospace organizations, 39
Aerospace software development, 4
Aerospace standards, 2
Aerospace systems, 3, 4, 9, 10, 19, 26, 27, 33, 39, 40, 54, 185
Agility, 40, 107
AI, 10, 33, 34, 122
Alternative autonomic behavior, 151
Alternative behavior, 164
Alternative paths, 125
Assistive autonomy requirements, 121
Assistive behavior, 139
Attributes, 25
Autonomic element, 23, 24, 137
Autonomic features, 33, 109
Autonomic system, 23, 33, 40
Autonomicity, 49, 52, 68, 107–109, 114, 140, 144, 161, 167
Autonomous, 23, 33, 34
Autonomous aerospace systems, 1
Autonomous agents, 18
Autonomous behavior, 107
Autonomous decision-making, 38, 39
Autonomous functions, 119, 121
Autonomous missions, 29
Autonomous mobile agents, 34
Autonomous process, 22
Autonomous software agents, 16
Autonomous spacecraft, 20, 34, 49

Autonomous system, 1, 10, 34–36, 38, 40, 51, 107–109, 112, 175, 176, 183
Autonomy, 52
Autonomy behavior baseline, 173
Autonomy features, 105
Autonomy requirements, 55, 109, 118, 121, 137, 139, 140, 142, 156, 169, 173
Awareness, 29, 53, 107, 141, 143, 169

B

Bandwidth, 35
BepiColombo, 105, 110, 115, 119, 122, 123, 126, 131, 136–138, 142, 144, 155, 156, 170

C

Central force field, 68
Certification, 1, 2, 4, 39, 185
Communication, 18
Communication interfaces, 80
Communication links, 34, 140, 143, 144, 148
Communication spacecraft, 63
Communications architecture, 116
Compositional verification, 173
Computational services, 23
Concept instances, 160
Concept tree, 157, 164
Constraints modeling, 109
Context-awareness, 53
Control loop, 23
Control software, 158, 161
Cooperation, 18
Cooperative, 23, 34
Cosmic impactors, 136

© Springer International Publishing Switzerland 2014
E. Vassev and M. Hinchey, *Autonomy Requirements Engineering for Space Missions*,
NASA Monographs in Systems and Software Engineering,
DOI 10.1007/978-3-319-09816-6

D
Decision making, 1, 40, 52, 167
Detection, 29
Diagnostics, 29
Distributed computing, 16
Domain modeling, 109
Dynamicity, 54, 109, 114, 123, 141, 144, 169

E
Earth-orbiting missions, 56
Embedded messaging, 82
Embedded software, 4
Embedded systems, 33
Environment monitoring, 169
Environmental conditions, 108
Environmental constraints, 122, 144
Equatorial low Earth orbit missions, 58
Execution semantics, 80
Exosphere, 58

F
Fault tolerance, 9, 118
Feedback learning, 52
Functional requirements, 106, 108, 109

G
General relativity, 135
Geostationary earth orbit missions, 61
Geostationary orbit missions, 58
Geostationary orbits, 142
Goal identification, 111
Goal satisfaction, 125
Goal-oriented autonomy, 49, 155
Gravitational forces, 57
Gravity assists, 126, 130
Gravity-assist maneuver, 140, 148
Gravity-assist manoeuvers, 68, 142
Ground-based systems, 28

H
Hazard analysis, 118
Hazards, 118
Health management, 1, 20, 28, 29, 40
Health monitoring, 20
Highly elliptic orbit missions, 62

I
Impacting factors, 56, 116
Implementation environment, 8

Inheritance, 33, 157
Intelligent swarm, 34
Interconnectivity, 2
Intermediate circular orbit missions, 58
Interoperability, 2
Interplanetary dust, 128
Interplanetary missions, 56, 64, 67, 68, 109,
        140, 142
Interplanetary trajectory, 148

K
Knowledge, 52, 156
Knowledge representation, 107

L
Latency, 35
Learning by observation, 52
Liveness properties, 48
Logical errors, 48
Low-thrust trajectories, 142

M
Mathematical algorithms, 29
Medium Earth orbit missions, 58
Mission objectives, 108, 131, 132, 165
Mission orbit, 116
Missions using low-thrust trajectories, 68
Mitigation strategies, 29
Mobility, 54, 109, 114, 142, 144, 169
Modularity, 33
Monitoring, 28, 107, 114, 121, 123, 141,
        144, 159
Multi-agent paradigm, 23
Multi-agent systems, 16
Multi-component systems, 10
Multi-tier specification model, 33

N
Non-functional requirements, 106, 108, 109,
        121
Non-gravitational accelerations, 136

O
Object tree, 160, 161
Ontology domain, 160
Operational requirements, 54
Orbit acquisition, 55
Orbit perturbations, 113
Orbital inclination, 143
Orbital perturbations, 57

P

Payload operational requirements, 115
Performance degradation, 113
Planetary atmospheric entry missions, 69
Planetary magnetic field, 134
Polar low Earth orbit missions, 58
Preliminary analysis, 111
Probabilistic beliefs, 164
Probability, 163, 166
Probability distribution, 166
Processing delays, 116
Prognostics, 29
Progress appraisal, 125
Progress metric, 125, 126

Q

Quality, 2

R

Reasoning, 107, 110, 114, 167
Redundancy, 116
Reinforcement learning, 168
Reliability, 2, 9
Remote-sensing satellite missions, 58, 61
Repeatability, 2
Requirements chunks, 119, 121
Requirements specification, 155
Resilience, 26, 27, 40, 54, 107, 109, 123,
        141, 144, 169
Reverse function, 158
Reverse requirements engineering, 120, 121
Robotic space-exploration systems, 40
Robustness, 54, 109, 123, 141, 144, 169
Rule-based mechanism, 52

S

Safety, 2, 3, 8, 9, 12, 19, 39, 48, 50, 54, 107,
        117, 118
Safety hazards, 6
Safety regulations, 3
Safety requirements, 1, 4, 8, 19, 39, 47, 106,
        117, 118, 185, 187
Safety standards, 8
Safety-critical systems, 6
Satellite constellation missions, 59
Satisfaction metric, 125
Self-* objectives, 118, 139, 148, 161
Self-* requirements, 25, 68
Self-adaptation, 23, 26, 32, 33, 35, 40, 47,
        51, 107, 185
Self-adaptive attributes, 52

Self-adaptive behavior, 137, 164
Self-adaptive objectives, 52
Self-adaptive systems, 35, 174–176, 183,
        185
Self-awareness, 40, 53
Self-configuring, 23, 107
Self-diagnosis, 23
Self-healing, 23, 107
Self-management, 18, 23–25, 33, 40, 52, 55
Self-management behavior, 32
Self-management objectives, 23, 25, 52, 107
Self-management policies, 80–82, 97, 98
Self-management policy, 97
Self-managing objectives, 23
Self-monitoring, 40
Self-optimizing, 23, 107
Self-protecting, 23, 107
Self-protection, 123, 140
Self-scheduling, 140, 145
Self-trajectory, 140
Service-level objectives, 80
Simulation, 186
Situational awareness, 169
Small object missions, 66
Soft goals, 114, 169
Software engineering for aerospace, 185
Software safety, 8
Software-intensive systems, 51, 109
Solar occultations, 135
Solar radiation pressure, 58
Space missions, 108, 109
Space-borne observatories, 62
Spacecraft orbit, 124
Specification flaws, 48
Spin-stabilized spacecraft, 128
Stability boundary capture, 143
Standards, 118
Steering law, 142
System behavior, 108, 117
System constraints, 19
System objectives, 109, 111
System optimization, 112

T

Technical readiness, 56
Test bed, 174
Testing, 1, 4, 39, 40, 50, 131, 174, 185, 186
Thrust vector, 142
Time schedule, 3
Time-tagged commands, 50
Trajectory maneuvers, 144
Trajectory parameters, 115

U
Uncertainty, 35, 51, 89, 179
Unmanned exploration, 99, 185
Unmanned mission, 94
Unmanned missions, 105
Unmanned space missions, 185, 186
Unmanned space systems, 186
Unmanned spacecraft, 40, 51, 173

Use case modeling, 109

V
Validation, 1, 4, 33, 39, 40, 110, 173, 185
Variability points, 122, 125
Verification, 1, 4, 33, 39, 40, 50, 110, 173,
    175, 185

Printed in the United States
By Bookmasters